DATE DUE

SEP 2 6 1989		
JUN 2 3 1993		
MAY 1 0 REC'D		

DEMCO NO. 38-298

D1116531

UNITED

The Divinity Library
The Jean and Alexander Heard Librar.
Vanderbilt University

Date _____

By _____

JOURNAL FOR THE STUDY OF THE NEW TESTAMENT SUPPLEMENT SERIES

17

Executive Editor, Supplement Series
David Hill

Publishing Editor
David E Orton

JSOT Press
Sheffield

THE PARADOX
OF THE CROSS
IN THE THOUGHT
OF ST PAUL

Anthony Tyrrell Hanson

Journal for the Study of the New Testament
Supplement Series 17

228 02

Fratri fidelissimo, doctissimo,
in vinculo caritatis.

Copyright © 1987 Sheffield Academic Press

Published by JSOT Press
JSOT Press is an imprint of
Sheffield Academic Press Ltd
The University of Sheffield
343 Fulwood Road
Sheffield S10 3BP
England

Typeset by Sheffield Academic Press
and
printed in Great Britain
by Billing & Sons Ltd
Worcester

British Library Cataloguing in Publication Data

Hanson, A.T.
    The paradox of the cross in the thought
    of St. Paul.— (Journal for the study of
    the New Testament. Supplement series,
    ISSN 0143-5108; 17).
    1. Bible. N.T. Epistles of Paul—Commentaries
    I. Title   II. Series
    227'.06   BS2650.3

    ISBN 1-85075-069-6
    ISBN 1-85075-068-8 Pbk

CONTENTS

ACKNOWLEDGMENT

I wish to acknowledge with gratitude the help of Dr J.E. Bickersteth, my former colleague on the staff of the Department of Theology in the University of Hull. She has read two sets of troublesome proofs with her usual scholarly accuracy and meticulousness.

A.T.H.

ABBREVIATIONS

BT	Babylonian Talmud
CBQ	*Catholic Biblical Quarterly*
ET	English Translation
ET	*Expository Times*
EVV	English Versions
JBL	*Journal of Biblical Literature*
LXX	The Septuagint
MT	The Masoretic Text
Nov. T.	*Novum Testamentum*
NTS	*New Testament Studies*
SJT	*Scottish Journal of Theology*
TDNT	*Theological Dictionary of the New Testament*
TWNT	*Theologisches Wörterbuch zum Neuen Testament*
ZNW	*Zeitschrift für die Neutestamentliche Wissenschaft*

The English version of the Bible used is the Revised Standard Version.

The text of the Hebrew Bible is that of G. Kittel, *Biblia Hebraica* (Stuttgart, 1945).

The LXX text of the Greek New Testament is that published by the United Bible Societies, ed. K. Aland *et al.* (Stuttgart, 1966).

Chapter 1

THE CROSS IN THE END TIME

I

This work has its origin in my reading of the Daily Office. I was reading in course Paul's first letter to the Corinthians, and I came to chapter four, verses six to thirteen. I was struck on this occasion by two things: first, the strangeness of the language. Why does Paul describe the activity of himself and his companions in a series of remarkable contrasts, indeed paradoxes? And secondly why is the language so reminiscent of an atonement? Much of vv. 9-13 could be very appropriately applied to the life, sufferings, and death of Jesus Christ. I could not recollect ever having read a commentary on First Corinthians which explored these questions in any depth. In particular I was interested by the use of περικαθάρματα and περίψημα in v. 13.

Subsequently another passage in my daily reading seemed to provide some sort of a link with 1 Cor. 4.9-13. It must have occurred in Holy Week, because only then do we read Lamentations. The verse was Lam. 3.45: 'Thou hast made us an offscouring and refuse among the peoples'. I explored this connection to some extent and published a brief article on it in the *Expository Times*,[1] an article which I make use of in a subsequent chapter. I later read a short paper on this passage in 1 Corinthians to a seminar at a conference. The hunt was now up, and I began to examine a number of other passages in the Pauline corpus where similar expressions occurred. I wanted to find out what was the theology behind these passages, why they were always expressed in terms of paradox, and whether the language really implied an atoning activity on the part of the apostles, a thought very much contrary to the theological tradition in which I had been brought up.

As I continued exploring I began to glimpse a connection with the teaching of Jesus. This demanded an explanation. The theme of cosmic conflict, or, as I prefer to put it, *militia Christi*, also kept appearing. This had to be included in my study as well. As soon as I began to read those scholars who had written on the same subject, or related subjects, I began to realize that in fact eschatology was the clue to Paul's thought in this area. Indeed I was able to prove for myself the truth of the principle which is often enunciated by modern scholars who are not too much under the influence of the Lutheran tradition, that the root of Paul's theology is eschatology rather than justification by faith. In this area tribute must be paid to E. Güttgemanns, whose book is absolutely essential reading for anyone who wishes to understand Paul's theology of the cross.[2] Naturally I refer to it in detail in a later chapter and indeed throughout this book. This does not mean that I accept all his conclusions.

From the point of view of one who is concerned with Christian theology, it is not satisfactory merely to elucidate Paul's theology of the cross. It is also extremely desirable that one should also attempt to see how that theology fared at the hands of his immediate successors; and also that one should try to make sense of that theology in the context of our church situation today, not the least significant of whose features is that the *parousia* has not arrived, as Paul believed it would arrive very soon. Both these tasks I have endeavoured to fulfil.

We begin, then, with an exposition of the theme by means of an examination of certain passages in 1 Corinthians, and of one particular passage in 2 Corinthians. We follow up with a detailed study of four key passages in Paul's letters in which the paradox of the cross is expounded as it relates to the life of the apostolic community. These are mostly from the Corinthian correspondence, though we do also consider a relevant passage from Philippians and others from Romans and Galatians. The scriptural background is examined and we relate these passages quite frequently to Jesus' own teaching. There follows a chapter on the *militia Christi* and its relevance for this theme. Next comes a review of this material in the light of what scholars have said about it, in which we try to answer five fundamental questions which seem to emerge. After this we briefly examine the rôle of the Deutero-Paulines and subsequent development as far as concerns the theology of the cross in relation to the apostolic community. In a final chapter we draw some conclusions about Paul's use of paradox, about the question of early Catholicism and eschatology, and about the relevance of our studies to the doctrine of the Church and of the ordained ministry.

When Aaron was taxed by Moses with having led the people into idolatry during Moses' absence on Mount Sinai, his answer, it has always seemed to me, was singularly ingenuous:

> And I said to them, 'Let any who have gold take it off'; so they gave it to me, and I threw it into the fire, and there came out this calf (Exodus 32.24).

I can say much the same thing as far as this study is concerned. I hope I may get off as lightly as Aaron did.

II

The theme of this book is the paradox of the cross, so by way of prologue we give some attention to two passages in 1 Corinthians and one in 2 Corinthians. The first two illustrate the nature of the paradox, and the second outlines the connection with the community which is, we believe, so central in Paul's thought. We shall try to clarify Paul's meaning by turning wherever possible to his sources in scripture.

We begin by drawing attention to an article by Professor Morna Hooker.[3] She is commenting on the obscure phrase τò μὴ ὑπὲρ ἃ γέγραπται which Paul uses in 1 Cor. 4.6, the verses leading up to the first of our four key passages which we examine in detail later on. She suggests that the phrase must refer to certain specific scripture passages, and she cites the passages quoted in 3.19-20 from Job 5.13 and Ps. 94.11. She also points out that there are other scripture quotations earlier on in this epistle, such as Isa. 29.14, quoted in 1.19 (a passage which we shall look at presently). 'The teaching which Paul gave to the Corinthians was the fulfilment of the scriptures', she writes (p. 130). The false teachers whom Paul is opposing were embroidering the message of the scriptures and thereby falsifying it. They were 'going beyond what is written'. This is a most illuminating suggestion. It implies that when we examine the scriptural background indicated for us by Paul's quotations we are not pursuing idle fancies but actually entering into the sources of Paul's theology of the cross.

Nowhere is the paradox of the cross more clearly stated than in 1 Corinthians 1.18-31. The most important part is contained in 1.18-25:

> For the word of the cross is folly to those who are perishing, but to
> us who are being saved it is the power of God. For it is written:
>
> I will destroy the wisdom of the wise, and the cleverness of the
> clever I will thwart
>
> Where is the wise man? Where is the scribe? Where is the debater
> of this age? Has not God made foolish the wisdom of the world?

Nearly all commentators emphasize the element of paradox here.
J. Weiss writes:[4] 'For those who are being saved Christ's death on the
cross is not now a sign of God's weakness or Christ's . . . but a proof
of God's supreme power', and he describes it as 'a supreme paradox'.
Conzelmann[5] defines 'the word of the cross' as 'an exhaustive
statement of the content of the gospel'. 'The foolishness', he adds, 'is
of a dialectical kind . . . Paul is playing with a positive and a negative
evaluation of σοφία'. On v. 21 he comments: 'The non-recognition of
God is not merely a negative act; it is the active refusal of
recognition'. He goes on: 'Preaching is not merely *considered* to be
foolish; it *is* foolish by God's resolve. He adds that τὸ μωρὸν τοῦ
θεοῦ means God's dealings with the world—revelation is not formal
communication of new knowledge about God, but an act of
salvation'. F.J. Ortkemper in a thoughtful article enlarges this
understanding of the passage:[6] 'For Paul', he writes, 'the cross is not
only an external symbol of Christian faith and life, it indicates an
understanding of the world and of ourselves. *The cross indicates the
relation of Christ to the world*' (his italics, p. 8). Further, '*The cross is
the criterion and norm of Christian thought and conduct* (p. 11)'. And
'*the death and resurrection of Jesus are for Paul no mere events of past
history*'. He goes on to explain that the crucified Lord acts in the
community in preaching, in baptism, and in the eucharist. H.
Lietzmann[7] coins the phrase 'die Umkehrung der Werte im neuen
Aion'. A.J.M. Wedderburn in an article on v. 21, ἐν τῇ σοφίᾳ τοῦ
θεοῦ,[8] says that the ἐν indicates 'the circumstances under which
something takes place'. This phrase has 'a similar function in the first
part of the verse to that of εὐδόκησεν ὁ θεός in the second'. And he
suggests that it indicates a dispensation. Only Robertson and
Plummer, writing from the comfortable security of the Edwardian
era, tend to play down the paradox:[9] 'God's wisdom', they write, 'at
its lowest is wiser than men's'. But in fact the cross is not a
demonstration of God's wisdom at its lowest but at its highest.
  Having thus outlined the central significance of the cross for Paul,

we may go on to examine his scriptural sources here. The only
explicit quotation occurs in 1.19:

ἀπολῶ τὴν σοφίαν τῶν σοφῶν, καὶ τὴν σύνεσιν τῶν συνετῶν
ἀθετήσω

This comes from Isa. 29.14b. This is a passage which was evidently a
favourite one among early Christians. The previous verse, which
refers to the purely external observance of God's commandments by
Israel, is quoted or echoed more than once in the NT; see Mark 7.6-7
(parallel Matt. 15.8-9); Col. 2.22. And Isa. 29.16 'Shall the potter be
regarded as the clay etc.' is quoted in Rom. 9.20. An earlier verse in
the same chapter, 29.10, is quoted in Rom. 11.8, 'for the Lord has
poured out upon you a spirit of deep sleep etc.' The MT expresses the
meaning of 29.14b more impersonally:

> the wisdom of their wise men shall perish,
> and the discernment of their discerning men shall be hid.

But the sense is no doubt that it is God who will destroy the wisdom
of the wise and obscure the intelligence of the intelligentsia. The LXX
has personalized it:

> 'I will destroy the wisdom of the wise,
> and I will hide the intelligence of the intelligentsia'.

Why Paul should substitute ἀθετήσω for the κρύψω of the LXX is not
clear. Robertson and Plummer refer to 'Paul's usual freedom of
citation'. Goudge[10] suggests that it may be due to the influence of Ps.
32.10 (LXX), where the LXX has κύριος . . . ἀθετήσει δε λογισμοὺς
λαῶν. Certain other verses in Isaiah 29 might well have appealed to
Paul. In v. 18 we read

> In that day the deaf shall hear the words of a book, and out of their
> gloom and darkness the eyes of the blind shall see.

Paul would understand this as a prediction of the acceptance by
Christians, Jews and Gentiles alike, of the fulfilment of prophecy in
the career of Jesus Christ. The LXX of v. 9 is literally 'and the poor
will rejoice because of the Lord in joy, and those among men who
have given up hope will be filled with joy'. This would emphasize the
bouleversement produced by the cross.

Moreover, the first half of the verse actually quoted by Paul here
(v. 14a) underlines the marvellous nature of God's dealings:

'therefore, behold, I will again do marvellous things with this people, wonderful and marvellous'.

In its translation of v. 14a the LXX omits altogether any reference to marvels; but Symmachus offers:

παραδοξάσαι τὸν λαὸν τοῦτον παραδοξασμῷ καὶ παραδόξως

This is a rendering which can hardly be accused of playing down the paradox.

Paul therefore, we may conclude, uses this quotation from Isaiah 29 because it comes from a passage in which he would trace the paradox and the wonder of the cross. He follows it with words which seem to echo another passage from Isaiah. 33.18. Paul writes:

ποῦ σοφός; ποῦ γραμματεύς; ποῦ συζητητής τοῦ αἰῶνος τούτου;

In Isa. 33.17f. the prophet promises his people that there will come a time when they will see the King in his beauty and then they will say: 'What has happened to the Assyrian bureaucrats who were reckoning up the booty of Jerusalem?' The RSV translates 18 thus:

'Where is the clerk? Where is the one who weighs, where is the one who counts the towers?'

The LXX renders the first phrase ποῦ εἰσιν οἱ γραμματικοί; But Symmachus is much closer to Paul's words, ποῦ ἐστιν ὁ γραμματεύς; The Targum[11] tends to loose it from the context of the Assyrian occupation and also to highlight the element of *bouleversement*:

The glory of the Shekinah of the everlasting king in his beauty shall thine eyes see; thou shalt observe and look on them that go down to the valley of Gehinnom. Thy heart shall muse on mighty things. Where are the scribes? ... Where are the reckoners? Let them come, if they can, to reckon the number of the slain of the chiefs of the armies of the mighty men.

Naturally editors have speculated as to whether Paul's 'wise men, scribe, and debater' refer to different categories of people. U. Wilckens[12] believes that σοφός refers to Greeks and γραμματεύς to Jewish rabbis (p. 522). Billerbeck[13] points out that συζητητής corresponds to דורש, one who searches the scriptures; and the rabbis certainly understood Isa. 29.14b in terms of searching the Torah. In much the same vein K. Müller suggests that the three words σοφός, γραμματεύς, and συζητητής all refer to Jewish defenders of the Torah (p. 251).[14] At least we may suggest that Paul saw in these two passages in Isaiah 29 and 33 respectively a prophecy of the wonder and the *bouleversement* that was to be caused by the cross, and the over-turning of the traditional Jewish understanding of the ways of God.

There may be a link between our passage, in which Paul lays such stress on the foolishness of the preaching and even writes of the foolishness of God, and the well-known passage in Matthew and Luke where Jesus rejoices that God has hidden these things from the wise and has revealed them to babes. See Matt. 11.26; Luke 10.21. The Greek vocabulary is different, since the Synoptic passages have νηπίοις, which is not the same thing as Paul's μωρία. On the other hand the suggestion of a dispensation is conveyed by οὕτως εὐδοκία ἐγένετο ἔμπροσθέν σου of Matthew and Luke, which reminds us of εὐδόκησεν ὁ θεός in 1 Cor. 1.21, and vv. 26-28 of the same chapter describe the low social status of the Christians in Corinth who have understood God's revelation in the cross. It would not therefore be far-fetched to suggest that Jesus speaking with prophetic inspiration of God's revelation of himself to the poor before the event of the cross and resurrection has its true counterpart in Paul's writing of that revelation now known after the event to those who were neither wise nor learned nor socially superior, but who had the simplicity of faith.[15]

Before leaving this passage we should notice two more points. W. Bender reminds us that the phrase ἐν Χριστῷ Ἰησοῦ in 1.30 should be taken in its full community sense.[16] He points to the parallel with 2 Cor. 5.21: the revelation of God in the cross is integrally bound up with the salvation which God has brought in Christ, and that is worked out in the community. And secondly R. Penna[17] claims that, despite the absence of explicit mention of the resurrection, it is implied in the phrase θεοῦ δύναμις which Paul uses in vv. 18 and 24. The word of the cross, writes Penna, can be called 'the power of God' because 'the genuine apostolic kerygma is nothing else but the prolongation, and in a certain sense the ritualization, of the divine work fulfilled in the historic Christ' (p. 292). Perhaps 'ritualization (*ritualizzazione*)' is not a very happily chosen word. 'Representation' might be better. But the point is surely valid.

We pass on to our second passage from 1 Corinthians, 3.18-21. But we should observe *en passant* that the mysterious verse 2.9, which has caused such perplexity to scholars, probably refers primarily at least not to future rewards but to that event of the cross and resurrection.[18] In 3.18-21 we have two quotations from scripture, the first from Job 5.13 and the second from Ps. 94.11. Paul must have connected these two quotations himself, for they would hardly be likely to figure in an early Christian *testimonia* collection. Paul's version of the Job citation is quite different from that of the LXX, though it renders the MT quite accurately. Héring thinks that Paul must have read the book of Job in a different translation from the LXX,[19] but B. Schaller[20] has recently argued very convincingly that what Paul was using was not another Greek translation but a revision of the LXX text. He writes of 'rezensionellen Bearbeitungen des Septuaginta-Textes in vorchristlicher Zeit' (p. 26).

If we look at both these OT passage we can see why they appealed to Paul. The Job passage comes from Eliphaz's first speech. It is a general disquisition on the unsearchable nature of God, a theme very congenial to Paul; witness Rom. 11.33-36, where Job is once again cited. Only two verses previous to the one quoted by Paul we read:

> he (God) sets on high those who are lowly,
> and those who mourn are lifted to safety.

The LXX translates the second line with

καὶ ἀπολωλότας ἐξεγείροντα

If Paul had this in his text it would speak to him of Christ's resurrection.

In his citation of Ps. 94.11 (LXX 93.11) Paul has substituted σοφῶν for the LXX ἀνθρώπων. The LXX is an accurate rendering of the MT, which has אדם here. Héring believes that Paul may have had ἀνθρώπων in his text and glossed it by altering it to σοφῶν in order to make his point. Weiss points out that the psalmist says men are vanity, but Paul applies it to their thoughts. He calls Paul's substitution of σοφῶν a targumic usage. The context of the psalm is one in which vengeance is called down on the unrighteous. The proud and wicked seem to be supreme, but they are really fools, for they do not realize that God is in control and will punish them. The psalm as read in the LXX could be looked on as an utterance of the Messiah, persecuted and done to death, but still looking by faith for God's deliverance. Verse 14 says that God has not forsaken his people, a point which Paul makes in Rom. 11.2. In v. 17 the psalmist declares that if the Lord had not helped him his soul would have dwelt in Hades. A literal translation of the LXX in v. 19 is:

'Lord, according to the multitude of pains in my heart, thy comforts have loved my soul.'

The theme of the wonderful nature of the cross whereby all calculations of men were upset and an unexpected deliverance was provided for the low and humble is thus illuminated for Paul by the scriptural background to his thought. We may now proceed to the second passage from the Corinthian letters which we have in mind, one in which both the eschatological and the community aspects of Paul's theology come to expression.

III

The passage we are now to consider is 2 Cor. 1.18-22, with special reference to v. 20. It is significant for our purpose because it contains so many of the themes with which we are to be concerned, all expressed in a short compass. Indeed v. 20 is perhaps the most compressed verse in the entire New Testament. The second clause in it contains more Pauline theology than any other half-verse in the entire Pauline corpus:

διὸ καὶ δι' αὐτοῦ <sc. Χριστοῦ> τὸ ᾽Αμὴν τῷ θεῷ πρὸς δόξαν δι' ἡμῶν.
That is why we utter the Amen through him to the glory of God.

The whole passage is an exposition of Paul's doctrine of the Church's existence in Christ. The eschatological element is clearly marked: Christians are living in the era in which God's promises are being fulfilled in Christ. But this is taking place in the Christian community. The Christ of whom Paul writes is the risen Christ, living in the Christian community. The tenses used all suggest an act in the past resulting in an existing situation. See γέγονεν in v. 19. The verb κηρυχθείς in v. 19 also refers to a past event, the proclamation of Christ in Corinth. But this in turn presupposes the event of the cross and resurrection. We could paraphrase v. 20b thus:

Because Christ has in his sufferings, cross, and resurrection fulfilled the promises of God recorded in scripture, the 'Yes' of faith is uttered by the worshipping congregation to God's glory through Christ present in the congregation as a result of our efforts, i.e. those of Paul and his companions who have preached the gospel in Corinth.

This is how Barrett[21] understands δι᾽ ἡμῶν, and he is probably right, though the sense could be the "Yes" is uttered in Christ by us Christians'.[22] But to take δι᾽ αὐτοῦ and δι᾽ ἡμῶν to refer to the same activity is awkward. Later Christian theology would probably prefer to say that the worshipping community acts 'through Christ in the Spirit' (cf. Eph. 2.18). But Paul does not always successfully distinguish between the activity of the risen Christ and the activity of the Holy Spirit, and he makes it clear in verse 22 that the Christians have the Spirit in their hearts.

Commentators have not perhaps accorded this passage all the attention it deserves. Goudge[23] suggests that Jer. 11.5 may be in Paul's mind. This is a passage in which God promises blessings on obedience and curses on disobedience, and Jeremiah responds by saying: 'So be it, Lord'. The Hebrew is אמן which the LXX renders with γένοιτο. Schlier[24] comments: 'To say Amen is the right of the baptised λαός' (p. 337). He compares Rev. 3.14. In connection with this Revelation passage, but not with 2 Cor. 1.20, he refers to Isa. 65.16. Strachan[25] merely observes that the Christian congregation utters 'amens' in worship.

J. Héring claims that Paul's repudiation of a 'Yes and No' approach is a repudiation of dialectic, and he amusingly adds 'ô Kierkegaard!'. But there is no real occasion for regret as there is plenty of dialectic in connection with the paradox of the cross. Many commentators emphasize that here Christ is a sort of Amen incarnate. Thus Lietzmann has 'das personifierte Ja'.[27] He adds, 'It is not a question of a Yes or No that Christ utters, but of the Yes that he is'. Torrance[28] describes Christ as 'the incarnate faithfulness of God' (p. 112), but also as the Church's response; he refers to our passage as being one 'according to which Jesus Christ is not only the faithful *Yes* of God to men, but *is also the faithful Amen* of man to God' (p. 114, italics his).

I suggest that a study of Isa. 65.15-16 in its context is the best way in which to approach this passage:

> (v. 15) You shall leave your name to my chosen for a curse,
> and the Lord God will slay you;
> but his servants he will call by a different name.
> (v. 16) So that he who blesses himself in the land
> shall bless himself by the God of truth,
> and he who takes an oath in the land
> shall swear by the God of truth;

because the former troubles are forgotten
and are hid from my eyes.

We should note first that what the RSV renders with 'a different name' is literally 'one name', שם אחר. The LXX translates with ὄνομα καινόν, 'a new name'. The Vulgate offers 'nomine alio'. In the MT the phrase translated 'by the God of truth' is באלהי אמן, 'by the God of Amen'. The LXX translates this with τὸν θεὸν τὸν ἀληθινόν, but the Vulgate offers the more literal version 'in Deo amen'. Commentators on the whole tend to claim that the use of Amen as a liturgical response is too late to be appropriate here, and they therefore want to point the Hebrew not אֹמֶן but אָמֵן. So Whitehouse, Duhm, Skinner, Box[29], Whybray. But Delitzsch[30] retains אָמֵן. Bonnard[31] offers the most theologically significant comment on Isa. 65.16. He writes:

> Amen is the word which guarantees the validity of oaths and the efficacy of blessings (and of curses) . . . The solid 'amen' is thus an attitude of God, just as are its synonyms derived from the verb aman, which means 'to carry', 'to be stable', and consequently 'to be true and faithful' . . . God's words, which are always expressed in acts, constitute 'the truest of the true'.

He describes Jesus Christ as 'l'Amen fait homme'.

The Targum renders 65.16ab with: 'He that blesseth in the earth shall bless by the living God, and he that sweareth in the earth shall swear by the living God'. The words translated 'by the living God' are in the Aramaic באלהא קים. In Aramaic קים can mean 'firmly established', but an alternative translation is 'living, existing', which is the one that Stenning has preferred. In view of the MT אמן and the LXX τὸν θεὸν τὸν ἀληθινόν the rendering 'reliable, truthful (in the Hebrew sense)' is perhaps preferable. Kissane thinks that in this context the phrase means not 'the God who fulfils his promises' but 'the true God as opposed to the pagan gods'.[32] Symmachus here translates with ἐν τῷ θεῷ ἀμήν, and this rendering was known to Eusebius.[33]

The suggestion that Isa. 65.16 is in the background to this passage is powerfully confirmed by an article by Brownlee.[34] He points to a passage in the Qumran documents, 1QS 10.1-4, which 'has a mystical interpretation of Isaiah lxv.16, when even the Masoretic text אמן is vocalised *amen* (amen) not *omen* (truth)'. He believes that Aleph is taken as referring to God and the Mem and the Nun refer to the coming priestly Messiah (p. 201). He comments: 'Paul may not have been ignorant of the messianic interpretation of the Amen in

Isaiah lxv.16 when he wrote that the 'Yes' and the 'Amen' are to be
found in Christ (II Cor. i.19-20)' (p. 206).

We may assume two things at least: firstly, that Paul knew the
Hebrew of the passage in the sense that he knew the original was 'the
God of Amen', whether the knowledge came to him direct from the
Hebrew text or from a Greek text such as that which Symmachus
presents. And secondly, whatever might have been the case when Isa.
65.16 was written, by Paul's day the phrase was understood as
meaning 'the God of Amen' and not just 'the faithful God'. Of course
Paul also knew that 'the God of Amen' also meant 'the faithful God'
because in 2 Cor. 1.18 he actually writes πιστὸς δὲ ὁ θεός. But he
must have read 'Amen' in the text because he calls Christ the one in
whom the Amen took place. Besides the references to Amen, there
are two other ways in which this Isaiah passage is very appropriate to
Paul's message. It is a highly eschatological passage. The verse with
which we are concerned occurs in the middle of what is to happen in
the future when God vindicates the righteous. And in the very next
verse we have the announcement that God will create 'new heavens
and a new earth'. The other remarkable point of similarity is that in
this Isaiah passage we read much about God's opponents, and in
2 Corinthians generally, and very specifically in 1.12, 17, Paul
certainly has in mind the accusations which his opponents in
Corinth have been making against him.

It may even be that Paul actually saw in this verse a reference to
God in another mode. He may very well have interpreted the passage
to mean that 'he who blesses himself on the earth will bless himself
by the God (who is called) Amen'. This is the 'one name' or the
'different name' (if we follow the LXX) to which Isa. 65.15 refers. In
other words, Paul does here what he does in other parts of his
writings, he finds here a reference to Christ as God, or at least to
Christ whom he recognizes as God. This no doubt explains partly at
least why Paul so early in the history of Christianity expounds so
exalted a christology. He believes that he finds in scripture
justification for ranking Jesus with God.

We may say therefore that we have in 2 Cor. 1.18-22 a passage in
which nearly all the characteristics of Paul's thought with which we
are to be concerned in this study appear. It is explicitly an assertion
that Jesus Christ fulfils all the promises of God. But that in its turn
reminds us that these promises are to be found in scripture. Hence if
we can identify the passage or passages in scripture which Paul has in

mind as he writes, we can be greatly helped to understand his thought. There is also a reference to the apostolic group in these verses. See v. 19, 'Silvanus and Timothy and I', not to mention the δι' ἡμῶν of v. 20, if Barrett's interpretation is correct. This does not, however, exclude the Christian community in Corinth as a whole, since they are certainly intended in ἡμᾶς σὺν ὑμῖν in v. 21, and the mention of the pledge of the Spirit being given in our hearts implies them also. The fundamental doctrine of Christians being 'in Christ' is surely implied in v. 20 also, since, though it is perhaps primarily the apostolic group through whom the Yes is pronounced through Christ by means of their proclamation of the gospel, the use of the liturgical phrase 'the Amen' must imply congregational worship, and this certainly includes the Corinthian Christians as a whole.[35]

The one outstanding feature which is lacking here is any mention of the cross, a lack which is amply made up for in the ensuing epistle. But that is why we have begun our main study not with this passage, appropriate though it would be as a proemium, but with two other passages in which the centrality and the paradoxical nature of the cross are fully expounded.

Chapter 2

RECONCILIATION BY ATONEMENT: 1 COR. 4.10-13

I

If Professor Hooker is right in the article referred to above (ch. 1, n. 3), Paul in 1 Cor. 4.6-13 is proceeding to describe, as far as concerns the life of the apostolic group, the consequences of the scriptural prophecies already set out in his exposition of the paradox of the cross. In the course of this exposition he contrasts the life of the apostles with the superior, patronizing attitude of the Corinthian Christians. One suspects that an influential element in the Corinthian church was claiming to be a spiritual élite, persons who had already triumphed once and for all, and who therefore had no need of the cross or of the sufferings and hardship endured by Paul and his companions. Paul describes by contrast the difficulties of the apostolic vocation, not in order to elicit sympathy, but in order to persuade the Corinthians to abandon their 'balcony' attitude and to come down into the arena in order to share his strenuous existence. The apostolic life is not something to be confined to the apostles; it is to be passed on to the church which they serve.

In the course of this description we encounter the first of these remarkable series of paradoxes which have occasioned this present work. As a matter of fact we have two literary forms here: a set of contrasts followed by a set of paradoxes. The contrasts are those between the situation of the Corinthians and that of the apostles. These contrasts are contained in v. 10; the paradoxes run from v. 11 to v. 13. But first of all in v. 9 Paul makes these mysterious references to himself and his companions as 'men sentenced to death etc.'. This properly belongs to the *militia Christi* and will be discussed there. There runs through the whole passage a strong emphasis on justification by faith: because God has through the cross and

resurrection of Jesus Christ brought about the salvation of mankind
in his own unexpected way, there is no room left for claims to
individual merit or achievement. It seems very probable that certain
persons in the Corinthian church were claiming superiority because
of their spiritual experience, their visions and revelations, or even
because of their remarkable powers of oratory. This is important to
bear in mind in view of that question which we must presently
discuss: does the activity of the apostolic group actually have atoning
value or not?

Héring, commenting on v. 10, says that the first half of each
contrasting couple expresses a cruel reality, and the second an
illusion. This does not do justice to Paul's subtle style, for in fact in
the third of the contrasts Paul reverses the order: the illusion comes
first. In any case, is 'cruel reality' a just description of the phrases
'fools for Christ's sake...weak...held in disrepute'? Paul at least did
not think of it as cruel. It is in fact an expression of that remarkable
exchange which we shall meet again in 2 Cor. 4.10-12, where also
there occurs a series of paradoxes, but this time they precede the
contrasts. The Corinthians are encouraged to exchange their
'wisdom', their 'strength', their 'respectability' (ἔνδοξοι) for the
weak, despised, and vulnerable position of the apostles, just as in
2 Cor. 4.2-10 the dying life of the apostles, whereby the Corinthians
are to gain the life of Christ, is to be reproduced in the Corinthians
themselves, so that they too can die in order that ultimately (at the
parousia) they may be raised with the apostles (see 2 Cor. 4.14).

In vv. 11 and 12a we have an apparently straightforward account
of the precarious and taxing life of the apostles. In vv. 12b-13 this
passes into the series of paradoxes to which we have referred, ending
with the remarkable nouns περικαθάρματα and περίψημα being
applied to the apostles. Here is most acutely posed the question: does
Paul deliberately use of the apostles language which would seem to
apply primarily to Christ, and does he therefore mean that the life of
the apostles has atoning value, as has the life of Christ? Billerbeck
compares Wis. Sol. 2.16ab, where the ungodly complain: 'We are
considered by him (the righteous man) as something base, and he
avoids our ways as unclean'. There is no common element of
vocabulary with 2 Cor. 4.9-13, and we doubt if Paul had this passage
in mind. He is describing a dialectical situation: not only does Paul
regard as worthless what traditional Judaism regards as valuable (see
Phil. 3.2-11 which we discuss in Chapter 5), and Paul regards as

supremely valuable what the Jews regard as scandalous (a crucified Messiah), but because Christ, who has the value of God, has allowed himself to be treated as offscourings, Paul and his companions are to be treated in the same way so that the effect of the divine salvation may be conveyed to the world, and the Corinthian Christians may themselves be drawn into the self-renouncing process. It seems to be in fact a three-tier process: first God in Christ through the cross and resurrection has reversed traditional values and demonstrated the sort of life he requires of those who believe. Next Paul and his companions (and also presumably any others who preach the true gospel anywhere) are commissioned to proclaim this message and in the course of the proclamation to represent in their lives the sufferings, death, and in some sense the risen life of Christ, though their own resurrection is still in the future. Thirdly, this suffering, dying, risen life is in turn to be reproduced in the lives of all baptized Christians.

We have therefore in these verses not only several major problems, but also all the main themes of our study. We must now investigate these verses in greater detail.

II

We begin with one of the two main problems to be met with in this passage, namely the connection both with OT scripture and with the teaching of Jesus. We will begin by setting out the text involved. In 1 Cor. 4.12b-13a Paul writes his three paradoxes:

λοιδορούμενοι εὐλογοῦμεν,
διωκόμενοι ἀνεχόμεθα,
δυσφημούμενοι παρακαλοῦμεν.

When reviled, we bless;
when persecuted, we endure;
when slandered, we try to conciliate.

This is reproduced in Romans in terms of paraenesis, thereby neatly demonstrating that Paul does not mean this sort of life to be restricted to the apostles. Rom. 12.14 runs:

εὐλογεῖτε τοὺς διωκόντας,
εὐλογεῖτε καὶ μὴ κατάρασθε.

Bless those who persecute you;
bless and do not curse them.

But, as has been pointed out by many commentators, this sentiment is found in the teaching of Jesus. Luke 6.27-28 has:

ἀγαπᾶτε τοὺς ἐχθροὺς ὑμῶν
καλῶς ποιεῖτε τοῖς μισοῦσιν ὑμᾶς.
εὐλογεῖτε τοὺς καταρωμένους ὑμᾶς,
προσεύχεσθε περὶ τῶν ἐπηρεαζόντων ὑμᾶς.

Love your enemies,
do good to those who hate you;
bless those who curse you,
pray for those who abuse you.

Matthew's version of this is to be found in Matt. 5.44:

ἀγαπᾶτε τοὺς ἐχθροὺς ὑμῶν
κὰι προσεύχεσθε ὑπὲρ τῶν διωκόντων ὑμᾶς.[1]

We should also note 1 Pet. 2.23:

ὃς λοιδορούμενος οὐκ ἀντελοιδέρει,
πασχων οὐκ ἠπείλει.

When he was reviled he did not revile in return;
when he suffered, he did not threaten.

This passage is no doubt later than any of the others, but it contains the essential reminder that the conduct required, or described, in these passages was originally exemplified in Jesus himself, and that is why it is enjoined on Christians. Indeed the author of 1 Peter himself enjoins it, for in 3.9 he writes:

μὴ ἀποδιδόντες κακὸν ἀντὶ κακοῦ ἢ λοιδορίαν ἀντὶ λοιδορίας,
τοὐναντίον δὲ εὐλογοῦντες.

Do not return evil for evil or reviling for reviling; but on the contrary bless.

But this sentiment was not original in Jesus' teaching. It seems that Jesus was himself adapting the language of Psalm 109. To those who are familiar with the Psalter this may come as something of a surprise, since Psalm 109 is the clearest example of a 'cursing psalm' that we have, so much so that vv. 6-20 are actually bracketed in some versions of the Psalter intended for liturgical use, as being unsuitable for public worship. They constitute indeed a ferocious and comprehensive series of curses on the psalmist's opponents, of which perhaps the most appalling is that to be found in v. 7b 'let his prayer be counted as sin'. But neither Jews nor early Christians viewed the

Psalter as we do today, and in fact this psalm was regarded as describing one who actually prayed for his enemies and showed love towards them.
Ps. 109.4-5 runs as follows:

> In return for my love they accuse me,
> even as I make my prayer for them.[2]
> So they reward me evil for good,
> and hatred for my love.

We should also notice v. 28a:

> Let them curse, but do thou bless.

The LXX (108.4) offers:

> ἀντὶ τοῦ ἀγαπᾶν με διέβαλλόν με,
> ἐγὼ δὲ προσευχόμην.
> καὶ ἔθεντο κατ᾽ ἐμοῦ κακὸν ἀντὶ ἀγαθῶν.
> καὶ μῖσος ἀντὶ τῆς ἀγαπήσεώς μου.

We should remember that ἀντὶ τοῦ ἀγαπᾶν με means 'instead of my loving', i.e. the love which I gave them, not 'instead of loving me'. For v. 28a the LXX has:

> καταράσονται αὐτοί, καὶ σὺ εὐλογήσεις.

There is some evidence that traditional Jewish exegesis regarded this psalm as giving an example of returning good for evil. In the *Midrash on the Psalms*[3] à propos Ps. 109.4 it is pointed out that at the festival of Tabernacles Israel offers up seventy bullocks for the seventy nations of the world, and prays for rain on all the earth. Of course it is assumed that the nations are persecuting Israel. It seems likely that at some point between the composition of Psalm 109 and the time of Jesus the sense of v. 28 had got changed to 'they curse but I bless'. This is shown both by Paul's λοιδορούμενοι εὐλογοῦμεν and Luke's εὐλογεῖτε τοὺς καταρωμένους ὑμᾶς.
In the Synoptic material Luke alone has

> εὐλογεῖτε τοὺς καταρωμένους ὑμᾶς

This is in fact verbally closer to 1 Cor. 4.12 and Rom 12.14 than is any of the other extracts from Jesus' teaching and is the only verbal link with Ps. 109.28a. It is relevant to observe that Luke is well acquanted with Psalm 109, assuming that he is the author of the book of Acts. In Acts 1.20b Peter quotes Ps. 109.8b (LXX 108.8b):

καὶ τὴν ἐπισκοπὴν αὐτοῦ λάβοι ἕτερος.
His office let another take.

The verse is applied to Judas Iscariot. If we look at another verse in its context in Ps. 109, we can see that only two verses previously it is said of the opponent:

Appoint a wicked man against him,
let an accuser bring him to trial.

The MT of v. 6b is literally:

and let Satan stand at his right hand.

The LXX renders this:

καὶ διάβολος στήτω ἐκ δεξίων αὐτοῦ
and a devil stand at his right hand.

Now according to both Luke and John this is exactly what happened to Judas Iscariot (Luke 23.3). John 13.2 says that the devil (τοῦ διαβόλου) put it into Judas' heart to betray Jesus. This is in fact one of the details in which Luke's special material and John's account agree. It seems that in one tradition of early Christianity Ps. 109.6-8 was seen as a prophecy of the fate of Judas Iscariot. Here then is another indication that early Christians were interested in Psalm 109. Jeremias, commenting on the language of Luke 6.27-28 and other Lukan passages, writes: 'Die im Nicht-Markusstoff begegnenden asyndetischen Imperative (z.B. Lk. 6.27f; 12.19; 15.23) sind vorlukanisch'.[4]

Bultmann, examining the two Synoptic passages that contain the logia about loving one's enemies, is uncertain whether Luke's difference from Matthew represents his own addition to the text of Q, or whether he had Q in a different form. Of Matt. 5.45 he says that it is one of those passages which are characteristic of Jesus' teaching.[5] C.G. Montefiore, commenting on the Lukan passage, remarks that the sentiment actually contradicts Psalm 109.[6] This is only so if we regard it from our modern point of view. As we have seen, the ancients saw it very differently. Billerbeck[7] compares Exod. 23.45, where the Israelite is ordered to rescue his enemy's ox or his ass if he finds it straying. Some rabbis said of this passage that the ox meant the non-Israelite. But they added that the animal must not be rescued if it was laden with wine for drink-offerings.

Weiss, commenting on 1 Cor. 4.12, compares Luke 6.27f. and suggests that Paul is echoing his master's words. Beyer also links together Luke 6.27-28, Matt. 5.44, Rom. 12.14 and 1 Cor. 4.12 and says of Christ's command: 'This has deeply stamped itself on early Christianity'. He believes that Paul is echoing Jesus' teaching (p. 761).[8]

It must be admitted that the only verbal echo of Jesus' words as recorded in the Synoptists is λοιδορούμενοι εὐλογοῦμεν. But Paul is well aware of the command to love one's enemies, as Rom. 12.17-20 makes clear. Also Luke's προσεύχεσθε περὶ τῶν ἐπηρεαζόντων ὑμᾶς is very much the same sentiment as Paul's δυσφημούμενοι παρακαλοῦμεν. Especially in view of 2 Cor. 5.20 ὑπὲρ Χριστοῦ οὖν πρεσβεύομεν, ὡς τοῦ θεοῦ παρακαλοῦντος δι᾽ ἡμῶν, 'So we are ambassadors for Christ, God making his appeal through us', we may say that the apostle's reaction to abuse and insult is to try to reconcile the opponents to God, an activity in which both prayer and love must have a part. It is premature to ask in what form Paul received this tradition of Jesus' teaching. That must be reserved for our discussion of 2 Cor. 6.3-10, where there are more parallels with Jesus' teaching to be examined.

Two important conclusions emerge from this study:

(a) Jesus based this part of his teaching on Psalm 109. He must have understood it as the psalm of the innocent sufferer who appeals to God to save him from his enemies. His sufferings have actually been brought on by his humble and loving behaviour. More than this, the behaviour of the righteous sufferer was to be a model for his followers. The citizens of the kingdom were to behave as the innocent servant of the Lord behaves.

(b) Paul not only knew of this element in Jesus' teaching, but he also applied it to the life-pattern of the apostolic community. It is remarkable that what appears in Jesus' teaching as instruction for the citizens of the kingdom appears in Paul's writings first of all not as instruction but as description. This is in fact the sort of life which the apostolic community is living. By 'apostolic community' I do not of course mean the twelve apostles or some supposed 'apostolic college' residing in Jerusalem and directing the destiny of the infant Church, as some theologians have fondly imagined. I mean the apostolic community in Paul's sense, that is those who in the end time have been commissioned to proclaim the saving act of God in Jesus Christ and have been thereby called to live the peculiar life of the apostolic community. It is very significant indeed that the life of the apostolic community can be described in terms which to some degree coincide with the description of the citizens of the kingdom. It suggests that there is a stronger link between Paul's teaching and the teaching of Jesus than has generally been allowed by modern scholars. Paul is related to the Jesus who lived and taught before the cross and resurrection. The members of the kingdom, or at least those who are being prepared for the coming of the kingdom, are now, after the great saving events, the members of the apostolic community in the dawning of the new age. This is a theme which we shall illustrate frequently throughout this work.

But the sequence does not end with Paul's description of the life of the apostolic community. In Romans the same teaching is applied to members of the Church. The original paraenesis of Jesus, which turned into description when applied to the apostles, has become paraenesis again when it is given in the context of Christian behaviour. The apostolic community does not exist merely for its own sake; its task is to pass on the message, and that means to pass on the life-pattern implied in the proclamation of the message. This is how the cross is woven into the very life of the Church; and this in turn brings up the question which we must now consider: is Christ's atoning work to be continued in the life of the apostles and ultimately in the life of the Church? Here too, as in the question of praying for one's enemies, we shall find ourselves being brought back to the Old Testament sources.

III

We are here concerned with two words, but we must quote them in their context:

> ὡς περικαθάρματα τοῦ κόσμου ἐγενήθημεν,
> πάντων περίψημα ἕως ἄρτι.

> we have become, and are now, as the refuse of the world,
> the offscouring of all things.

These two words περικαθάρματα and περίψημα are very remarkable. Both seem to have a strong overtone of expiation; they apply to persons, animals, or things that are thrown away or destroyed in order to avert divine displeasure. The word περικάθαρμα occurs in the LXX of Prov. 21.18.

περικάθαρμα δὲ δικαίου ἄνομος.

This translates the MT (כפר לצדיק רשע) which the RSV renders: 'the wicked is a ransom for the righteous'. C.H. Toy comments on the verse as follows:[10] 'when punishment is inflicted by God on a community, it is the bad man, and not the good on whom it falls . . . the thought appears to be simply that the bad and not the good suffer, a fact which is practically represented as a substitution of the former for the latter'. Nevertheless the notion of expiatory substitution must have clung to the word, and those who read their Bibles in Greek will certainly have read an element of substitution into it. The word περικαθάρματα means literally sweepings off the floor. The noun κάθαρμα can be used as a term of abuse. Hauck defines περικάθαρμα as an intensification of the profane κάθαρμα. It means 'an offering laden with guilt'.[11] He adds that such an offering in order to be effective must be voluntary. The word can also be used as a term of abuse meaning 'worthless'. A third meaning is 'that which is removed by means of the cleansing process'.

The word περίψημα means literally dirt scraped off the body. Photius writes that it was used of a human victim who was offered in order to placate Poseidon in time of great danger. It is used by Ignatius of Antioch to mean 'devoted servant' (*Eph.* 8.1), and he also uses the obscure phrase 'my spirit is a περίψημα of the cross' (*Eph.* 18.1), which may mean 'I am an abject and devoted servant of the cross'. See also *Ep. Barn.* 6.5. In the third century AD 'your *peripsēma*' became conventionalized so as to mean nothing more than 'your humble servant'. Stählin[12] says that the word could be a synonym for ἀντίλυτρον or ἀντίψυχον. He quotes a papyrus (P Michigan VIII 1951) as follows:

ὡς ἔβλαβές με χιλίας διακοσίας δραχμάς, περίψημά μου τοῦ υἱοῦ ἀπελθῶσιν.

Since you have cost me the loss of one thousand two hundred drachmas, write them off as a sacrifice in return for my son's safety.

It seems probable that behind these two words lies a passage from scripture. Lam. 3.45 runs as follows in the MT:

סחי ומאום תשימנו בקרב העמים

Thou hast made us offscouring and refuse among the peoples.

This looks very like περικαθάρματα and περίψημα, but it is very difficult indeed to find any verbal connection. As far as a sense parallel is concerned, περικαθάρματα τοῦ κοσμου and πάντων περίψημα correspond neatly to the MT's 'among the peoples'. The LXX has misunderstood the passage, not surprisingly, since סחי is a *hapax legomenon* in the Hebrew Bible. It offers:

καμμύσαι με καὶ ἀπωσθῆναι ἔθηκας ἡμᾶς ἐν μέσῳ τῶν λαῶν

The verb סחה 'to scrape away' is used in Prov. 2.22b for the treacherous being 'rooted out from' or 'scraped away from' the earth. Here then the idea of 'offscouring' is applied to the wicked. In Lam. 3.45 מאוס is an infinitive absolute of the quite common verb מאס 'to reject'. Symmachus gets nearer the correct sense in rendering the phrase with κοπρίαν καὶ κιβδηλείαν.[13] The Targum of Lam. 3.45 is

כניעתא ומאיסותא תשוי יתנא בחובנא ביני עממיא

Thou hast made us as a mockery and refuse among the peoples.

The second noun is of course cognate with the Hebrew verb מאס. If the first one is connected with the Hebrew root נוע, it can mean 'to shake the head in mockery'. Thus Symmachus's translation suggests he may have known the targumic tradition. The Vulgate is perhaps the most accurate rendering of all: 'Eradicationem et abiectionem posuisti me in medio populorum'.

    If we may assume as a working hypothesis that Paul had Lam. 3.45 in mind, perhaps using a Greek text nearer to that of Symmachus, or even translating directly from the Hebrew, we can see that this whole chapter would have appealed to him as depicting the sufferings of the Messiah, to be shared by faithful Israel. There is in this chapter an alternation between the first person singular and the first person plural which would have encouraged him to apply what was said about the Messiah to his servants also; vv. 42-43 are in the first person plural. Verse 30a, describing the condition which the sufferer should accept, runs: 'let him give his cheek to the smiter'. This is very reminiscent of Isa. 50.6a, which describes the suffering servant of the Lord.[15] We recollect that Jesus was struck on the cheek by those who arrested him (Mark 14.64 and pars.), and that Paul says that he and his companions are 'buffeted' (1 Cor. 4.11). The word is κολαφίζειν both in the LXX of Lam. 3.30 and in 1 Cor. 4.11. Then in v. 53 of Lamentations 3 the writer says:

    they flung me alive into the pit,
    and cast stones on me

which would well be taken by an early Christian as a prophecy of the death and burial of the Messiah. Verse 58 would be taken as a prophecy of the resurrection:

Thou hast taken up my cause, O Lord,
thou hast redeemed my life.

Given the belief which was certainly held by many early Christians, including Paul, that the sufferings, death, and resurrection of the Messiah were prophesied in many of the scriptures, this passage from Lamentations would seem a very likely one to have inspired the language of 1 Cor. 4.13. Paul would see in it the description of the atoning sufferings, death, and resurrection of the Messiah, to be reproduced in the lives of the apostolic community. Paul's strange language is accounted for by the words of Lam. 3.45.

Commentators on the whole have not easily accepted the conclusion that Paul by using this language is describing the life and sufferings of himself and his companions as having atoning efficacy, despite the strongly expiatory associations of the words he uses. Thus Allo does not believe that the apostles accepted like Christ the rôle of victims for the sins of the world.[16] Straub denies that one should read the meaning of 'scapegoat' in these two words.[17] Billerbeck seems to agree, since he translates περικαθάρματα with 'excrement', 'rubbish' and περίψημα with 'dirt', with no suggestion that Paul and his companions are substitutes for others. Stählin (pp. 89-90) is inclined to agree that they see themselves as having been appointed as substitutes. The aorist ἐγενήθημεν confirms this, and he well compares ἀπέδειξεν in v. 9.[18] The words, he says, must have conveyed to Paul's readers the thought of people who were destined to die on behalf of others (p. 90). He adds however 'but naturally Paul does not want to usurp the rôle of the crucified' (p. 91). This is hardly a satisfactory solution to the question. We have already noted the three meanings which according to Hauck the word can bear. περικάθαρμα can mean 'an offering laden with guilt', 'something worthless' and 'dirt removed'. He suggests that the word bears all three meanings in 1 Cor. 4.13. Güttgemanns specifically denies that Paul's life is atoning or is that of a martyr.[19] But he also writes 'Die Leiden des Apostels sind lediglich eine Form der Offenbarung des Christus'. H.D. Betz, in his discussion of the meaning of imitation in Paul's thought, describes baptism as a ὁμοίωμα τοῦ θανάτου τοῦ Χριστοῦ, not as a μίμησις. The Christian life is not a mystery drama but a *Vergegenwärtigung* of the historical events of Christ's suffering and death, a representation or realization.[20]

As we review this passage in 1 Corinthians 4, we must conclude, if the evidence presented above has any force, that Paul, in describing the life of the apostolic community, has in mind the tradition he knew of Jesus' teaching about the life and characteristics of the citizens of the kingdom, that he consciously modelled this description on the pattern of the sufferings and death of Jesus Christ, and that in doing so he was frequently inspired by his interpretation of scripture. We cannot avoid the conclusion also that Paul regarded the sufferings and possible death of the apostles as possessing an atoning, reconciling, salvific value. This does not mean, however, that he held some doctrine that ascribed salvation to man's unaided powers, nor that he believed the sufferings and death of Christ to have been somehow inadequate, so that they had to be supplemented by the sufferings and death of the apostles. All that Paul and his companions did and suffered they did and suffered *in Christ*. It was only because they were in Christ that their sufferings could be regarded as expiatory and reconciliatory. Paul is as far as possible from holding any doctrine which suggests that Christians could save themselves or others by their own efforts. As he read the scriptures he believed he found in them evidence that the Messiah was to suffer and die (and be raised from the dead), and that he would thereby bring about God's salvation promised in the last days. But in most of the passages in scripture where he found this evidence the language alternated between singular and plural, so that Paul had no difficulty in finding in scripture that extension of the Messiah's activity to that of his disciples which we have been examining. It is not a question of the Messiah ceasing to function and his disciples taking over; it is rather the Messiah active by means of the activity of his servants.

We have written above about God's saving activity taking place at three levels. It may be helpful to specify these levels once more, since we shall be meeting this feature of Paul's thought throughout the rest of this book. The salvific suffering of the Messiah and of his faithful followers is first prophesied in scripture. Then the Messiah appears, and in his teaching about the nature of the kingdom and of those who are to accept it he gives a description of that suffering, dying life which God can use for this redemptive purposes. Then in his suffering, death, and resurrection he gives the perfect pattern which itself effects the salvation. Then the apostolic community, heirs of the kingdom in the new age, manifest the same pattern of life, and, because Christ lives in them, continue God's saving activity based on the once-for-all events of Jesus Christ's career. Finally this pattern of life is to be reproduced in every new generation of Christians.

Purists might maintain that this is really a five-level process, but the last three levels are the most important: the Messiah's pattern of life, the apostolic community's representation of that life in the end time, the acceptance of this pattern of life by the Christian Church as it gradually realizes the necessity of living on in history. We have perhaps sufficiently clarified the nature of this pattern by means of a study of the first major passage in the Pauline letters. We must now trace and evaluate it through the other passages.

Chapter 3

THE LIVING AND THE DYING
OF THE APOSTOLIC COMMUNITY:
2 CORINTHIANS 4.7-15

I

Our next passage is even more directly and explicitly concerned with the apostolic ministry than was 1 Cor. 4.9-13, because it is set in the context of an exposition of what the apostolic ministry means. Whereas in 1 Corinthians Paul had gone on from an account of the significance of the cross to a discussion of the internal problems of the Corinthian church, which itself prompted the description of the ministry in 4.6-13, in 2 Corinthians Paul seems to be facing a more direct challenge to his authority. A group of persons within the church is claiming that they are true apostles, probably on the basis of special revelations, outstanding spiritual gifts, and fidelity to the Mosaic tradition. Paul responds by setting out the superiority of the ministry of the new covenant (ch. 3), then in 4.1-6 he refers to the nature of the message which the ministers have to proclaim, emphasizing (v. 5) that the message concerns not themselves but what God has done in Christ. The account of the ministry rises to a new point of tension and emotion in the passage we are to consider, in which the element of the cross, which has remained in the background since the beginning of the epistle, comes to the fore. The theme of the apostolic ministry continues to dominate for the next two and a half chapters, culminating in 6.3-10, which is the third main passage that we have to examine.

In 4.7-15, as in 1 Cor. 4.6-13, as the emotional temperature rises Paul seems to slip naturally into expressing himself in paradoxes and contrasts. The paradox of the cross has, it appears, to be expressed in paradoxical terms as it works itself out in the life of the ministry. Verse 7 states the paradox in terms of the contrast between the greatness of the message and the poverty of the means; vv. 8-9 revert to that paradox style which we have already encountered in 1 Cor. 4.10-13; and vv. 10-12 express the paradoxical exchange between life and death that goes on in the work of the ministry and the life of the Church. In vv. 13-14 we have an entirely characteristic appeal to scripture and a theologically necessary reference to the resurrection, without which the cross would be incomprehensible. So we have here a passage which seems to exhibit all the features of those elements in the Pauline letters with which we are concerned in this book.

We must begin however by deciding whether there is any special significance in the use by Paul of the word 'treasure'.

ἔχομεν δὲ τὸν θησαυρὸν τοῦτον ἐν ὀστρακίνοις σκεύεσιν.

But we have this treasure in earthen vessels.

This is the only place where Paul uses the noun θησαυρός.[1] There are a number of passages in scripture where the word σκεῦος with a disparaging adjective is used in the LXX to describe someone who is rejected or oppressed. One such is Jer. 22.28ab:

Is this man Coniah a despised, broken pot, a vessel no one cares for?

The LXX renders:

ἠτιμώθη Ἰεκονίας ὡς σκεῦος, οὗ οὐκ ἔστιν χρεία αὐτοῦ.

The MT is:

העצב נבזה נפוץ האיש הזה כניהו אם־כלי אין חפץ בו

The word עצב is rendered by Symmachus with περίψημα. But it is difficult to visualize Jeconiah as a type either of Christ or of Christ's apostles. Codex Marchalianus in the margin adds καὶ τὸ σπέρμα αὐτοῦ after ἐξερρίφθη (which it has instead of LXX ἠτιμώθη). This would certainly come nearer to Paul's context: Christ is the Davidic seed. Nearer still perhaps may be Lam. 4.2b in the LXX:

πῶς ἐλογίσθησαν εἰς ἀγγεῖα ὀστράκινα ἔργα χειρῶν κεράμεως

How have they been reckoned as earthen vessels, the work of mens' hands!

The reference is to 'the precious sons of Zion'. If our contention is correct that Lam. 3.45 lies behind 1 Cor. 4.13, this may be nearer the mark.[2] Billerbeck cites various rabbinic parallels: as wine is best kept not in silver or gold vessels, but in pottery, so the words of the Torah are only retained by those who abase themselves. Similarly the rabbis draw the analogy of wine being kept in earthen vessels to apply to a very ugly rabbi who was full of great wisdom. Schmiedel suggests that the earthen vessels are the apostles' bodies.[3] But Lietzmann rightly contends that we should think of them rather as 'menschliche Persönlichkeiten'. Bultmann says that the earthen vessels are 'weak ephemeral bodies' and the treasure is the διακονία τῆς δόξης. This seems a little inaccurate: the ὀστράκινα σκεύη correspond to ἡμεῖς. Lietzmann is right in saying that it is the persons of the apostles, not merely their bodies, that are contrasted with the treasure. In view of the scriptural background we have just referred to, it is likely that there is an overtone of contempt and rejection in the word here. Also Bultmann can hardly be right in saying that the treasure is the ministry. The treasure is surely 'the knowledge of the glory of God in the face of Christ' referred to in the previous verse. Collange has a different suggestion (p. 146): the phrase could indicate man as an instrument in the hand of God, and he compares the parable in Jer. 8.1-11. He agrees that the treasure is 'the light of the knowledge of God', which means in effect the proclamation of the gospel, an interpretation which brings him close to Bultmann. Windisch points out that ὀστράκινον σκεῦος is a regular expression in the LXX for a vessel used in Temple worship.[4] It refers here, he says, to the outer man, not the inner man of v. 16. This last comment is questionable; in vv. 16f. Paul is perhaps thinking of the spiritual bodies laid up for faithful disciples at the *parousia*; here he is contrasting not the outward appearance or bodily presence of the apostles with the glory of the knowledge of God in Christ which they have to communicate, but the apostles themselves, men exposed to every sort of danger and risk of death, men despised and rejected by the world, as Christ was. Barrett is therefore right when he comments that is the insignificance of God's servants that is emphasized.[5]

We must now pursue the possible link between this phrase and the logion attributed to Jesus about treasure. Matt. 6.19-21 runs:

> Do not lay up for yourselves treasures (μὴ θησαυρίζετε ὑμῖν θησαυρούς) on earth, where moth and rust consume and where thieves break in and steal, but lay up for yourselves treasure in heaven, where neither moth nor rust consumes and where thieves do not break in and steal.

/ Luke's version (Luke 12.32-34) is somewhat different:

> Fear not, little flock, for it is your Father's good pleasure to give
> you the kingdom. Sell your possessions and give alms; provide
> yourselves with purses that do not grow old, with a treasure
> (θησαυρόν) in the heavens that does not fail, where no thief
> approaches and no moth destroys. For where your treasure is, there
> will your heart be also.

It is interesting that Luke places the logion immediately after the
promise of the kingdom, thereby suggesting that the kingdom is the
treasure, a thought which, *mutatis mutandis*, brings him within
measurable distance of Paul in 2 Cor. 4.7.

This logion, which has all the characteristics of authenticity, may
have been influenced by a verse in Sir. 29.11. We can only quote it in
Greek, since the Hebrew has not survived:

> θὲς τὸν θησαυρόν σου κατ᾽ ἐντολὰς ὑψίστου
> καὶ λυσιτελεῖ σοι μᾶλλον ἢ τὸ χρυσίον.

> Lay up treasure according to the commandments of the Most High,
> and it will profit you more than gold.

But Box and Oesterley prefer the Syriac version, which they
translate:[6]

> Lay up for yourselves a treasure of righteousness and love,
> And it shall profit thee more than all that thou hast.

They maintain that this version seems more original than the Greek,
which 'reads as though it were merely explanatory'. Certainly this
version is nearer the spirit of the Synoptic logion. Even if direct
influence by Ben Sira on Jesus is not very likely, it indicates that this
sort of sentiment was quite in the tradition of late Judaism. We have,
however, yet to consider more carefully what Jesus meant by the
treasure.

There is a considerable difference between Matthew's version of
the logion and Luke's. McNeile believes that Matthew's is nearer the
original because it is more Hebraic.[7] Beare remarks of Luke's version
that the material 'must have come to him in a source which was not
used by Matthew'.[8] Creed says 'The heavenly purses which do not
wear out are peculiar to Luke, and are perhaps his own addition'.[9]
Klostermann is of the same opinion.[10] Bultmann puts the treasure-
sayings under the category 'Logia (Jesus as the Teacher of Wisdom)'.
The final sentence 'where your treasure is . . .' could originally, he

thinks, have been an independent maxim.[11] He gives Luke 12.33 as an example of Luke recasting parallelisms. On the whole it seems likely that Matthew is nearer the original,[12] though we should not ignore Luke's association of the logion with the kingdom.

What exactly does the treasure mean in this context? Commentators on the whole assume that it means accumulating a credit account with God in the world to come. So Plummer,[13] Lagrange,[14] Klostermann, Beare. E. Schweizer however is more discerning.[15] He writes: 'To say that "riches" bind our hearts is not simply to distinguish transitory riches from eternal ones. It is also to criticize the man who tries to lay up riches in heavenly acts of devotion. Its terseness makes it easily conceivable as a saying of Jesus, although we have no idea in what context it was originally spoken'. Like Bultmann, he thinks that Matt. 19.21 (= Luke 12.34) may originally have been a separate logion. He realizes that the language of this saying need have no relation to storing up a credit account with God. He writes: 'Ultimately, then, the riches in heaven can only be the kingdom of heaven itself, not specific rewards for specific acts'. This interpretation, which is surely correct, brings the logion closer both to Luke's context and to 2 Cor. 4.7.

In Jesus' teaching, then, the treasure is the kingdom, and in Paul's thought the treasure is the knowledge of God in Christ attainable by the coming of the kingdom through the life, death, and resurrection of Jesus Christ. Once more we seem to have arrived at the conclusion that those who are prepared to receive the kingdom during the period of Jesus' ministry are to be recognized after Jesus' death and resurrection as the apostolic group whose task it is to proclaim the gospel.

One is tempted to ask the very difficult question, in what form did the tradition of this logion of Jesus reach Paul? It is easy to say that it must have come from the Q source, because it is found in slightly different forms in Matthew and Luke but does not appear in Mark. But that does not help us very much to answer our question. Perhaps we might institute a tentative comparison between Matt. 6.19-34 and 2 Cor. 4.1–5.10. We will put the Pauline material on the left hand side, since it is written in a form that precedes Matthew by at least a generation. The question of the form of the Lukan material we will discuss later. The comparison might be laid out thus:

2 Cor. 4.1–5.10	*Matt. 6.19-34*	
4.1-5	serving two masters	6.24
4.6 God in Christ as light	the light of the body	6.22-33
4.7	treasure	6.19-21
4.16-5.10	living by faith	6.25-34

It is only fair to point out that Luke has all the same material as we
encounter in Matt. 6.19-34, but he has distributed it very differently.
Matt. 6.19-21 corresponds to Luke 12.32-34; Matt. 6.22-23 corresponds
to Luke 11.34-36; Matt. 6.24 corresponds to Luke 16.13; Matt. 6.25-
34 corresponds to Luke 12.22-32. This does not necessarily imply
that Matthew's order is secondary. Luke may have had his own
reasons for breaking up the material which in Matthew constitues a
solid block.

Paul, having made this reference to the treasure which is the
knowledge of God, goes on to give a graphic description of the
distractions of the apostolic calling, but concludes that it is all well
worth while for the sake of the knowledge of God in Christ, that is, of
the things that are eternal. A great deal of the teaching contained in
Matt. 6.19-34 is about the danger of distractions and the importance
of concentrating on what is essential, real, and eternal. If Paul knew
of this teaching in a form at all comparable with that in which
Matthew knew it, it was probably still in an oral form and had not yet
been written down in the form which it assumed in Q—if indeed Q
ever was a document and did not itself consist of oral tradition. But it
seems to me by no means beyond the bounds of possibility that as
Paul wrote the fourth chapter of Second Corinthians he had in mind
a corpus of dominical teaching known to him by oral tradition, and
that he is transposing into the conditions of the new age, after the
death and resurrection of the Messiah, teaching that was originally
given by Jesus to his disciples to prepare them for the coming of the
kingdom.[16]

II

The next natural section consists of vv. 8-9, including four antitheses,
which Héring calls 'les célèbres antithèses des v. 8 et 9', each
containing a first half which indicates a condition of difficulty or
danger, and a second half which limits the extent of the difficulty.
Windisch and Bultmann contrast 2 Cor. 1.8, where Paul says that
'we were so utterly, unbearably crushed that we despaired of life
itself'. The last phrase is in Greek ὥστε ἐξαπορηθῆναι ἡμᾶς καὶ τοῦ

ζῆν, exactly the verb which Paul here uses to describe the limit of suffering which the apostles do not reach. Bultmann explains this by saying that in 1.8 Paul is looking at things 'from a human standpoint'. This is no doubt right in the sense that in the experience referred to in 1.8 (probably a very dangerous brush with the authorities at Ephesus) though Paul despaired of life he was not justified in doing so since he was in fact delivered. With διωκόμενοι ἀλλ᾽ οὐκ ἐγκαταλειπόμενοι Windisch compares Ps. 37(36).25, 28, where the psalmist declares unequivocally that he has never seen the righteous abandoned, that the Lord will not abandon his holy ones. The LXX uses the verb ἐγκαταλείπειν here.[17] Bultmann profoundly comments that Jesus was not delivered in the sense which Paul intends here, and Collange (p. 151) compares Jesus' cry on the cross, which echoes Ps. 22.1, 'why hast thou forsaken me?' In the deepest sense we must say that Jesus was not *ultimately* forsaken in the sense that God raised him to life on the third day, and no doubt this is the way in which Paul would interpret Psalm 22. But the example of Jesus certainly challenges the facile optimism of the author of Psalm 37. Allo insists that the image in vv. 8-9 is that of a man-hunt. Collange (p. 148) points out that others have suggested a game or a fight. À propos these two verses Allo agrees with Plummer that Paul as he describes the life of the apostles has in mind the whole career of Jesus, not merely the passion and death. The apostles, he says, are to be delivered from all perils until the moment when God wills their death, and he draws a comparison with the way in which Jesus saved himself until the moment of God's providence arrived. This is perhaps a rather Johannine way of viewing Jesus' ministry. It would be more accurate to say that God preserved him, as he does the apostles. This fits in with Collange's remark (p. 149) that the sequence of passive participles is a Semitic way of indicating that the ultimate actor is God. Windisch points out that καταβάλλω could mean to 'throw' an opponent in wrestling. Paul is often thrown but never knocked out.

It is perhaps worth bringing to light a possible scriptural background to these two verses, Isa. 8.22-23. The LXX runs thus:

v. 22:   καὶ εἰς τὴν γῆν κάτω ἐμβλέψονται
          καὶ ἰδοὺ θλῖψις καὶ στενοχωρία καὶ σκότος ὥστε μὴ
          βλέπειν,
v. 23:   καὶ οὐκ ἀπορηθήσεται ὁ ἐν στενοχωρίᾳ ὢν ἕως καιροῦ.

This we may translate

And they shall look down towards the earth and behold tribulation
and oppression and darkness so that they cannot see, and he who is
suffering oppression for a period will not be without resort.

The context is one in which the coming trials and sufferings of Israel
are described. The LXX has misunderstood the Hebrew, which is as
follows:

ואל־ארץ יביט והנה צרה וחשכה

מעוף צוקה ואפלה מנדח

v. 23a   כי לא מועף לאשר מוצק לה

and they will look to the earth, but behold, distress and darkness,
the gloom of anguish. But there will be no gloom for her that was in
anguish.[18]

The LXX has borrowed the first phrase of v. 23b in the Hebrew and
mistranslated it. The phrase is כעת הראשן 'in the former time', but
LXX has made it mean 'for a time'. The Targum has no hint of any
respite before the beginning of ch. 9. It paraphrases thus:

For none that come to oppress them shall be wearied: as at the
former time the people of the land of Naphthali have been carried
into exile; and their remnant shall a mighty king carry into exile,
because they remembered not the mighty act *which was done* at the
sea, the miracles of Jordan, the war of the cities of the peoples.

It is interesting that the Targum makes this prophecy apply to both
the exiles, that of Samaria in 721 BC and that of Jerusalem of 697-687
BC. It therefore brings together the two great disasters of Israel
related in scripture and contrasts them in the ensuing chapter with
the messianic age. This might well appeal to an early Christian as
applicable to the experiences of the Messiah and his people.

There is quite a considerable coincidence of language between the
LXX of Isa. 8.22-23 and 2 Cor. 4.8-9: θλῖψις, στενοχωρία, ἀπορεῖσθαι
are all in the Isaiah passage. We have here what Paul would regard as
a description of the sufferings of the people of God, followed in ch. 9
by what everyone, Jews and Christians alike, regarded as a messianic
passage. Isa. 9.1-2 is actually applied to the ministry of Jesus in Matt.
4.15-16. Moreover Isaiah 8 was a favourite scripture with early
Christians. It contains the famous 'stone of stumbling' passage in
8.14, quoted by Paul in Rom. 9.32 (the preceding verse is echoed in
1 Pet. 3.14-15); 8.14 is also behind Luke 2.34 and is explicitly quoted
in 1 Pet. 2.8. Even more significant is the fact that Isa. 8.13 in its LXX

form is quoted in Heb. 2.13: 'Here am I and the children God has given me'. The author of Hebrews quotes it in order to show that the Son when he entered into the world intended to share fully in humanity and that he was destined to gather round him God's elect, a theme very close to that which Paul is treating here.

We may therefore reasonably suggest that in writing vv. 8-9 Paul had this Isaiah passage in mind. He would understand it as a prophecy of the condition of the apostolic community between the times, when the Messiah had come in the flesh but before he returned in glory. He would see in the earlier part of the chapter several prophecies of the cross, and in ch. 9 a prophecy both of the Messiah himself and of his reign with the faithful at the end of history. This passage would describe the situation of his faithful followers during the present epoch. Perhaps Paul regarded the ἕως καιροῦ of the LXX as indicating that epoch.

In vv. 10-12 Paul takes his theme a step further: so far in this passage we have only had a description of the apostolic life, with in the background the life of Christ. But now we have language that is definitely atoning or substitutionary: the apostles, by means of carrying about in the body the νέκρωσις of Jesus, bring life to the Corinthian church. This is not a simple exchange of death (on the part of the apostles) for life (given to the Corinthian church), as v. 12 by itself might suggest. The situation is more complicated than that: the apostles by dying (or by leading a life which is always liable to come to a violent end) not only bring life to the Corinthians, but also in some sense to themselves: the life of Jesus is to be manifest in their mortal flesh (v. 11). Moreover since the whole process is a representation of the pattern of Jesus' death and life, the resurrection is not to be excluded. The resurrection of both apostles and Corinthian Christians is mentioned in v. 14; and, as we shall be seeing, the resurrection of Jesus is implied by the scripture quotation in v. 13.

We must therefore carefully examine this mysterious word νέκρωσις. Schmiedel and Plummer both claim that it must mean 'process of dying'. The latter writes: 'They (the apostles) shared (Christ's) sufferings including the process which in his case ended in death and at any time might so end in their case'. Windisch emphasizes this further: νέκρωσις is not the state of being dead, but the constantly repeated dying. Paul represents his life as a progressive reproduction of the passion of Jesus. Windisch also introduces a nuance of meaning which later scholars take up: dying is here a 'dying from'. Héring underlines the word περιφέροντες, 'carrying around'. It refers to the missionary journeys of the apostolic group, he says. Windisch had pointed out that Greeks often wrote about men as carrying around dying bodies or bodies doomed to death, but this is not Paul's thought. Bultmann, however, inclines to this meaning. νέκρωσις, he says, does not mean being in danger of death but the actual decay of the body. Paul uses the term sacramentally for a process that continues throughout the Christian life, one which is not completed at baptism. The process is not of course an ascetic discipline.[19] Collange however holds that the word must denote a state and not a process. Paul does not say that he dies with Christ but that he carries in his body the νέκρωσις of Christ, something objective (pp. 154-55). Ahern defines νέκρωσις as 'the state of death which is the permanent effect of baptised death with Christ'(p. 22).[20] Güttgemanns believes that νέκρωσις is not a process, but 'a divine act' (p. 115). Baumert prefers the definition 'Nicht das "Töten Jesu" sondern das "Töten an Jesus", also das "Getötetwerden Jesu"',[21] which approximates him to the position of Windisch. Barrett's comment is interesting: νέκρωσις, he says, does not simply mean death; the process of Paul's life is analogous to the killing of Jesus. The life of Jesus is visible now, but will be fully manifested at the *parousia*. Finally we should notice Proudfoot's view: he defines νέκρωσις as 'putting to death'.[22]

We can to some extent check the accuracy of these various opinions by means of the lexicographical evidence. The word is used for the first time in extant Greek literature by Paul.[23] It occurs in Rom. 4.19 to describe the sterility of Sarah's womb, where the thought of the resurrection is in the background, as indeed it is here. It occurs also as a variant reading in Mark 3.5 in D, the Old Latin and the Sinaitic Syriac, where it denotes the deadness of the hearts of Jesus' hearers. Most editors prefer the reading πωρώσει. Bultmann calls the meaning in our passage 'sakramental'. He adds: 'The word is plainly used here instead of θάνατος because here it is a question of the dying of Christ not in as much as this has been basically fulfilled in the act of baptism, but in as much as it is continually enacted in the concrete life of the apostle'. Thus Paul's life becomes a continual killing off (*Abtötung*) or dying from (*Ersterben*). In profane Greek νέκρωσις means 'mortification' in a medical sense. Moulton and Milligan[24] have a quotation from Photius's *Bibliotheca*: οἱ γὰρ κόκκοι μετὰ τὴν ἐκ σήψεως νέκρωσιν καὶ φθόραν ἀναζῶσιν, 'for seeds come to life again after the deadness and corruption of decay'. Liddell and Scott offer a quotation from Atrampsychus' *Oneiro-criticus*,[25] a second century AD book on dreams: νεκροὺς ὁρῶν νέκρωσιν ἕξεις πραγμάτων 'if you see corpses (sc. in a dream) you will have a deadness in your business affairs'.

— From this one conclusion at least emerges: the translation 'process of dying' for νέκρωσις is not justified by the lexicographical evidence. The word must mean 'a state of being dead' or 'deadness'. This would seem to confirm the view of those who speak about 'a divine act' (Güttgemanns) or 'something objective' (Collange). Paul uses it instead of θάνατος because he wanted to indicate a present state of affairs (not a process to be completed) resulting from an event in the past. When therefore he writes that the apostles are 'always carrying in the body the νέκρωσις of Jesus', he does not mean that Jesus' death is somehow or other being achieved by means of the development of their spiritual lives, or that as their careers unfolded a process of gradual dying could be perceived, ending in their physical death. He means that as the apostles go about their task committed to them by God, this activity is only justified and upheld by the death of Jesus on the cross, and that therefore his deadness is to be manifested in their deadness to the world. In this respect the meaning 'dying from' commended by Windisch and Bultmann is correct.

It is in fact a strange and mysterious idea which Paul is trying to express here. The death of Jesus (followed of course by his resurrection) has taken place and this in itself constitutes an all-important event, the event which has ushered in the new age in which Christians are living. The apostles primarily, and after them their converts, are to manifest this death, more exactly the fact of Jesus having died, by their proclamation of the event and by their representing in their lives Jesus' sufferings, ending of course in their actual physical death. By so doing the life of the risen Jesus is proclaimed by their preaching, manifest in their lives, and passed on to their converts. Thus when the author of Colossians writes νεκρώσατε οὖν τὰ μέλη τὰ ἐπὶ τῆς γῆς (Col. 3.5), 'Put to death therefore what is earthly in you', he is slightly simplifying his master's teaching, as he does in other respects also. The nearest Paul gets to this is in Rom. 6.11, λογίζεσθε ἑαυτοὺς [εἶναι] νεκροὺς μὲν τῇ ἁμαρτίᾳ 'so you must also consider yourselves dead to sin'. But here he is alluding not to a process that he hopes is taking place in

Christians, but to something that has already happened to them in virtue of their baptism. The word νέκρωσις therefore underlines the *Einmaligkeit*, the once-for-allness, of the event of the death of Christ.

Commenting on these three verses 10-12, Proudfoot (p. 155) says that life can come to the Corinthians by means of Paul's precarious life because that life is 'a sort of illustration of or commentary upon his preaching of the gospel'. This is accurate enough. On the other hand we must definitely disagree with Dupont when he says that the life to which Paul refers in v. 11 will only be seen at the *parousia*.[26] Because the death and resurrection of Jesus is a past event, his life can be manifest now in the mortal flesh of the apostles. Bultmann entitles the whole passage 4.7-12 'Die Paradoxie' and connects it closely with the concept of the cross as the revelation of God's glory. Paul's opponents, he says, have been demanding ostentatious signs. They only see a dying life. We may well add that the paradox of the cross is at the very heart of this passage; the mysterious exchange between the dying of the apostles and the life of the Corinthian church, the apostolic experience, patterned on Jesus' experience, of being handed over to the worst that the world can do, though never ultimately abandoned by God—all this is part and parcel of the paradox of the cross, the strange revelation of God's very nature by means of events and persons who would seem to the outside world to be the very antithesis of all that one would naturally associate with the divine. Baumert (p. 31) rightly says that this description of the apostolic office must not be understood in an exclusive sense: Paul is speaking for himself and his fellow-workers. We may add that ultimately it must include all other Christians as well. Collange well remarks (p. 160) that Paul's paradoxes have a triple root, Paul's own life, the experience of the righteous sufferer in the Psalms as understood in Jewish tradition, and the career of Jesus delivered to death on the cross. If God's design was to be carried out, the suffering and weakness both of Jesus and of his disciples was necessary. Barrett expresses very much the same thing when he writes: 'The pattern of Christian existence, which becomes particularly clear in the life of an apostle, is determined by crucifixion and resurrection'.

This is undoubtedly vicarious suffering; death works in the apostles and thereby life in the Corinthians. But we must not conclude that life does not also work in the apostles, nor that the

Corinthians are exempt from the strenuous 'life in death' existence of the Christian disciple. Quite the reverse! Witness our exposition of 1 Cor. 4.9-13. It is indeed vicarious suffering, but it is only effective when those for whom it is undertaken enter into the process themselves. This of course is equally true of Christ's sufferings. And all is done 'in Christ'. There is no suggestion that the sufferings of the saints in some mysterious way make amends for the fact that those Christians who are not saints, or who are still on the way to becoming saints, have not suffered at all or have not suffered enough. Christ's sufferings become manifest in Paul and in his companions, and become effective in as far as those to whom they appeal themselves enter into those sufferings. And all from beginning to end is done in Christ. There is no suggestion of merit or reward.

The last element in the passage we are concerned with is the psalm citation in v. 13 and its significance.[27] The majority of commentators conclude that when Paul writes (literally) 'having the same spirit of faith, according to what is written, "I believed and therefore I spoke"', he means 'according to the same spirit of faith as the psalmist had'. This is the opinion of Plummer, Lietzmann, Allo, Bultmann, and Collange (p. 162). Windisch also prefers this interpretation, though he does mention a possible alternative, the same spirit as Paul's readers have. It seems to me that such a conclusion ignores the way in which early Christians understood scripture. If you say that Paul is claiming the same spirit of faith as the psalmist had, you are in effect saying that Paul is claiming the same spirit of faith as David had. That is how Paul would see it, and such a conclusion is alien to everything else we know about Paul's method of interpreting scripture. Far more likely is Goudge's explanation: Paul, he says, thinks of the Lord himself as uttering this psalm. Paul therefore is claiming the same spirit of faith as the Lord himself. Goudge goes all through the psalm (Ps. 116) finding in it words applicable to Jesus' career, and ends by finding in it 'the agony of Gethsemane . . . and the joy of Easter'. If we are to understand Paul's use of this psalm we must do the same thing.

Paul quotes the LXX version, where it is 115.1. In fact the LXX has cut what is one psalm in the Hebrew into two, making 116.1-9 in the Hebrew into Psalm 114 in the Greek, and 116.10-19 in the Hebrew into 115 in the Greek. The MT of 116.10 is:

האמנתי כי אדבר אני עניתי מאד

The RSV translates: 'I kept my faith, even when I said "I am greatly afflicted"'. The LXX rendering (115.1) is:

ἐπίστευσα, διὸ ἐλάλησα· ἐγὼ δὲ ἐταπεινώθην σφόδρα.[28]

Thus the Greek has given the sense that the psalmist spoke because he believed despite his being greatly humbled.[29] When we read the psalm as a whole, especially if we confine ourselves to 115 in the Greek (116.10-19 in the Hebrew and EVV), we can see how appropriate the psalm would be on the lips of the suffering and triumphant Messiah. I will translate most of the psalm direct from the LXX, since this is probably the form in which Paul read it. Verse 1 we have already quoted: the Messiah affirms his faith in God despite his deep humiliation. Verses 3 and 4:

> What shall I repay to the Lord
> for all wherewith he has repaid me?
> I will take the cup of salvation
> and I will call upon the name of the Lord.

The Messiah gives thanks to God for the salvation he has received through the resurrection. It is impossible for a Christian not to associate these verses with the cup of salvation in the eucharist, the feast wherein God's great salvation in Christ is celebrated. Verse 6:

> Precious in the presence of the Lord is the death of his holy ones.

This would be seen as a reference to the salvific death of Christ. Verse 7:

> O Lord, I am thy servant (δοῦλος),
> thy servant and the son of thy handmaid;
> thou hast burst my bonds asunder.

This would certainly indicate to Paul the resurrection of Christ. Verses 8-10:

> I will sacrifice to thee the sacrifice of praise,
> I will pay my vows to the Lord
> before all his people
> in the courts of the house of the Lord,
> in thy midst, O Jerusalem.

This would convey to Paul the thanksgivings of the people of God which he regarded as being offered to God through Christ; see our exposition of 2 Cor. 1.20 above.

If this is what the psalm must have meant to Paul when interpreted messianically, we can see that it would also have a deep meaning for him in the context in which he quotes it. He is claiming for the apostolic group, and for those whom they persuade to become Christians, the same sentiments and the same experiences to which, he believes, the Messiah has given voice in the inspired scriptures. Just as Christ still believed in God despite the deep humiliation of his days on earth, so do the apostles believe despite their humiliating situation. They too know the value of the death of Christ and therefore of the death of all his faithful. They look forward to the resurrection which God has already accorded to Christ, and they too pay their thanksgivings to God in the fellowship of the Church. The Targum of Ps. 116.13 is 'I am sure that I will speak in the community of the righteous',[30] so in Jewish tradition it is seen as a psalm of the one and the many. When we look again at the context of the citation in 2 Cor. 4.4-15, we can see that Paul's discourse follows the pattern of the psalm. First he speaks of the suffering and death of the apostolic community in Christ; then he looks forward to their resurrection to come. Finally in v. 15 he mentions the thanksgiving which will be uttered to God by the Christian community. There can be few examples of a scripture reference in Paul which, when carefully examined in its context, can tell us more about Paul's theology.

We have seen how the theme of the one and the many runs through this psalm. This, and many other passages like it, help to explain how Paul can pass so easily from language about Christ to very similar language about Christians. Another point of great interest arises from our consideration of this psalm. In Paul's view, the Messiah expressed faith in God. We are to understand, I believe, that in Paul's hermeneutic the psalm is a prophetic utterance inspired by the Holy Spirit expressing the sentiments of the Messiah when he should appear on earth. We may therefore safely assume that Paul thought of the historical Jesus as having expressed faith in God. This is a big subject, one which we cannot explore here. But it is at least an indication, very much in line with the evidence we have discussed, that Paul knew traditions of Jesus' teaching, that Paul was not wholly uninterested in anything to do with Jesus except his sufferings, death, and resurrection. To live by faith is a life-long process. If the Messiah expressed his faith in God at the moment of his deepest humiliation, and if he is here held up as a pattern for the Christian life, then it is more than likely that Paul could appeal to the example of Jesus' whole life and ministry as an inspiration to Christians.

With this, the second of our four main passages, we have penetrated deep into our subject. The paradox of the cross has now been shown to affect not only the life of the apostolic community, but also of the Church which it is their task to found. Connections have appeared running back to Jesus' own teaching. The atoning or substitutionary nature of the apostolic community has been clearly outlined, together with an absolutely explicit relation with the sufferings and death of Christ. The place of the resurrection has been established in a way which did not clearly appear in earlier passages; and all is undergirded and illuminated by the scriptural background. We now turn to another passage further on in the same epistle in which these themes are further elaborated.

Chapter 4

THE ONE AND THE MANY:
2 COR. 6.1-10; ROM. 8.35-37; 15.3

In the third of our main studies we pursue the same themes, the paradox of the cross, the scriptural background to Paul's thought, the link with the teaching of Jesus. All three themes appear in an intensified form in the passages which we must study now. For convenience's sake we will take them in a slightly different order: we begin with the scriptural background; then comes an exploration of the paradox of the cross in the detailed study of 2 Cor. 6.2-10; and finally the links with Jesus' teaching.

I

Our passage begins with a citation of Isa. 49.8 in 2 Cor. 6.2:

καιρῷ δεκτῷ ἐπήκουσά σου
καὶ ἐν ἡμέρᾳ σωτηρίας ἐβοήθησά σου.

At the acceptable time I have listened to you,
and helped you in the day of salvation.

Paul reproduces our LXX exactly. The LXX in its turn gives a very fair translation of the MT:

בעת רצון עניתיך
וביום ישועה עזרתיך

A consideration of the entire passage Isa. 49.1-8 very much illuminates Paul's meaning here.[1] This is a 'servant' passage; it begins in vv. 1-3 by describing God's calling of his servant. Then in v. 4 the servant protests that his mission has been unsuccessful, but he appeals to God for vindication:

But I said, 'I have laboured in vain,
I have spent my strength for nothing and vanity;
but surely my right is with the Lord,
any my recompense with my God'.

In the ensuing verses God answers his servant by saying, first that the servant's mission is to be extended beyond Israel to the whole world (v. 6), and then that the servant will be vindicated. God will answer him, save him, and make him a covenant for the nations. Paul would certainly understand this passage as applying primarily to Christ, the original servant. He too was uniquely called. When he was put to death on the cross he seemed to have laboured in vain. But by raising him from the dead God has saved him, vindicated him, and is now making him the means of salvation to non-Jews as well as to Israel.

In the context of 2 Cor. 6.2, however, Paul is applying the citation to Christians as well. In the previous verses he has been expounding the mysterious exchange whereby the sin of humanity has been assumed by Christ and Christ's righteousness imparted to us. He now emphasizes by means of this citation that Christ's vindication also belongs to Christians: now is the time of our salvation. The Targum version of this passage is significant, because it actually interprets the second person singular in Isa. 49.8 as a second person plural, just as Paul does:

> At the time that you do my pleasure I will receive your prayer
> and in the day of distress I will raise up salvation, and will help
> you.

Of course the Targum has postponed the day of salvation till the future, as neither scripture nor Paul does, and has made its coming dependent on Israel obeying God's will. But the change of person is interesting. The same change is carried on throughout vv. 6 and 7, so that it is made plain that Israel is being addressed.

We may therefore understand that Paul is using this Isaiah citation in order to assure the Corinthians that as they share in the sufferings of Christ so they are also to share in his vindication. But there is another interesting cross-connection to be found. This Isaiah passage contains the phrase 'at an acceptable time'. The LXX has καιρῷ δεκτῷ, rendering בעת רצון in the MT. The same phrase occurs in Ps. 69.13b:

> At an acceptable time, O God,
> in the abundance of thy steadfast love answer me.

The MT (69.14b) has עת רצון. The LXX here translates with καιρὸς εὐδοκίας. These two texts are connected in rabbinic tradition, for we find the following in the Babylonian Talmud in *Berakoth*:

For R. Yohanan said in the name of R. Simeon b. Yohai 'What is the meaning of the verse *But as for me, let my prayer be made unto Thee O Lord, in an acceptable time?* When is the time acceptable? When the congregation prays.' R. Jose b. R. Hanina says, '(You learn it) from here, *Thus says the Lord, In an acceptable time have I answered thee*'.[2]

We find here both a connection between the two passages and an application of the Isaiah passage to the congregation.

Now Psalm 69 is a favourite with early Christian writers. It is quoted twice by Paul, first in Rom. 11.9-10. But it is the second quotation that bears a special interest for us, since it has a christological significance. It occurs in Rom. 15.3:

> For Christ did not please himself; but, as it is written, 'The reproaches of those who reproached thee fell upon me'.

The Greek is

οἱ ὀνειδισμοὶ τῶν ὀνειδιζόντων σε ἐπέπεσαν ἐπ᾽ ἐμέ.

This is a quotation of Ps. 69.9. Paul has exactly reproduced the LXX, where it is Ps. 68.10b. The LXX has correctly translated the MT (Ps. 69.10b). It is a psalm in which the righteous sufferer describes in detail the afflictions which he has to endure because of the persecution of the ungodly. He frequently calls on God to rescue him and vindicate him. He points out (as here) that his sufferings are largely due to his faithfulness to God. Towards the end of the psalm he begins to give thanks to God for help received. For example v. 29 runs:

> But I am afflicted and in pain;
> let thy salvation, O God, set me on high.

But the LXX (v. 30) renders this with:

> I am poor (πτωχός) and in pain,
> And the salvation of your countenance, O God, has come to my help.

The word πτωχός is significant, for it occurs in 2 Cor. 6.10, and the LXX, we note, represents the victory as already won. The entire psalm is written in the first person. By any well-informed early Christian this psalm would have been regarded as the utterance of Christ, who describes his sufferings, cries to the Father for help, and gives thanks when help is received in the resurrection. There can be no doubt that this is how Paul understood the psalm. He quotes it in Rom. 15.3 in order to show that what Christ suffered he suffered because it was the Father's will. Of course Paul interprets σε as referring to the Father. What is not quite clear is how the insults heaped on Jesus were really intended for God. The two previous verses describe how the psalmist has suffered reproach because of God; for God's sake he has become alienated from his own people. This might well be applied to Jesus' repudiation of his own family for the sake of the ministry, as recorded in the Gospels. The previous verse, 'The zeal of they house has eaten me up', is quoted in John 2.17 to indicate that Jesus' cleansing of the Temple was ultimately responsible for the hostility that led to his death. It seems likely therefore that Paul's meaning in Rom. 15.3 is this: Jesus, in order to carry out God's will, did not live a life pleasing to himself, but boldly accepted a career of insult and suffering. We Christians likewise must not seek to please ourselves, but must accept such element of suffering and abuse as is inevitable for those who seek to live the Christian life. It is remarkable that Paul applies the words of the psalm to Christ, but draws from them also an application to the community.

For anyone who studies Paul's use of scripture there can be no doubt that σε in this citation refers to God.[3] This is accepted by Lagrange, Michel, Cranfield, and Käsemann.[4] The exception to this is provided by Sanday and Headlam,[5] who think that Christ is addressing 'a man'. Lagrange for some reason calls this the Protestant view. It can more accurately be described as the view of those who have not carefully studied Paul's method of scripture interpretation. Käsemann does not think that Christ is necessarily regarded as the suffering servant in this passage. This seems to be going to an extreme of scepticism, especially in view of the extensive use of the psalm in a messianic sense in the NT as a whole. D. Worley has devoted a whole article to the use of Psalm 69 in Rom. 15.3.[6] He agrees that the sufferer in the psalm is taken by Paul as referring to Christ, and that σε must mean God. He makes the surprising claim: 'In none of Paul's writings is the suffering of Christ a major theme'. In view of our study of 1 and 2 Corinthians this must appear as a questionable statement. He adds: 'The desire of Christ to please God involved the suffering of reproaches, as well as his own humility' (p. 9). This is perfectly true. It is possible however that Paul meant something more than this by his use of the citation: in reproaching

Christ those who uttered the insults were, without knowing it, insulting God. The third Pauline passage to be brought into comparison is Rom. 8.35-37:

> Who shall separate us from the love of Christ? Shall tribulation, or distress, or persecution, or famine, or nakedness, or peril, or sword? As it is written:
>
> For thy sake we are being killed all the day long
> We are regarded as sheep to be slaughtered
>
> No, in all these things we are more than conquerors through him who loved us.

It will be sufficient to reproduce the Greek of vv. 35-36:

> τίς ἡμᾶς χωρίσει ἀπὸ τῆς ἀγάπης τοῦ Χριστοῦ;[7] θλῖψις ἢ στενοχωρία ἢ διωγμὸς ἢ λιμὸς ἢ γυμνότης ἢ κίνδυνος ἢ μάχαιρα; καθὼς γέγραπται ὅτι
>
> > ἕνεκέν σου θανατούμεθα ὅλην τήν ἡμέραν,
> > ἐλογίσθημεν ὡς πρόβατα σφαγῆς.

There is an interesting parallel to be traced between the list of afflictions here and those mentioned in 2 Cor. 6.1-10, and elsewhere in the Corinthian letters. We could list them as follows:

Rom. 8.35	*2 Cor. 6.1-10*	
θλῖψις	θλίψεσιν	v. 4
στενοχωρία	στενοχωρίαις	v. 4
διωγμός	cf. 1 Cor. 4.12	
λίμος	cf. 2 Cor. 11.27	
γυμνότης	cf. 1 Cor. 4.11; 2 Cor. 11.27	
κίνδυνος	cf. 2 Cor. 11.26	
μάχαιρα	ἀποθνήσκοντες	v. 9
θανατούμεθα	cf. 2 Cor. 4.11	

If we draw on all the passages in the Corinthian correspondence in which Paul details the hardships of the apostolic life, we can parallel every one of the afflictions listed in the Romans passage. But in Romans Paul is writing to ordinary Christians whom he does not even know personally. It is clear therefore that these afflictions, a partaking in the sufferings of Christ, are not confined to the apostolic group, but are to be shared by all Christians.

In this passage from Romans Paul quotes Ps. 44.22. He coincides exactly with the LXX (Ps. 43.23), which is a good translation of the

MT (Ps. 44.23). The psalm would be regarded by Paul as uttered by the suffering Messiah on behalf of the faithful in Israel. In the LXX v. 25b runs:

ἐπιλάνθῃ τῆς πτωχείας ἡμῶν καὶ τῆς θλίψεως ἡμῶν;

Why hast thou forgotten our poverty and affliction?

Here occur two words which also appear in the description of the apostolic life in 2 Cor. 6.1-10. In vv. 24 and 27 in the Greek we have the words ἐξεγέρθητι and ἀνάστα, 'rouse thyself' and 'arise', addressed to God.[8] Paul would think of these words as predicting the resurrection of Christ. He uses ἐξεγείρειν himself in 1 Cor. 6.14 of the Christian resurrection, and ἀνίστημι of Christ's resurrection in 1 Thess. 4.14. If we take Psalm 44 with Psalm 69 we find that the first psalm is expressed entirely in the first person plural and the second is cast entirely in the first person singular. Paul uses both psalms to refer to both the sufferings of Christ and the sufferings of Christians. Obviously for him the alternation of the one and the many in the passages in scripture dealing with the righteous sufferer meant that both the sufferings of Christ and the sufferings of Christians were predicted in scripture.[9]

As we might expect, Psalm 44 was regarded in Jewish tradition as applicable to Jewish martyrs, especially to the martyrs in the Antiochean persecution in the second century BC.[10] In the *Midrash on the Psalms* it is said that those who are ready to suffer death for their belief suffer from a 'sickness unto death'.[11] This means that they are sick with love for God, so much so that they are ready to die for him. In Rom. 8.31-39 Paul has changed things round in a way entirely consonant with the paradox of the cross: because God has shown us his love in the death of Christ we must be ready to die for our belief in him.

Michel well compares with Rom. 8.36 both 1 Cor. 15.31 and 2 Cor. 4.11. Of these two references, the first applies to Paul's own individual experience, and the second to the experience of the apostolic group. All in some sense die daily. Here in Rom. 8.36 the reference is to the experience of Christians as a whole. We could not have a clearer indication that the sufferings of Christ, though they are mediated to the Church by the apostolic group, are not the burden (or the prerogative) of the apostles alone, but are to be passed on to all Christians. Cranfield writes of 8.36 that the point of the citation is to show that 'the tribulations which face Christians are nothing new or unexpected, but have all along been characteristic of God's people'. We may add that such tribulations are closely connected with the sufferings of the Messiah. In a footnote Cranfield disagrees with C.K. Barrett, who had argued that in this passage there is no cross-reference to the servant of Isaiah 53 on the grounds that if the servant passage had already been applied to Jesus that would be a good reason for not applying it to his people. Cranfield is surely in the right here: after examining how Paul uses the various scripture citations which we have been considering in this chapter, it must be clear that there is nothing exclusive about such citations. If a passage applies to the Messiah this is no reason why it cannot apply to his people. On the contrary, Paul has no hesitation in applying messianic passages from scripture (or rather passages which he believes to be messianic) both to Christ and to the apostolic group and to Christians generally. Far from being something merely incidental or accidental, this is a basic part of his doctrine of the cross. The belief in the one and the many is built into the very foundations of his theology. As further evidence of the link between Psalm 44 and Isaiah 53 in Paul's mind we may refer to an article by Delling.[12] He claims, no doubt rightly, that in Rom. 8.32 there is an echo of Isa. 53.6, 12 (p. 83): ὑπὲρ ἡμῶν πάντων παρέδωκεν αὐτόν 'he (God) delivered him up for us all' echoes the LXX κύριος παρέδωκεν αὐτόν 'the Lord delivered him up' and παρεδόθη εἰς θάνατον ἡ ψυχὴ αὐτοῦ 'his life was handed over to death'.[13] Delling also points out (p. 91) that in Rom. 8.35 there are seven circumstances that might in theory but do not in fact separate us from the love of God, just those that are characteristic of what he calls 'the apostolic existence'. He goes on (p. 92) to compare the citation of Ps. 44.22 with 1 Cor. 4.9: 'God has exhibited us apostles as last of all, like men sentenced to death', a verse which we shall examine in Chapter 6.

Münderlein has a relevant article in which he discusses the afflictions listed in Rom. 8.35f.[14] He points out that in the Old Testament the afflictions to which Israel or individuals in Israel are subject are often regarded as punishments for Israel's apostasy, but never as disciplinary.[15] Paul is making use of two views of suffering to be found in Israel's religious tradition: the first concerns the sufferings of the righteous, whose cause is known only to God. The supreme example of this is to be found in the life and death of Jesus Christ, who came as revealer of God. The second tradition is that referred to already: sufferings are punishment for wrongdoing. This

tradition Paul radically alters; according to him the sufferings of the
righteous (not that Paul would use that word in this context) can lead
to victory because they are suffered for the sake of God and Christ.
This is an example of how the coming of Christ has radically altered
the situation; he turns curse into blessing, death into life; and so here
in Romans 8 he turns affliction into victory (see *art. cit.*, pp. 140-41).
Münderlein emphasizes the fact that in view of the event of the cross
Paul has not hesitated to modify the tradition he received. Thus
Münderlein has brought us back once again to the paradox of the
cross, which radically alters received traditions and projects
Christians into a new world where new standards and new concepts
of God prevail.

In this section we have had a good opportunity of seeing how
various passages in scripture underlie Paul's thought. We have
observed the way in which one passage will connect with another, so
that what is quoted of the Messiah can also be held to apply to his
people and *vice versa*. And we must surely conclude that when Paul
quotes scripture he does not mean it in a purely 'accommodatory'
sense. He does not mean merely to say 'what I have been writing
could well be expressed in the words of scripture'. He means that the
events and the experiences of the life and death of the Messiah and of
his faithful followers have been prophesied in scripture, so that when
the appropriate passage in scripture is cited one can recognize that
those events were all foreseen and foreordained in God's providence.
It also proves in Paul's eyes that the Christians to whom he is writing
are living in the last time, the end of the age, the epoch of fulfilment.
The eschatological element in Paul's thought should never be
overlooked; it explains, as we hope to show later, a great deal that is
obscure in his work. Above all, the eschatological age is ushered in by
the paradoxical event of the cross. And finally we should not forget
that Paul does not normally cite scripture entirely disregarding the
context of the citation. This is not to claim that Paul understood
'context' in the sense that we do today. He was not concerned with
establishing at what point in Israel's history any given extract was
written, or who wrote it under what circumstances, or with what
purpose. But it is never safe entirely to disregard the context from
which a quotation is taken. Frequently by reading on or reading back
we can understand why Paul has chosen this quotation, what exactly
it means to him, and how it is related to his other quotations. Careful
examination of Paul's use of scripture enables us to comprehend the
sources and history of Paul's thought.

As well as all this there remains for the student who has any concern for Christian theology in our own day a number of difficult questions to be answered. If this is how Paul believed and how his thought developed, what does it mean for us today, both in understanding scripture and in interpreting the significance of Jesus Christ? These are questions which we must attempt to answer, but the attempt must be postponed until towards the end of this book.

II

We now go through 2 Cor. 6.2-10 in detail, bringing out what is relevant to our theme. The passage comprises in fact a description of the ministry. In 5.18 Paul has already described this ministry as one of reconciliation, and has portrayed the ministers as acting as God's ambassadors; God is making his appeal through them (5.20). If we compare this description with the other two descriptions which we have examined, 1 Cor. 4.6-13 and 2 Cor. 4.7-15, we can perhaps conclude that what sparks off these descriptions of the apostolic ministry in paradoxical terms is a sense of contrast between Christian living and the standards of the outside world. In 1 Corinthians 4 Paul is contrasting the uncommitted, spectator-like behaviour of the Corinthians with the strenuous, committed life of the apostles. In 2 Corinthians the contrast is between the weakness, obscurity, and humility of the apostles in the eyes of the world and the greatness of the message which they proclaim. Here the contrast lies between viewing things 'after the flesh', i.e. as the outsider would see them, and understanding them in the light of faith. Always the side of the comparison which Paul favours is expressed in paradoxical terms, as if the sphere of divine action could only be understood in some such way. One might almost say that in Paul's thought God's saving activity can only be expressed by means of paradoxes.

Bultmann provides this passage with a most appropriate heading; he calls it 'the apostle in the power of the eschatological event'. Windisch, likewise commenting on v. 2, compares Jesus' claim that the time is fulfilled in Luke 4.21, and remarks that we are now in the end time. Collange (p. 292) in a striking phrase describes this passage as 'une sorte de "bréviaire du serviteur de Dieu"'. May we translate this as 'a sort of handbook for the servant of God'? Beyer notes that this διακονία can also be called ἡ διακονία τοῦ πνεύματος (2 Cor. 3.7-9) and in the same passage ἡ διακονία τῆς δικαιοσύνης. This may well throw light on the meaning of δικαιοσύνη in v. 7 below.

His conclusion is 'Das Apostelamt ist Dienst'.[16] Bultmann rightly points out that here the ministry is not just Paul's own activity; it is the apostolic ministry.

Verses 4 and 5 describe the precarious and dangerous conditions in which the ministry is carried out. Both Collange (p. 294) and Fiedler believe that in Paul's mind there was a category which they call περιστάσεις into which Paul's apostolic experiences fitted. Collange writes:

> (a) there existed a precise scheme of apostolic *peristaseis* which is disclosed to us in 6.5 and to which the record of 11.23f recurs; (b) this scheme had been elaborated by Paul as the fruit of his reflections on life and on his experiences as an apostle (my tr.).

Fiedler (p. 74), presumably following Collange's lead, writes of a 'Peristasenkatalog'.[17] It is not easy to see why these two scholars should have chosen the noun *peristaseis* to describe this phenomenon. It is not one used anywhere in the NT. It can mean 'circumstances, condition, state of affairs'. It is often used by Polybius. No doubt Collange wishes to emphasize that Paul's apostolic sufferings are in some sense continuous with the eschatological woes expected before the coming of the end in Jewish apocalyptic literature. In view of the close connection between the sufferings of Christ and the sufferings of the apostles, it might be more satisfactory to link Paul's accounts of his precarious life with the sufferings of the righteous sufferer in the Psalms, rather than going outside early Christian vocabulary altogether for a technical term.[18] What had been, in the minds of Jewish apocalyptic writers, thought of as the woes which should come before the end were surely for Paul to be regarded as the sufferings of the Messiah who had already come.

There is some disagreement among scholars as to the meaning of νηστείαις in v. 5. Allo suggests that the fastings may be voluntary, a view supported by Goudge. This suggestion is rejected by Schmiedel, Héring, Bultmann, Barrett, and Behm.[19] Paul is detailing the sufferings and dangers which he has had to undergo as an apostle. To include in the list the fact that he chose voluntarily to fast in the course of his adventures would be quite pointless and indeed much more akin to the character of the Pharisee in the parable than to Paul the ex-Pharisee converted to a belief in justification by faith. No doubt Paul did fast voluntarily on occasion, but it is the last thing he would have wished to include in a list of apostolic sufferings.

In vv. 6-7 the description passes into another mode, though exactly the same preposition, ἐν, is used. Here we have an account of the apostle's spiritual armoury. We leave the discussion of v. 7b till Chapter 6. The phrase ἐν γνώσει is slightly surprising. What sort of knowledge is this? Windisch thinks it is a pneumatic sort of knowledge. This seems reasonable in view of ἐν πνεύματι ἁγίῳ which follows. But what does 'a pneumatic knowledge' imply? Dupont in his great work on Gnosis is very helpful here (pp. 381, 402). He points out that γνῶσις is included in a list of qualities which Paul attributes to the Romans in Rom. 15.13-14, and in a list of qualities which he attributes to the Corinthians in 2 Cor. 8.7. He maintains that the meaning is simply the possession of a good understanding of scripture. This is something which is obviously necessary for those who are undertaking the apostolic ministry, and, since that ministry is to be handed on to each newly founded church, it is not surprising to find it in a list of qualities possessed by well-established communities. Hence the knowledge is only 'pneumatic' in the sense that the guidance of the Holy Spirit is necessary in order to understand the scriptures rightly. From this it follows that ἐν πνεύματι ἁγίῳ later on in v. 6 must refer to the Holy Spirit, not, as Barrett maintains, to Paul's sanctified behaviour: 'it is certainly unlikely', he writes, 'that Paul should throw in a reference to the Third Person of the Trinity in the midst of a series of human ethical qualities'. But if we read the list right through from the beginning of v. 6 to half way through v. 7, we will realize that it does not consist simply of human ethical qualities. Paul, having in vv. 5-6 described the external circumstances of the apostolic life, now turns to its internal circumstances. This certainly includes some moral qualities essential for the successful maintenance of that life, but it also includes 'the word of truth' and 'the power of God'. Bultmann holds that the Holy Spirit is meant here 'in as much as the Holy Spirit makes himself known in the particular moments of the apostolic work'. Collange insists (p. 295) that the reference is to the Holy Spirit, not just to a spirit of holiness, and he mentions several other places in Paul where the Holy Spirit is connected with ἀγάπη. Windisch, accepting the same view, compares 1 Cor. 2.4, where Paul claims that he was with the Corinthians 'in demonstration of the Spirit and power'.

Now in vv. 8-10 come the true paradoxes. Paul has described the external and internal circumstances of the apostolic ministry. He now expounds its true significance in a series of striking paradoxes. Commentators have striven to pinpoint the exact differences between the two sides of each of the paradoxes. Lietzmann rightly says that ὡς does not indicate an apparent situation different from the true one: 'ὡς, wie zeigt v. 9f, nicht "als ob" vom Anschein, sondern "als" vom tatsächlichen Zustand'. We may compare 5.19, where Paul does not mean that God gives the impression of making his appeal through the apostles though he is in reality not doing so. He is actually making his appeal through them. Allo writes that in these antitheses the first member indicates the reputation Paul and his colleagues have, what they are held to be. The second member indicates what they are in reality. But this does not explain everything. In the first place, διὰ δόξης καὶ ἀτιμίας and διὰ δυσφημίας καὶ εὐφημίας is a factual description. The apostles are held in low esteem by some and honoured by others. Then in v. 10 we may say that both λυπούμενοι and χαίροντες truly apply to the apostles all the time. We know from his witness in this epistle that Paul could be grieved; cf. 2.1f. Again there is a genuine sense in which the apostles are poor, materially poor. Allo's explanation takes the paradox out of the contrast. Bertram expresses the matter better: 'He (Paul) sees a connection between the external experiences of his life, which must appear to him and to others as death, as chastisement, as affliction, and the inner certainty of life, of the conquest of death, of joy'.[20] Héring, like Allo, tends to remove the paradox when he writes of 'le contraste entre l'aspect phénomenal et l'essence profonde de la vie de l'apôtre'. Paul perhaps would have protested that there was nothing 'phénomenal' about his chastisement, his grief, his poverty, any more than there was anything phenomenal about Christ's sufferings. Allo and Héring are in danger of introducing a sort of Docetism into the apostolic life. C.K. Barrett is much nearer the truth when he says: 'each of the two descriptions that stand together in pairs may in a paradoxical sense be said to be true'. Bultmann as usual offers a series of penetrating comments on the paradoxes. We must admit that ὡς πλάνοι καὶ ἀληθεῖς does present a straightforward antithesis between the world's opinion and the true state of affairs, as Bultmann points out. The phrase 'dying and behold we live' is uttered from the standpoint of the believer: he knows of the hidden life. But the outward man really is in a state of dying. Bultmann connects the phrase with 2 Cor. 10f., which we have already examined. There certainly was no question of a contrast between appearance and reality. As for λυπούμενοι, that, says Bultmann, is from the human point of view of Paul himself. This, we may object, hardly puts the phrase into clearest focus. Paul himself argues in 7.9-10 that there is a κατὰ θεὸν λυπή which he contrasts with ἡ τοῦ κόσμου λυπή. The first brings repentance and thus salvation; the second leads to death.

In v. 9, as many commentators have pointed out, Paul appears to be echoing scripture. The relevant phrase is ὡς παιδευόμενοι καὶ μὴ θανατούμενοι, 'as punished, and yet not killed'. This is an echo of Ps. 118.18 (LXX 117.18). The LXX is

παιδεύων ἐπαίδευσέν με ὁ κύριος,
καὶ τῷ θανάτῳ οὐ παρέδωκέν με.

The MT is יסר יסרני יה ולמות לא נתנני. The LXX is therefore perfectly accurate in rendering with τῷ θανάτῳ. This psalm is echoed elsewhere by Paul in Rom. 8.31 εἰ ὁ θεός ὑπὲρ ἡμῶν, τίς καθ᾽ ἡμῶν; which is a very loose paraphrase of the MT

יהוה לי לא אירה מה־יעשה לי אדם

With the Lord on my side I do not fear,
what can man do to me?

We could, I suppose, claim that Paul's ὁ θεὸς ὑπὲρ ἡμῶν is nearer the MT than the LXX's translation κύριος ἐμοὶ βοηθός. But Psalm 118 is a favourite with early Christians, being very frequently quoted in the NT. It contains among other things the famous verse about the stone that the builders rejected becoming the top stone of the corner. When we read the psalm as a whole in the LXX we see how strongly it would appeal to Paul as being an utterance of the Messiah. The two previous verses translated from the LXX run:

The right hand of the Lord has exalted me,
the right hand of the Lord has done an act of power.
We do not die but we shall live,
and I shall tell forth the works of the Lord.

This would be understood by Paul as primarily the proclamation of his resurrection by the exalted Messiah, but it passes over into the first person plural and this would be seen by Paul to apply also to the faithful. Verses 22-23 narrate the elevation of the rejected stone and the wonder of the event. Verse 24 runs:

This is the day which the Lord has made,
let us rejoice and be joyful in it.

This echoes Isa. 49.8, which Paul has quoted above, with its reference to the day of salvation. In v. 9 therefore Paul is echoing a messianic psalm, in which the Messiah declares the way in which God has chastened him, but has not given him over to (ultimate) death. Paul and his companions in the apostolic ministry can join in this psalm because they are in Christ and mediate his redemptive sufferings to believers. We may note in addition that 'the word of truth' mentioned in 2 Cor. 6.7 implies the proclamation of the mighty acts of God, which is exactly what the psalmist says he will do in the verse immediately before that which Paul quotes.

On the whole, commentators, while often noting the echo of Psalm 118 in v. 9, do not make very much of it. But Collange has a relevant comment (p. 299): 'One can see, in addition, how much Paul considers his own existence from the point of view of ('à travers le projet de') the righteous sufferer in the Psalms'. But one should add perhaps that he can only do so because Christ is the original sufferer. Paul, his fellow-apostles, and ultimately all believers can only claim to fulfil this rôle because Christ has first fulfilled it and they are 'in Christ'.[21] Collange also suggests that Paul applies παιδευόμενοι ('chastised') to himself and his colleagues because in the eyes of his adversaries their suffering is a sign of God's punishment. This would seem to be doubtful; in the original context of the psalm certainly the author regarded himself as having been punished by God, and it is not likely that Paul means to represent Christ or himself as not really having been chastened by God even though the bible said they had been. Surely the λύπη κατὰ θεόν which leads to μετάνοια of 7.9-11 is a form of chastening.

III

We turn now to the remarkable links which can be traced between our passage and Jesus' teaching as recorded in the Synoptic Gospels. These links have of course been observed frequently by those who have commented on 2 Corinthians. Windisch, for example, à propos vv. 8-10, points out very significantly that similar paradoxes are to be found in the Sermon on the Mount. He suggests also that the word πλάνοι in v. 8b may be a term of abuse applied to Paul by his opponents; Jesus is so described by the Jewish authorities in Matt. 27.63; and Windisch also compares 2 John 2. Barrett, likewise, commenting on v. 10, compares Luke 6.20; Matt. 5.3. In order to begin with a synoptic view of all the parallels to be found, it will be convenient to tabulate them as follows:

2 Cor. 6.4-10		Synoptic Parallels	
v. 4	ἐν θλίψεσιν, ἐν ἀνάγκαις	μακάριοι οἱ δεδιωγμένοι	Matt.
	ἐν στενοχωρίαις	ἕνεκεν δικαιοσύνης	5.10
v. 6	ἐν ἁγνότητι, ... ἐν	μακάριοι οἱ καθαροὶ	Matt.
	ἀγάπῃ ἀνυποκρίτῳ	τῇ καρδίᾳ	5.8
v. 8	διὰ δόξης καὶ ἀτιμίας,	μακάριοι ἐστε ὅταν	Matt.
	διὰ δυσφημίας καὶ	ὀνειδίσωσιν ὑμᾶς	5.11
	εὐφημίας		
		μακάριοι ἐστε ὅταν	Luke
		μισήσωσιν ὑμᾶς ...	6.22
		καὶ ὅταν ὀνειδίσωσιν	
v.10a	ὡς λυπούμενοι, ἀεὶ	μακάριοι οἱ πενθοῦντες	Matt.
	δὲ χαίροντες		5.4
		μακάριοι οἱ κλαίοντες	Luke
		νῦν, ὅτι γελάσατε	6.21b
v.10bc	ὡς πτωχοὶ πολλοὺς	μακάριοι οἱ πτωχοὶ	Matt.
	δὲ πλουτίζοντες,	τῷ πνεύματι	5.3
	ὡς μηδὲν ἔχοντες	μακάριοι οἱ πτωχοί	Luke
	καὶ πάντα κατέχοντες		6.20b

Some of this material has already been commented on; compare p. 28 above, where the parallel between 1 Cor. 4.12-13 and various passages in Luke has been explored. If we take the first parallel listed above to begin with, we may note a tendency among scholars to suggest that Matt. 5.10 is secondary, the product of the early Church rather than an authentic logion of Jesus. Thus Schweizer calls it 'a late inclusion'. Bultmann describes it as 'a Matthaean formulation intended to bring the number of the beatitudes...up to seven'.[22] Beare contents himself with remarking that 'the rhythmical structure of the initial sequence (three in Luke, eight in Matthew) is abandoned for this beatitude, which would seem to indicate that it was transmitted as a separate saying in the oral tradition'. Hill describes Matt. 5.11 as 'a specific application of verse 10 to the persecuted disciples and the Church', which implies that he regards v. 10 as authentic. Lohmeyer has a most interesting treatment of the logion.[23] He considers that Matt. 5.10-11 and Luke 6.22-23 are 'the variants of one and the same utterance, which both may go back to Jesus'. He compares Ps. 44.23, which of course we have already examined in connection with this passage; he mentions the eschatological nature of the disciples' sufferings, and he describes them thus: 'The disciples of Jesus—and the disciple means every eschatological believer—are the contemporary prophets'. He also calls them 'the future community in God's kingdom'. Lohmeyer's view confirms in a remarkable way our thesis that the citizens of the kingdom are the apostolic community in the time of the early Church.

It is true no doubt that the language of Matt. 5.10-11 and Luke 6.22-23 has been influenced by the experience of persecution suffered by contemporary Christians. But there is no need to conclude that these were invented by the early Church and that Jesus had no idea that his disciples would be persecuted. Nauck has claimed in an article that trials were an expected element in the eschatological afflictions, and that the experience of the Antiochean persecution and the Maccabean struggle strengthened this belief.[24] He himself passes over Jesus' teaching and attributes the references to persecution in the NT to the early Church's awareness that persecutions were to be a feature of the last days. But there is no reason to except Jesus from a knowledge of this apocalyptic tradition. His was an eschatological message. Nothing is more likely than that he should warn his disciples to expect persecution in the last days. Much more realistic on this topic is Pobee.[25] He shows that there was a strong martyr tradition in late Judaism. Legends grew up purporting to show that all the prophets were martyred. Jesus died a martyr's death because of his devotion to the will of God. In view of the very early attestation (in Paul's letters in fact) of the belief that suffering and persecution is the lot of the Christian apostle, we are surely justified in concluding that behind Matt. 5.10-11 and Luke 6.22-23 there stands authentic teaching of Jesus known to Paul.

When we consider the next verse on our list, 2 Cor. 6.6, we must be content with a simple comparison. The phrase 'pure of heart' comes in Ps. 24.4 (LXX 23.4). It is a translation of the Hebrew בר־לבב, rendered by the LXX with καθαρὸς τῇ καρδίᾳ. It is interesting that in the psalm the 'pure of heart' is promised a blessing from the Lord and 'righteousness' (MT צדקה) from the God of his salavation, i.e. vindication by God who is a saviour. In the very next verse to that in which Paul speaks of purity and love unfeigned, v. 7, he claims that the apostles have available to them the power of God and the weapons of righteousness. This could be an echo of the psalm. Compare also Phil. 1.17, where Paul's opponents are accused of proclaiming Christ οὐχ ἁγνῶς, which in the context seems to mean 'insincerely'.

Next comes v. 8 with its echo of 1 Cor. 4.10c. This we connect with Matt. 5.11 and Luke. 6.22. Plummer underlines the paradoxical nature of this beatitude, well in line with Paul's paradoxes here. Hill observes that the 'reward' mentioned in both Matthew and Luke may possibly here denote 'good repute' or 'glory', which would bring the sentiment very close to 2 Cor. 6.8a διὰ δόξης καὶ ἀτιμίας.

We must take v. 10 with its three clauses as a whole, because the two concepts grieving yet rejoicing and being poor yet really rich come together in the synoptic logia. There has of course been much discussion as to which of the two versions of the Synoptic logion about poverty is original, Matthew with his 'poor in spirit' or Luke with his 'blessed are you poor'. It is generally agreed that Jesus is not thinking of the economically deprived, but of the 'poor' of the Psalms, the ענוים. Montefiore (I, pp. 32f.) believes that Luke's version is nearer the original logion, and that Matthew's τῷ πνεύματι was added in order to make the meaning plain. W.C. Allen makes this explicit: 'The editor of the First Gospel probably thought that the simple πτωχοί would be misrepresented by Greek readers unacquainted with Semitic idiom'.[26] Schweizer explains that in 'the Judaism of Jesus' time "poor" had also become a sort of title of honour for the righteous (Ps. Sol. 5.2,11; 10.7; 15.1; 18.2)'. He adds that these beatitudes fall into the category of most NT beatitudes, which depict the unique eschatological age that dawns in Jesus. Matthew's version, he points out, underlines the danger of thinking that poverty is an honour. In Luke 'the statement becomes simply the legalism that in heaven all conditions are reversed, so that the poor become rich and the rich poor'. The contrast, says Lohmeyer, is not with those who have riches but with those who have power: 'Die Armen sind die Frommen'. Billerbeck (on Matt. 5.3) says that the same group is indicated by both Matthew and Luke. He commits himself to the statement that the phrase עני רוח is not found. In any case, he says, it should be עני ברוח. Since his day however the phrase ענוי־רוח has turned up in the Qumran documents, which only goes to show the perils of trying to turn the Synoptics into Hebrew.[27] D. Hill describes the category of the poor as 'the poor and afflicted saints of God', and adds that in Qumran the phrase means 'the humble poor who trust in God's help'.

What we have gathered so far would be sufficient in itself to establish a strong link between 2 Cor. 6.4-10 and Jesus' teaching as recorded in the Sermon on the Mount. But there are two scripture passages which establish the link still more firmly. They are Ps. 34.18 (MT 34.19; LXX 33.19) and Isa. 61.1-2. We must explore both these passages. Ps. 34.18 runs:

The lord is near to the broken-hearted,
and saves the crushed in spirit.

The MT has for these two nouns נשברי לב and רוח הכאי respectively.
The LXX offers συντετριμμένοις τὴν καρδίαν and ταπείνους τῷ
πνεύματι. This does not provide any very close verbal parallel,
though it could be said to correspond to all of the first three
beatitudes in Matt. 5.3-5, the poor in spirit, those who mourn, and
the meek, as well as covering generally the meaning of 2 Cor. 6.10.
But it also provides a link with the second scripture passage, Isa.
61.1-2, with which there are plenty of verbal links.
In the MT Isa. 61.1ab runs:

רוח אדני יהוה עלי יען משח יהוה אתי
לבשר ענוים שלחני לחבש לנשברי לב

The Spirit of the Lord God is upon me,
because the Lord has anointed me
to bring good tidings to the afflicted;
he has sent me to bind up the broken-hearted.

The LXX has:

πνεῦμα κυρίου ἐπ᾿ ἐμέ, οὗ εἴνεκεν ἔχρισέν με· εὐαγγελίσασθαι
πτωχοῖς ἀπέσταλκέν με,
ἰάσασθαι τοὺς συντετριμμένους τῇ καρδίᾳ.

The word for 'poor' here, ענוים, is exactly the word which scholars are
agreed lies behind the πτωχοί of Matt. 5.3; Luke 6.20. E. Bammel
comments that Matt. 5.3 refers to the ענוים whose hopes are fixed on
true eschatology.[28] The emphasis is on religious and not material
poverty. He describes 2 Cor. 6.4-10 as containing 'seven paradoxical
formulae which describe the essence of the apostolic life and service'
(p. 909). Hauck and Kasch associate Paul's enriching others through
his poverty with Christ, who was in the μορφὴ θεοῦ, taking the
μορφὴ δούλου.[29] Paul, they say, demonstrates 'ein heilsgeschichtliches
Gesetz' whereby a renunciation of one's own rights brings about
riches for others.

We are thus brought back to the citation from Isaiah 61, which
would certainly have been regarded as messianic by an early
Christian (cf. Matt. 11.5; Luke 4.18-19). The poverty to which both
Jesus and Paul refer belongs to the eschatological era, when God's
faithful servants will receive their reward. The association of the ענוים
with the saints is attested in rabbinical tradition. See *Abodah Zarah*

20b, where R. Joshua ben Levy is recorded as claiming that meekness is the greatest virtue of all.[30]

> Scripture says, *The Spirit of the Lord God is upon me, because the Lord hath anointed me to bring good tidings unto the meek*. It does not say 'unto the saints', but 'unto the meek', from which you may learn that meekness is the greatest of all these.

There is also an interesting tradition about Isaiah in connection with this passage to be found in *Pesikta Rabbati*.[31] It is pointed out that all the other prophets prophesied by means of another prophet, e.g. the spirit of Elijah rested upon Elisha. But God says to Isaiah: 'thou alone wilt prophesy from the mouth of the divine Power, so that thou canst say . . .'. Then follows Isa. 61.1. Is this tradition perhaps reflected in the Targum? It omits any reference to anointing and renders the opening sentence thus: 'The prophet said, The spirit of prophecy from before the Lord Elohim is upon me . . .'. In the same passage in *Pesikta Rabbati* Isaiah is warned by the example of the other prophets that he will suffer for his prophesying. He replies in the words of Isa. 50.6: 'I am ready to give my back to the smiters'.

The same theme is treated in *Piska* 33.3.[32] With that occasional disregard for historical sequence which is characteristic of rabbinical exegesis, God, detailing the sufferings of the prophets, says: 'When I sent Jeremiah they threw him into a pit'. Isaiah is then represented as quoting Isa. 50.4. In the *Pesikta de Rab Kahana*[33] the same tradition appears. Here it is linked with Isaiah 52.7: 'How beautiful upon the mountains are the feet of him who brings good tidings'. The messenger of good tidings is identified both with the prophet himself and with the redeemer mentioned in Isa. 59.20, presumably the Messiah. This casting of Isaiah in the rôle of the servant of the Lord is not without significance for our theme. It shows that Isa. 61.1f was associated in rabbinic tradition with one who had received the Holy Spirit in outstanding measure, one who had to suffer for his message, and one who was to be expected in the end time. Perhaps Paul thought of himself and his companions as 'the poor' in the sense that they had received the eschatological gospel (good tidings) from the one designated in this prophecy, and that they were obliged to hand it on to others. As themselves recipients of the Spirit, which was a mark of the end time, they also shared in the activity of messianic prophecy.

Billerbeck quotes both Isa 61.1 and Ps. 34.19 as passages which
may lie behind Matt. 5.3. We should also point out another
interesting feature of this passage from Isaiah: it gives us one more
instance of a reference to the acceptable time. Isaiah 61.2a says that
the prophet has been anointed in order 'to proclaim the acceptable
year of the Lord'. The MT is לקרא שנת רצון ליהוה. The LXX offers
καλέσαι ἐνιαυτὸν κυρίου δεκτόν. This of course marks the passage
as apocalyptic, looking to the end time, and also gives a remarkable
link with 2 Cor. 6.2, at the beginning of the passage with which we
are concerned.[34]

As we look at 2 Cor. 6.10 in the light of the extracts from Jesus'
teaching considered above, there would seem to be good reason to
conclude both that Paul was well aware of this teaching and that he
believes the apostolic group in his day to be the recipients of the
promises as we have them in the Sermon on the Mount. Moreover
behind this teaching of Jesus lie the scriptural passages we have
reviewed, and Paul was also aware of this. In this connection
Windisch's comment is relevant: he says that the word χαίροντες has
an eschatological ring about it. The inner riches of which Paul
disposes consist in the fulness of charismatic gifts or the access to the
heavenly heritage. This must not be understood, we would want to
add, as something different from possession of the gospel referred to
in 4.7: the knowledge of the gospel is the essential preliminary to the
receiving of charismatic gifts. Windisch well compares 2 Cor. 8.9,
where Christ is described as having been poor that Christians
through his poverty might become rich. It is not implied that Christ
is now permanently poor. It is the same paradoxical life-in-death,
riches-through-poverty, glory-through-suffering that runs all through
Paul's theology of the cross.

The link with Jesus' teaching that we will be examining in the next
chapter has no connection with the Q tradition, but is of a quite
different character. It is appropriate therefore to bring up here once
more the question as to whether it is possible to identify the
knowledge which Paul betrays of Jesus' teaching with any existing
body of material.[35]

There has recently been quite a lot of discussion on this point,
some of which we may relevantly review. Furnish allowed the most
obvious links between Paul and Jesus' teaching, such as the relation
of 1 Cor. 9.14 to Luke 10.7, of Rom. 12.14 to Matt. 5.44 and Rom.
12.17 to Matt. 5.39.[36] He does not however note any parallels with

2 Corinthians. Dungan sees a parallel between 1 Cor. 9.14 and the Lord's command that apostles should be supported by their audience, a point which we shall meet again presently.[37] His general conclusion is that Paul was acquainted with a wide area of Jesus' teaching (p. 150). Fjärstedt makes a more systematic attempt in his book to trace connections between 1 Corinthians and Jesus' teaching.[38] He therefore explores in detail the connection between 1 Corinthians 9 and Jesus' missionary discourse in Luke 10.1-20 (pp. 66f., 99). He allows a connection between 1 Cor. 4.12-13 and Matt. 5.44; Luke 6.27f. (p. 105). He draws an interesting comparison between 1 Cor. 1.17-2.16, the language about wisdom and folly, and Luke 10.21-24 (= Matt. 11.25-27), the so-called 'Johannine thunderbolt', or as the Germans call it the 'Jubelruf', a point we have already touched on on p. 17 above.[39] He concludes that Paul must have had access to some written traditions of Jesus' teaching, part of which anyway later appeared in the document called Q (pp. 173f.).

More recently Allison has treated the same subject in a very convincing manner.[40] He allows that Fjärstedt has made his case for a close parallel between 1 Cor. 9 and Luke 10. Paul did know Jesus' mission discourse (pp. 9-10). On the strength of 1 Cor. 4.12-13 he concludes that Paul knew of the teaching preserved for us in Luke 6.27-28 (pp. 11-12). But he is rightly sceptical about the possibilities of drawing any conclusions concerning Q from this evidence: 'The existence of a special "Q community" that had no interest in the passion of Jesus is probably a myth of modern scholarship' (p. 29). He will not commit himself to any theory that Paul knew Q or L or M or Ur-Mark: 'But that Paul did know blocks which finally found their way into Q and the second gospel indicates that he was no stranger to the circles eventually responsible for the corpus of logia and Mark' (p. 19). He also concludes that the tradition of the works and words of Jesus was much more independent of the needs of the early Church than the first Form Critics imagined. He writes: 'the persistent conviction that Paul knew next to nothing of the teaching of Jesus must be rejected' (p. 25). Tuckett has very recently examined J.A.T. Robinson's suggestion that there could be a connection between 1 Corinthians and Q.[41] He asks however whether it is Paul or the Corinthians who are using Q. He allows the connection between 1 Corinthians 9 and the mission address of Jesus found in Q. He also allows with some hesitation the 'Jubelruf' connection, but says it comes from Paul's tradition, not that of the Corinthians. His general conclusion is that the evidence does not prove any firm connection with Q.[42]

If we add to the evidence connecting 1 Cor. 4.12-13 with Jesus' teaching about loving one's enemies the evidence which we have been examining in the last two chapters, it greatly strengthens the case for the theory that Paul was acquainted with a good deal of Jesus' teaching. What is more, all the teaching material which we have in Paul's references in 2 Corinthians seems to come from those parts of the Synoptic Gospels which are common to Matthew and Luke but not to Mark—in other words from the source known as Q. It looks very much as if Paul knew a source of Jesus' teaching which later (or quite possibly at the same time) contributed to the Q source used by Matthew and Luke. But we must pay heed to Allison's careful language. We must not say that Paul knew Q, only that the teaching of Jesus known to Paul seems to have also found its way into the Q source. We must certainly refrain from writing about 'a Q community'. I am not at all sure that we should commit ourselves to the belief that Q was a written, and not an oral, source. But certainly the case for a connection between Jesus' teaching as reflected in 1 and 2 Corinthians and the source known as Q has been greatly strengthened.

Finally we may just glance at a question which we must discuss at greater length later: since Paul was certainly acquainted with a substantial portion of Jesus' teaching, why does he not acknowledge it? Why does he never say explicitly that the teaching given by Jesus concerning the citizens of the kingdom now applies to the apostolic community? Furnish's explanation is this: 'Paul does not appeal to Jesus as an earthly teacher or to his sayings as to the instruction of a distinguished rabbi. His appeals are to the risen, reigning Christ, the Church's Lord' (p. 56). I believe that this is correct, though I think it could be expressed more precisely. Otto Betz, writing in a completely different context, comes to a very similar conclusion.[43] He suggests that the reason why Paul does not use the phrase 'Son of Man' is that there is no further need to refer to the exalted Lord by means of what was a mysterious word. Wedderburn has very recently devoted an article to our problem.[44] He makes the interesting suggestion that in Paul's day Jesus' teaching was in enemy hands, i.e. was being constantly quoted by Judaizing or Gnosticizing Christians. To quote Jesus explicitly would be for Paul to subordinate himself to the Jerusalem church (pp. 190-91). Again, perhaps too frequent references to the kingdom of God in Corinth by Paul had already given rise to false ideas, e.g. 1 Cor. 4.8 (p. 201). He concludes that 'It is the new and different situations in which Jesus' followers later and subsequently found themselves that called for new language' (p. 203). The speculation about Jesus' teaching being in enemy hands is interesting but unsupported by very much evidence. It is quite true that Paul and his fellow-workers were in a quite different situation from that of the earthly Jesus. The great event had taken place (Wedderburn does not mention eschatology). But the surprising feature is not the difference but the parallelism of language. What has to be explained is why the teaching was not explicitly attributed to Jesus.

All the parallels with Jesus' teaching which we have discussed in these last two chapters have to do with his teaching concerning the kingdom. They are descriptions of those who are fit to be citizens of the kingdom. When we transpose this teaching into a post-Easter situation, the obvious candidates for the rôle of citizens of the kingdom are the apostles themeselves, the apostles of course in the sense in which Paul understood the term, that is those who are charged with the task of preaching the gospel of God's act in Jesus Christ. This may well explain why Paul does not write 'The Lord Jesus said this is what we should be like, this is how we should behave'. Paul was trying to persuade his converts to live out the life of Christ in their lives because the kingdom had already dawned. Moreover, they were not merely externally related to Christ, imitating him as an artist draws from a model; they were ἐν Χριστῷ, in Christ. Hence the language which the earthly Jesus used to describe the life of the kingdom can be freely used, illuminated by the Christian's knowledge of how Jesus had lived out that teaching in his own sufferings and death. But, since Paul wanted to turn their minds towards the present living Christ, whose sufferings are in some sense represented in the sufferings first of the apostles and then of their converts, he does not revert to the earthly Jesus. The teaching which the Lord while on earth had given about the citizens of the kingdom had now been fulfilled in the life of the apostles. Paul owes a great debt to the teaching of Jesus, just as he owes a great debt to the writings of the prophets in scripture. But he is no more interested in the context in which the teaching of Jesus was originally given than he is interested in investigating the circumstances in which the various prophecies recorded in scripture were composed and uttered.

In both cases he concentrates on the period of fulfilment.

Chapter 5

WHO ARE THE DOGS?
PHIL. 3.2-16; GAL. 6.17

In this chapter we enter new territory, in the sense that we leave the Corinthian correspondence in order to examine a passage in Philippians. Since our theme is the paradox of the cross, we cannot afford to ignore this passage. Yet at first sight it does not seem to fit into the pattern of the three key passages which we have considered so far. It does not offer a series of striking paradoxes, and it does not appear to be a description of the apostolic ministry. What is more, there seems to be a total absence of scriptural references. We hope to show, however, that, though there is no series of paradoxes, all turns on the one great paradox of the cross, which has reversed traditional values. We shall try to show that the situation is closely parallel to that in Corinth, and we shall spend at least half our time tracing a connection with the teaching of Jesus that is remarkably different from any which we have encountered hitherto.

I

The study of St. Paul's Epistle to the Philippians has not been made easier by the recent tendency on the part of scholars to regard the Epistle as a collection of fragments of letters rather than as an integrated whole. It would be beyond the scope of this work to examine in detail the various reconstructions that have been proposed. We are chiefly concerned with 3.2-16, which everyone agrees is all part of one letter. But we shall not hesitate to cite other parts of Philippians as evidence in favour of the interpretation of this passage which we advance. In any case it is not likely that, however various may have been the contexts in which the various fragmentary letters were written (if Philippians is really a collection of fragments), the quality of the opponents with whom Paul was dealing varied greatly from one context to another.

The significance of Phil. 3.2-16 for our theme is that it is a passage in which Paul is very explicit about his sharing in the sufferings of Christ. Paul actually mentions 'the fellowship of his sufferings', and writes about himself as 'being made conformable to (Christ's) death'. Moreover he lists his apparent advantages 'according to the flesh' in a way reminiscent of 2 Cor. 11.22-29. In both contexts he is telling of subjects about which he could legitimately have boasted, though he has no intention of doing so. In 2 Cor. 11.22 he begins with the same sort of reasons for boasting as he details in Phil. 3.5-6, his privileges as a Jew, and a scrupulous and zealous Jew at that. But in 2 Corinthians he goes on to give a list of his sufferings in the course of his apostolic ministry, something which we do not find in Philippians. At the same time, the circumstances in which Philippians ch. 1 at least seems to have been written are very similar to some of the predicaments listed in 2 Corinthians 11.

There are however other features of Phil. 3.2-16 which distinguish it from the descriptions of the ministry in the Corinthian letters which we have been considering. In the first place, there does not seem to be any explicit reference to the apostolic ministry in Philippians; Paul seems to be concentrating exclusively on his own experience. Then again, the resurrection, which plays a prominent part in the Philippians passage, seems to be a purely future event. Paul looks forward to his own resurrection in the future, as he does in all his genuine letters, but there does not seem to be any clear mention of the life-through-death teaching which we find in 2 Corinthians. Thirdly, as we have already noted, there is a remarkable absence of references to scripture in this Philippians passage. Whereas in the three passages from the Corinthian letters with which we have been concerned Paul's doctrine of the paradox of the cross and the apostolic ministry is supported by plentiful references to scripture, here there appears to be none at all. If we are to include Phil. 3.2-16 in the list of passages in which Paul expounds the paradox of the cross and the apostolic ministry, we must try to answer these questions.

We will do so by examining first what Paul means by κοινωνία παθημάτων αὐτοῦ, 'the fellowship of his sufferings' in Phil. 3.10. Then we shall try to show that the opponents in Philippi were very like the opponents in Corinth, to that extent equating the two situations. Beyond this of course lies our exposition of the connection of this passage with the teaching of Jesus himself.

J.B. Lightfoot seems to equate Paul's sharing in Christ's sufferings simply with living the Christian life.[1] He writes:

> The conformity of the sufferings of Christ implies not only the endurance of persecution for His name, but all pangs and all afflictions undergone in the struggle against sin either within or without. The agony of Gethsemane not less than the agony of Calvary will be reproduced, however faintly, in the faithful servant of Christ.

No doubt this is true homiletically. We would be quite justified in putting this gloss on St. Paul's words if we were apply them to the life of the modern Christian in the Western democracies. But is this what Paul meant? Does he ever list his own spiritual struggles among the sufferings he endures for Christ? Would not 2 Cor. 12.1-10 rather point in the opposite direction? Lipsius, writing at very much the same period as Lightfoot, seems nearer the mark.[2] He expounds the phrase we are concerned with as 'a participation in the suffering and death of Christ through the experience of actual suffering in the course of his apostolic work'. Lohmeyer on the other hand would equate Paul's sufferings with martyrdom.[3] He actually claims that in this passage the apostolic calling is eclipsed by the call to martyrdom. He adds that Paul's martyrdom is also linked with that of believers. This seems to be going beyond the evidence. We may refer to Pobee's work which we have mentioned above.[4] He suggests that Paul's prospect of martyrdom is interpreted in terms of his apostolic ministry rather than *vice versa*. Though it is quite true that the martyr motif in Judaism helps to explain much of Paul's doctrine of the atonement, Paul does not, unlike Ignatius of Antioch later, positively welcome the prospect of martyrdom. He is too much concentrated on his relationship to Christ in the course of his apostolic ministry to concern himself with whether in fact it matters that ultimately he should be put to death for Christ's sake. He is ready to die for Christ, but that is all in the day's work, not a separate achievement.

Lohmeyer believes that the phrase ἐξανάστασιν τὴν ἐκ νεκρῶν in 3.11 does not refer to the general resurrection, but to a special resurrection of the faithful in Christ. Collange on the other hand, on the strength of the phrase τὴν δύναμιν τῆς ἀναστάσεως αὐτοῦ in v. 10, says that this cannot be confined to the final resurrection, but has an element of present experience in it.[5] This experience, he claims, is well expressed in 2 Cor. 4.7-10, the passage in which Paul explicitly asserts that life for the Corinthians is to come through the operation of death among the apostles. But in the same passage of course Paul also says that the life of Jesus is to be manifested in their mortal flesh. Martin[6] however remarks that the rare word ἐξανάστασις, unique here in biblical Greek, emphasizes that Paul means the final resurrection.[7] Both scholars may well be right: Paul held that one could experience the power of Christ's resurrection before one's own bodily resurrection. He links knowing Christ with experiencing the power of his resurrection and sharing the fellowship of his sufferings, obviously a contemporary process. The goal of the process was his own resurrection from the dead.

It is true that in Philippians Paul does not underline the corporate nature of the apostolic life, as he does in the Corinthian letters. But, if we may bring in evidence from parts of the Epistle outside this passage, we may note that it is writen in the name of Paul and Timothy, who are both indifferently described as slaves of Christ (1.1). Again, in 1.29-30 Paul writes as follows:

> For it has been granted to you that for the sake of Christ you
> should not only believe in him but also suffer for his sake, engaged
> in the same conflict which you saw and now hear to be mine.

Here certainly is the corporate element. The sufferings are described as taking place 'for the sake of Christ', and are identified with Paul's. The identification of the Philippians' sufferings with Christ's sufferings is not actually made here, but they are identified with Paul's sufferings, and 3.10 certainly identifies those with Christ's. What is lacking is any specific reference to the apostolic ministry. There is, however, no lack of mention of the apostolic ministers. In 2.19-23 he tells the Philippians of his intention to send Timothy to them; and in 2.30 his assistant Epaphroditus is described thus: 'he nearly died for the work of Christ, risking his life to complete your service to me'. We might almost say that the apostolic ministry is here, but Paul has not fully integrated it into his theological thought. We know that in 2 Corinthians his opponents were describing themselves as true apostles and were casting doubts on Paul's apostolic credentials. Perhaps this new element in the opposition which he encountered at Corinth instigated Paul to work out a theology of the apostolic ministry.

One other resemblance between Philippians and 2 Corinthians may be pointed out. In Phil. 1.28 Paul exhorts the Corinthians thus:

and (be) not frightened in anything by your opponents. This is a
clear omen to them of their destruction, but of your salvation, and
that from God.

This is very like 2 Cor. 2.15-16, a text which we will be examining in
detail in our next chapter. Both the passages use military metaphors,
and both assert that the same process indicates salvation to believers
and perdition to unbelievers. In Paul's mind as he wrote Philippians
(however he wrote it) the same theology of salvation was present.

At this point we must step aside for a moment to examine a
passage from Galatians. Gal. 6.7 qualifies for inclusion in our study
because in it Paul asserts his unity with the cross of Christ in such
startling language that some commentators have been tempted to
take him with absolute literalness. In Gal. 6.12-15 Paul has been
referring to the opponents who have been troubling the Galatians.
He uses language remarkably like that used in Phil. 3.2-11, or indeed
that of Phil. 1.15-17. They only urge circumcision on the Galatians
in order to exploit them for their own advantage. What matters is not
circumcision but the new creation. Paul declares that through Christ
he has been crucified to the world and the world to him. Then in
v. 17 he concludes with:

τοῦ λοιποῦ κόπους μοι μηδεὶς παρεχέτω, ἐγὼ γὰρ τὰ στίγματα τοῦ
Ἰησοῦ ἐν τῷ σώματί μου βαστάζω.

Henceforth let no man trouble me; for I bear on my body the marks
of Jesus.

Naturally there has been much speculation as to Paul's exact
meaning here. Commentators have referred to Isa. 44.5, where those
who belong to Yahweh are told that in the end time they will have
written on their hands 'belonging to Yahweh'. In Isa. 49.16 Yahweh
has written Jerusalem on the palms of his hands. There was a
practice in contemporary pagan religion of branding on one's body
the name of one's chosen deity. Criminals were also brand-marked to
prevent their escaping.[8] Betz admits that Paul's reference could
mean that he was brand-marked as Jesus' slave. But he considers that
this is not what Paul means. The στίγματα were the marks on his
body consequent on his sufferings for Jesus Christ (p. 663). In
profane Greek στίγμα can mean a tattoo mark, inscribed laws, a
mark or spot (as on a dragon's skin), or a colour. In late Greek it can
denote a cicatrix, i.e. the mark of an old wound. In fact it never
means the mark of a wound *tout simplement*. In Gal. 6.17 therefore it

cannot mean that Christ's wounds were somehow reproduced on Paul's body, as in the case of St. Francis' stigmatization. When doubting Thomas in John 20.25 demands to see the marks of the nails, the word is τύπος, not στίγμα.

Luther in his commentary on Galatians roundly denies that Francis really received the stigmata: 'he printed them on himself through some foolish devotion'.[9] Calvin maintains that Paul's claim is not to be taken literally.[10] The 'marks' are 'imprisonments, bonds, floggings, blows, stonings, in fact every form of ill usage which he had borne on behalf of witness for the gospel'. Lagrange agrees that the maltreatment Paul had received is the brand-mark distinguishing him as a slave of Jesus.[11] He adds that since the grace accorded to St. Francis of Assisi the word has taken on a new meaning. Straub says that the reference is not to a brand-mark voluntarily imposed, but to the injuries received during Paul's missionary labours.[12] Schlier[13] well quotes Thomas Aquinas as saying that the verse means 'Nullus super me ius habet nisi Christus', 'No man has any rights over me except Christ'. Schlier agrees with the almost universal interpretation that the στίγματα are the marks of injuries received during Paul's ministry. At first sight Güttgemanns seems to dissent from the general view.[14] The verse does not refer to the beatings or maltreatment that Paul had suffered at the hands of his enemies, nor to some sort of physical illness which he had endured. They are Jesus' στίγματα, and βαστάζω here is analagous to the περιφέροντες of 2 Cor. 4.10. He concludes, 'In the maltreated body of the apostle is the crucified Jesus present as Lord' (p. 134). No doubt Güttgemanns is justified in insisting on the primary meaning of the presence of Christ in Paul's life, but it comes to very much the same thing as the general interpretation. Bligh has a slight modification of this view.[15] The stigmata, he says, are 'the spiritual counterpart of circumcision; they mark Paul as the servant of Christ; they are a spiritual badge of freedom'. One might protest on behalf of Paul that there was nothing very spiritual about the wounds left on his body by the beatings and other maltreatment which he had received, a point which Bligh acknowledges when he adds that Paul is probably also thinking of 'the scars left on his body by the persecutions he underwent during his mission to the Gentiles'.

W. Klassen has drawn attention to a passage in Josephus's *Jewish War*, 1.197, where Antipater, on being accused of disloyalty to Caesar, stripped off his clothes and exposed his numerous scars.[16]

His loyalty to Caesar needed no words, he said, 'his body cried it aloud, were he to hold his peace'. So Paul's plea is that the wounds he has gained proved his loyalty to Christ. But was anyone doubting Paul's loyalty to Christ? In any case, Paul has just specifically repudiated boasting about anything except what Christ had achieved and was achieving by his death. Emphasising his own loyalty would be a form of boasting.

Borse has not very long ago written an important article on the subject of the stigmata.[17] They refer, he says to the wounds Paul acquired during his apostolic labours. He suggests three possible interpretations, which he regards as mutually incompatible:

(a)   The wounds of Paul and Jesus are identical (stigmatization presumably).

(b)   The scars on Paul's body are the signs of his fellowship in suffering with Christ.

(c)   By Jesus' will Paul has received wounds in his service which are comparable with those of Jesus.

He rejects (a) and inclines to (c).[18] He believes Paul is referring to the dangerous situation in which he had found himself in Asia, to which both 1 Cor. 15.32 and 2 Cor. 1.8 refer. The circumstances are very obscure and it may be that Luke deliberately omits them in Acts 19.21-40 (though Borse does not hold this view, see p. 107), but it looks as if before writing either 1 or 2 Corinthians Paul had been in danger of his life in Ephesus. Borse finds cross-connections between Gal. 6.17 and most of the passages in the Corinthian letters with which we are concerned. He holds, on the basis of 2 Cor. 4.12, 'So death is at work in us but life in you', that other Christians are not regarded as sharing in the process of life-in-death (p. 102). But he admits that they could if they shared Paul's sort of life. In any case we may claim that our studies in the last chapter have made it clear enough that this was Paul's meaning. Borse has in fact brought Gal. 6.11-17 well within the area of the subject we are considering.

We may finally cite Ebeling on behalf of the view that the stigmata are the marks of the ill-treatment which Paul had received according to Christ's will: they are the sign of his apostleship.[19] And also we refer once more to Pobee.[20] The stigmata, he says, are the scars which Paul received as a result of the persecutions which accompanied his apostolic ministry. Thus our latest commentator strongly supports the general opinion.

When we take Gal. 6.11-17 as a whole we can say that it fits into the general pattern of passages about the paradox of the cross. It is not as effectively presented as the Corinthian passages with their brilliant series of antitheses, and Paul is not here concerned with the apostolic ministry. But the paradox of the cross is central to this passage, and so is the representation of Jesus' sufferings by his disciple. One might conjecture that whenever Paul faced opposition in the form of teaching markedly different from his own he fell back on the doctrine of the cross, and this is always expressed in terms of paradox.

We must now undertake a brief review of the opinions of recent scholars on the subject of the nature of Paul's opponents in Philippi, in order to decide how far the position there was similar to that which prevailed in Corinth. Lohmeyer holds that the opponents in Philippi must have been Jews not Christians; perhaps they came from the Jewish synagogue in Philippi. This does not on the whole seem very probable. The word ἔργαται ('workers'), which Paul uses of them suggests that they were missionaries, and this points towards Christian Jews (a point made by Koester, p. 320). In 1961/2 Koester published an article[21] in which he maintained that the opponents were 'Jewish Christian apostles who boasted of their special spiritual qualities'(p. 321). He thinks they claimed that a spiritual resurrection had already taken place (p. 323). He calls them early Gnostics but not libertines (p. 324). They are not necessarily to be identified with the opponents in Corinth (p. 332). Klijn in 1965 maintained, in line with Lohmeyer, that Paul's opponents in Philippi were Jews and not Christians.[22] The γνῶσις they propagated was knowledge of the law. This plays down the Gnostic element, but somehow does not exactly fit the situation. Paul does not give the impression that he is facing people who denied Christ altogether, as Jews would have done. He seems to be arguing against people who misunderstand Christ rather than repudiating him. In the same year Gnilka published an article which treated the question more thoroughly.[23] The opponents, he believes, were Christian Jews. They proclaimed Christ but also preached circumcision (p. 261). They claimed to be pneumatics though it is not clear what they taught about the resurrection (p. 270). Perhaps they described Jesus as a θεῖος ἀνήρ ('divine man'). They must in fact be described as Gnostics (pp. 271-72). Moses was also such a divine man, they claimed. They blurred the line between the earthly Christ and the risen Lord; hence the cross became unimportant. They were very like the opponents in Corinth (p. 276).

Two years later H.D. Betz in his important work on the imitation of Christ in the NT devoted some pages to the question of Paul's opponents in Philippi.[24] He disagrees with Schmithal's view that they are Gnosticizing Jews (p. 149). He also discounts the accusation of Libertiniism or Antinomianism which they have incurred because of Phil. 3.18-19. This is the regular theme of the Greek diatribe and need not be taken seriously. Paul in fact attacks two quite separate groups in Philippi, Gnosticizing Jewish Christians and a group of profligate livers (p. 151). Collange in his commentary on Philippians expresses the belief that Paul had been called a 'dog' by his opponents because he did not fully observe the law. Glasswell in 1973/4 published an article in which he claimed that in Philippians we have an attack on people who performed physical circumcision,[25] 'probably Jewish Christian Gnostics' (p. 332). He adds: 'The play on words (περιτομή=κατατομή) in 3.2 is bitterly ironical and reminiscent of Gal. 5.12, where Paul wishes his opponents would go too far and fall under the condemnation of Deut. 23.2, thus revealing their actual state of conflict with God's will'. We may question this conclusion as far as concerns the situation in Philippi. The word κατατομή itself does not recall Deut. 23.2, where the LXX uses ἀποκεκομμένος,[26] unlike Gal. 5.12 where Paul writes ὄφελον καὶ ἀποκόψονται οἱ ἀναστατοῦντες ὑμᾶς. All Paul is doing in Phil. 3.2f. is asserting the superiority of faith over circumcision, and claiming that Christianity is Judaism spiritualized, much as he does in Rom. 2.28-29. R.P. Martin in his commentary on Philippians already referred to suggests that the opponents are Jewish Christians. Lastly we may cite A.T. Lincoln, who holds that the opponents are 'Judaising propagandists'.[27]

I conclude from this review that Paul's opponents in Philippi were Jewish Christians, ardent defenders of the Torah, who taught an early form of Gnosticism in which the cross played a very insignificant part. I do not think that we need necessarily conclude that they insisted on circumcision for all converts, though no doubt they boasted of being circumcised themselves.

When we sum up the impression we gain of Paul's opponents in Philippi, we cannot fail to remark how similar they are to those in Corinth. The opponents in Corinth were Jewish Christians influenced by Greek philosophy,[28] pneumatics;[29] they represented a form of early Gnosticism;[30] they held that a spiritual resurrection had already taken place.[31] When we turn to 2 Corinthians 3 we can see there are clear traces of the presentation of Moses in the teaching Paul is opposing as something like a 'divine man'. That these opponents were Christian Jews we have already argued. The one point of apparent difference between the opponents in Philippi and those in Corinth is that there is no suggestion in the Corinthian correspondence of any concern about circumcision. In Philippi there certainly is. But we believe that we have shown that the evidence in Philippians does not necessarily require that the opponents have been demanding circumcision from their converts. Another, minor, point of difference may be that in Corinth the question of apostolic authority seems to have been in debate. There is no sign of this in Philippi.

Robert Jewett in his book on the chronology of Paul's life published in 1979 has suggested a chronological sequence which would place the writing of Philippians in Ephesus in the year AD 55, while Paul was in imprisonment there.[32] He adopts the view we have already referred to in discussing Borse's article (see p. 85 above) that the trouble in Ephesus was far more serious than Luke implies in Acts 19. Jewett places the writing of the Corinthian letters in the years 55-56, after Paul's release. This schema would allow the two passages 1 Cor. 15.32 and 2 Cor. 1.8 to refer to the trouble in Ephesus. It would also fit in with the view that Philippians is, so to speak, a dress rehearsal for the Corinthian correspondence as far as concerns Paul's theology of the apostolic ministry and its relation to the cross. Paul's encounters with the Corinthian church must have made him think. The theology of the apostolic miistry which he sets out in the two epistles is the fruit of his pastoral experience. But the materials for it are nearly all there in Philippians: the close association of Paul's sufferings with Christ's, the references to Paul's fellow-workers, the necessity to defend his teaching against Judaizing opponents, the repudiation of any boasting on Paul's part, the association of the church to which he is writing with similar sufferings which they are to undergo or are undergoing—above all the paradox of the cross at the centre of it all. What was present in the Philippian correspondence has been integrated and worked out in the Corinthian. But Philippians provides us with a genuine example of the pattern of thought which we are engaged in studying.[33]

The outstanding difference between the two sets of correspondence which we have left unresolved is that there does not seem to be any scriptural background to the theology of the cross in Philippians. One can only conjecture that as Paul thought over the significance of the apostolic ministry he began to see the light which the scriptural theme of the one and the many that he had learned to distinguish in the Psalms and elsewhere could throw upon the relation of the crucified Christ to the apostolic ministers and to Christians as a whole. When he set out his theology of the cross in greater detail in the Corinthian correspondence he was able to incorporate these references to scripture and thus to enhance and amplify his theme.[34] It may even be that his close brush with death in Ephesus drove him back to study his bible more carefully.

II

The remarkable reflection of Jesus's teaching which we encounter in Phil. 3.2-16 is to be found in vv. 2 and 8. It is this: in verse 2 Paul refers to his Judaizing opponents as 'dogs'. These are the people who are demanding that their Gentile converts become almost Jews if they are to join the Christian Church. In v. 8 Paul says that he has now come to regard precisely those Jewish privileges which he formerly prized, and which his opponents still prize, as σκύβαλα, a word that could mean 'leavings of a meal only fit to be thrown out'. In Mark 7.24-30 we have a story in which Jesus, asked to cure a Gentile woman's daughter, replies

> it is not good to take the children's bread and throw it to the dogs.

The reflection of Jesus' teaching here is a mirror image: the values have been exactly reversed. Those whom Jesus regarded as dogs are now the true circumcision, the true Jews, the renewed people of God. That which is really only fit to be thrown to the dogs is what in Jesus' day distinguished Jews from Gentiles and therefore made Jesus hesitate to grant the Gentile woman's request. The question, which I have ventured to use as a title for this chapter is, who are the dogs? Gentiles? Or those who would demand that Gentiles become Jews before receiving the bread of life? Does Paul know of this tradition about Jesus? Is he deliberately underlining the reversal of values?

This question cannot be answered without a careful evaluation of the pericope Mark 7.24-30. This in turn requires a consideration of the Matthaean parallel Matt. 15.21-28. Nor can we ignore the very relevant logion in Matt. 7.6:

> Do not give dogs what is holy; and do not throw your pearls before swine, lest they trample them under foot and turn to attack you.

— We will begin by considering the way the commentators on Philippians have treated the parallel. We will then examine what scholars have made of the pericope about the Gentile woman's daughter. Finally we will try to draw some conclusions.

Lightfoot in his commentary on Philippians has noted the contrast. Paul, he says, has reversed the situation of orthodox Judaism: orthodox Jews thought that the Gentiles might receive the leavings. He defines σκύβαλα in v. 8 as 'the refuse or leavings of the feast'. Straub[35] tells us that Suidas paraphrases σκύβαλα with κυσίβαλόν τι ὄν, τὸ τοῖς κυσὶ βαλλόμενον, 'something that is thrown to the dogs', a false etymology but a correct interpretation. Straub suggests that Paul may have deliberately used σκύβαλα as a word of abuse used among Jews to denote opponents. Michel compares Matt. 7.6, and speculates whether Paul knew of this logion.[36] His conclusion is that Paul did know it and is echoing it here in reverse. On the other hand he thinks Jesus' use of κυνάρια in Mark 7.27 (par. Matt. 15.26) is a reference to domestic dogs, not to the wild 'pi-dogs' who roamed the streets. So he must be classed among those who accept the 'soft option': Jesus is not using insulting language towards Gentiles here. Beare in his commentary on Philippians gives three possible meanings for σκύβαλα: 'street-sweepings', 'refuse of the table', and 'excrement'. Lohmeyer holds that Jesus did apply the word 'dogs' to Gentiles in the full pejorative meaning of the term. Paul turns back on Jews the term they use for Gentiles. What Paul so completely rejects is what has been consecrated by the history of the Jewish people. Lang points out that Philo uses σκύβαλα for the remains of food (*Sacr. Abelis*, 109).[37] He comments on our passage in Philippians thus: 'The God-given precedence of Israel and the spiritual character of the law are not hereby denied'. Gnilka[38] claims that in calling his opponents 'dogs' Paul did not mean that they were immoral, but that they did not hold the right faith. We may remark that if there is a reference to Jesus' logion on the subject, the epithet 'dogs' means more than 'heretics'. Martin in his commentary gives a reference to Matt. 15.21-28, but only concludes that Jesus called Gentiles 'dogs'. Lastly we note that

Lincoln has seen the remarkable reversal;[39] he compares Phil. 3.2 with Mark 7.27. Paul, he writes, is 'turning his Judaising opponents' description of the uncircumcised against themselves'. We now turn to the pericope. But we should first observe that the passage already alluded to, Matt. 7.6, the prohibition against throwing what is holy to the dogs, is peculiar to Matthew. Matthew's treatment of the pericope about the curing of the Gentile woman's daughter exhibits some peculiar features also, so much so that some scholars have questioned whether Matthew is really following Mark here and have suggested that his account of this incident comes from his own tradition. The only point where Matthew and Mark exactly agree is in the words

οὐκ ἔστιν καλὸν λαβεῖν τὸν ἄρτον τῶν τέκνων καὶ βαλεῖν τοῖς κυναρίοις
It is not right to take the children's bread and throw it to the dogs.

We will begin with the scholars who dismiss the historicity of the episode of the Syro-Phoenician woman altogether, regarding it as a creation of the early Church. The first is Burkill, who in two articles published in consecutive years argued that Mark uses the incident to show that Jesus was unhampered by Pharisaic rules about defilement by contact with Gentiles and therefore represents him as deliberately entering Gentile territory.[40] The passage, presenting Jesus as the bread of life, may have had a eucharistic association. 'Dogs' must be taken in its strictest sense. He mocks at commentators who regard the pericope as recording an actual happening, accusing them of ignoring the cultural background: 'We may safely assume', he writes, 'that any intelligent Hellenistic woman, addressed in such terms by a barbarian, would have immediately reacted by slapping the man's face'.[41] It must be said that this remark itself shows great insensitivity to the accepted rules of behaviour in relations between men and women in public both in the ancient and in the modern East. Dermience published an article which largely follows Burkill's lead:[42] Mark, he says, has invented the whole thing; the pericope is a pastiche of phrases borrowed from the healing of Jairus's daughter and a number of formulae which do not fit into traditional forms of narrative. We rejoice indeed that our Roman Catholic brethren are now free to study scripture without the supervision of censors in the Vatican, but we cannot fail to regret that some of them have chosen to follow the will-o'-the-wisp of extreme reductionist criticism.

Now we follow the other commentators in roughly historical order. We begin with a penetrating remark by George Salmon in a posthumously published book.[43] Commenting on Matt. 7.6 he writes: 'If it had been a Jewish habit to regard the Gentile nations as dogs, the application of the word seems to have been inverted in the Christian community'. Gould in his commentary on Mark[44] holds that 'dog' is always a word of contempt, but adds that there is a place for dogs in the household, and that therefore Jesus held that there is a place for Gentiles in God's world. He also suggests that Jesus is ironically reproducing current Jewish sentiments. This impresses one as being an unjustified attempt to save Jesus from the responsibility of uttering a thoroughly anti-Gentile logion. Gould also notes that Matthew has transferred the incident to Jewish soil and has removed the modifying sentence ἄφες πρῶτον χορτασθῆναι τὰ τέκνα 'Let the children first be fed'. Billerbeck on Matt. 15.27 has no doubt that to call a woman a dog is the greatest insult. It could be used of a Samaritan and of those unlearned in the Torah. *Megillah* 7b is quoted, where 'It shall be for you a solemn assembly' is glossed 'for you and not for foreigners; for you and not for dogs'. And there is a story quoted from *Baba Bathra*, where a disciple of a rabbi, pretending to be ignorant of the Torah, asks, 'Give me what is fallen on the ground, as you would a dog or a raven'. Rawlinson is a 'soft option' man: the diminutive κυνάρια shows that the saying is half humorous; they are domestic dogs.[45] Swete most appropriately quotes Jerome's comment on the logion: 'o mira rerum conversio!' He thinks that Matthew and Mark are using different sources.[46] The Jews as God's children had first claim. Branscomb believes that Mark did not invent the episode.[47] It is a true reflection of the thought of Jesus; indeed we see Jesus in some uncertainty; he did not want to be known. Was he to give to a Gentile what he was denying to Jews? Vincent Taylor points out that 'Several linguistic features suggest that the narrative reflects Aramaic tradition'.[48] 'Gentiles', he says, 'are sometimes described as dogs by Jewish writers, generally with a reference to their vices'. He accepts the soft option because of the diminutive κυνάρια. He agrees with Branscomb that Jesus is working out his own position.

In 1956 Jeremias published a work devoted to the question of Jesus' relation to the Gentiles.[49] Jesus, he reminds us, lived during a period of intense missionary activity on the part of Jews. Jeremias regards the logion in Matt. 23.15 about Pharisaic proselytizing as very old, since it has Aramaic features. Jesus forbade his disciples to preach directly to Gentiles; see Matt. 10.5 (pp. 12-19). Thus Jesus in his lifetime did not envisage a Gentile mission (p. 24). Jeremias writes, 'When Jesus heals his act has eschatological significance, and is always the sign and pledge of the breaking-in of the Messianic age, an anticipatory participation in its blessings' (p. 28). He then examines the two occasions on which Jesus is represented as healing Gentiles. The other is of course the healing of the centurion's servant in Matt. 8.5-10 (Luke 7.1-10; ?John 4.43-54). Jeremias suggests that a third example may be the episode of the Gadarene swine. He holds that in Mark 7.27 πρῶτον is a mitigation of the harshness of Jesus' answer to the Gentile woman, and that Mark found it already in his source: 'The insertion of πρῶτον precludes the suggestion that Jesus was definitely opposed to the Gentile mission' (p. 29n). In the same note he adds that the diminutive κυνάρια cannot be reproduced in Aramaic and hence should not be cited on the side of the soft option. He actually considers the possibility that Jesus changed his mind about the Gentile mission in view of increasing hostility towards him on the part of Israel, but he does not think this probable (p. 32). He concludes that Jesus never envisaged himself as undertaking a ministry among the Gentiles. Paul calls him a διάκονος περιτομῆς, 'a servant of the Jewish people' in Rom. 15.8. Jeremias quotes Rabbi Eliezer ben Hyrcanus (c. 90 AD) as holding that 'No Gentile will have a part in the world to come' (p. 41). But Jesus did envisage Gentiles having a share in the resurrection; the Ninevites, the Queen of Sheba etc. were their representatives (p. 47); thus Gentiles would share in God's eschatological salvation (p. 51). Matt. 8.11 (to which Luke 13.28 is a parallel) is an authentic logion, in which Jesus says that many will come from the east and the west to recline with the patriarchs in the kingdom, but the children of the kingdom will be cast out. He concludes 'We have to do with two successive events, first the call to Israel and subsequently the incorporation of the Gentiles in the kingdom of God'. Before the eschatological message could be delivered to all, two things had to happen, it had to be delivered to the Gentiles, and Jesus had to die (pp. 71-72). This seems to be a most convincing reconstruction of Jesus' attitude towards the Gentiles, one which fits in very well with the evidence of Mark 7.24-30.

Remarkably enough, Butlmann regards the whole episode of the Syro-Phoenician woman in Mark as a variant of the story of the healing of the centurion's servant in Matt. 8.5-10.[50] Matt. 15.34 is 'a church product' because it refers to Jesus' mission, which Jesus (it seems) never did. All the materials therefore which establish a connection with Phil. 3.2, 8 are church products and do not bring us back to Jesus. Johnson thinks the narrative of the episode may have come to Mark in oral form.[51] He agrees with Branscomb that Jesus may be almost talking to himself. The bread refers more naturally to teaching than to healing; in its original context the saying may have referred to teaching—a good and valid point. Lagrange is one of those who adopt the soft option: the dogs are domestic animals, and they do not even have to wait for their meal till the children have finished, since they eat the crumbs as they fall from the children's table.[52] Lohmeyer agrees that Jesus' original words did not belong to the narrative of a healing.[53] Matthew has passed the episode through a Jewish sieve: it happens in the street, where Jesus would not be compromised as he would by entering a Gentile house. Jesus is the householder who must feed the children first. He has the bread of life to give to his hungry children.

Schmid agrees with the Branscomb–Johnson's suggestion that Jesus is being persuaded to change his mind: 'the one who is vanquished in the argument is Jesus himself.'[54] The logion in Mark 7.27 shows harshness but not contempt. He thinks that Matt. 15.24 'I was sent only to the lost sheep of the house of Israel' is a substitute for Mark 7.27a 'Let the children first be fed'. Flammer in an article expresses the view that κυνάρια simply means κυνές. The harshness should not be modified.[55] It reflects Jesus' own belief that there was a divinely ordained difference between Jews and Gentiles (pp. 465-66). The principle enunciated in Rom. 1.16b Ἰουδαίῳ τὲ πρῶτον καὶ Ἕλληνι is perhaps one which Paul inherited from the early Church. Flammer sees a parallel with John 6 and 12. In the Fourth Gospel also Jesus is not ready to receive the Gentiles till after the resurrection. And there is a hint of Jesus as the bread of life (p. 476). Our pericope may have a eucharistic significance (p. 477). Haenchen[56] holds that Matthew shows his Jewish-Christian milieu by bringing Jesus into the street and making the Gentile woman address him as 'Son of David'. The word κυνάρια does not modify the harshness of the sentence. Matthew is dependent on Mark for his version of the event.

Schweizer on the other hand is a strong advocate of the soft option; he does not think the word κυνάρια is insulting at all.[57] The woman is typical of the Gentiles during the early period of the Church, because she has nothing to offer and comes full of faith and of reliance on God's mercy. Klostermann suspects that Mark's πρῶτον might be a redactional weakening of the original saying.[58] He quotes another anti-Gentile utterance from Rabbi Eliezer: 'He who eats with an idolater is like one who eats with a dog'. Derrett insists that the episode is historical,[59] though he sees the influence of various scripture passages, such as Pss. 45.12; 87.4, and the story of the widow of Zarephath in 1 Kings 17 (pp. 164-67). 'Dogs' of course refers to Gentiles here in no complimentary sense (pp. 169-70). He differs from Lohmeyer when he writes: 'Jesus is not the householder . . . God is' (p. 171). For the principle 'the Jew first and then the Gentile' he quotes Isa. 42.5-7 (p. 184). This is quite significant; it suggests that this principle was not invented by the early Church, but goes back to Jesus himself, who found it in scripture. Finally we note a brief article recently published by Schwarz.[60] In it he argues that the original Aramaic of the description of the Syro-Phoenician woman in the pericope must have been כנעניתא. This lies behind both traditions. This would suggest that the story goes back to an Aramaic original, and brings it that much closer to an historical origin, weakening the theories such as those of Burkill, Dermience, and perhaps Bultmann, who regard the whole as a construction of the early Church.

What conclusions may we draw from all this discussion of the evidence? First, as to the text of the pericope itself: we conclude that Matthew's version does not owe anything to a source of information peculiar to himself. He is adapting Mark to his own context, in which it would be compromising to represent Jesus as having voluntarily entered a Gentile household, and in which Jesus' mission is known to have been to Israel. The admission of the Gentiles is a later event in the eschatological programme. Matthew does, however, know independently of a logion in which the disciples are told not to throw what is sacred to the dogs, and 'dogs' here probably includes Gentiles as well as misunderstanding Jews. Mark's half-verse 'Let the children first be fed' we conclude to be not Mark's addition, nor the invention of the early Church. It goes back to the mind of Jesus himself. Indeed he found it in scripture. The early Church inherited this principle and acted on it, as can be seen in Rom. 1.16; Acts 13.46. The bread logion probably originated independently of the incident of the Syro-Phoenician woman and applied originally to Jesus' teaching about the kingdom. This is not to say that the incident is fictional: the Gentile woman did gain Jesus' favour by her witty answer. 'Dogs' in its original context had its full pejorative meaning. To attempt to mitigate it by suggesting that they were really dear little domestic doggies is to miss the point. Jesus began from the traditional Jewish attitude to Gentiles of his time. Whether this incident helped him to change his mind, as some editors have suggested, we do not know. Jeremias has made out an excellent case for believing Jesus to have held the view that Gentiles would be admitted to God's eschatological kingdom when it came.

Paul knew the tradition of Jesus' word about not giving the children's bread to dogs, i.e. to Gentiles, though we cannot say whether he knew of the incident of the Syro-Phoenician woman. He also knew the tradition that messianic salvation was to be offered to Israel first and then to the Gentiles, a tradition which goes back to Jesus' day. Paul stands at the farther side of the great eschatological event, the suffering, death, and resurrection of the Messiah. That event has effected the great reversal of values which runs through all Paul's theology of the cross. Here the reversal is more remarkable than ever, because it has reversed rôles. Those who in the time when the Messiah was on earth were dogs, outside the privileges of Israel, are now the inheritors of the privileges. And those who used to be the privileged people, marked out by the signs of membership of Israel, are now to be described as 'dogs' as long as they cling to their old distinctiveness and claim their old privileges on the basis of that. Those who previously could only claim the leavings of the feast are now to be partakers in the messianic banquet, and what used to be regarded as the fare of the privileged turns out now to be mere leavings. The dogs are now not the Gentiles, but Jews who cling to their former distinctiveness and make it a ground of boasting. So great is the change that has been brought about by the death and resurrection of the Messiah that the teaching of the Messiah himself has been transformed.

We do not know from what source Paul learned of this piece of Jesus' teaching, but it was not from the source later used by Matthew and Luke, which scholars call Q. It must have come independently to Mark and to Matthew. In Mark it appears in the incident of the Syro-Phoenician woman, in Matthew at Matt. 7.6, though he reproduces it again when he gives his version of the Marcan pericope. Paul uses it with brilliant effect in his exposition of the meaning of the cross, which is what Phil. 3.2-16 essentially is. He applies it to the renewed people of God in the end time, without bringing in the apostolic ministry. Perhaps his later experience with the Corinthians made him realize more fully the part which the apostolic ministry must play in the mediation of the meaning of the cross to the people of God.

Chapter 6

MILITIA CHRISTI:
2 COR. 10.2-6; 2.14; 1 COR. 4.9; 15.32; 2 COR. 6.7

We propose in this chapter to attempt to show that Paul included in his theology of the cross the conviction that he and his fellow-workers were waging a campaign against the powers of evil, a battle that must be engaged in by all active Christians. This campaign was a continuation of that which Christ was waging during his ministry on earth, one which reached its climax on the cross. We begin with a study of 2 Cor. 10.2-6, the passage in which this campaign is most fully described. We then examine a number of passages connected with the same theme, two of which are single verses in contexts we have already considered, though we have noted in each place that they are to be reserved for fuller treatment. That treatment they receive here. Finally, we trace the theme back to the teaching of Jesus himself.

I

The tenth chapter of Second Corinthians is written in a mood of deep indignation. Some scholars have suggested that it is in fact the opening part of the painful letter referred to in 7.8f. It is therefore appropriate that Paul should make an extended reference to the warfare which he wages on behalf of Christ, that *militia Christi* with which we are concerned in this chapter. We will examine in order the phrases which he uses, showing how they are related to the background of scripture.

Perhaps we should begin by quoting the passage in question:

> (3) 'For though we live in the world we are not carrying on a worldly war, (4) for the weapons of our warfare are not worldly but have divine power to destroy strongholds. (5) We destroy arguments

and every proud obstacle to the knowledge of God, and take every thought captive to obey Christ, (6) being ready to punish every disobedience, when your obedience is complete.

The phrase, 'carrying on a worldly war' translates κατὰ σάρκα στρατευόμεθα; 'the weapons of our warfare' renders τὰ ὅπλα τῆς στρατείας ἡμῶν; 'to destroy strongholds' represents πρὸς καθαίρεσιν ὀχυρωμάτων; and 'we destroy arguments' λογισμοὺς καθαιροῦντες; 'every proud obstacle' is πᾶν ὕψωμα ἐπαιρόμενον; and 'taking every thought captive' is αἰχμαλωτίζοντες πᾶν νόημα. Our intention is to demonstrate the rich scriptural background to this passage by examining the words στρατεία, ὀχύρωμα, λογισμοί, ὕψωμα and αἰχμαλωτίζοντες.

Strictly speaking, there are two distinct words in Greek, στρατεία 'an expedition', and στρατία 'an army'. But the two are frequently used interchangeably. The Greek bible uses στρατία only once (or στρατεία, for it does not distinguish the two) to give the meaning 'warfare, labour'; everywhere else in the Greek bible the word means 'army'. But that one exception is very significant. It occurs in Isa. 40.2, where the MT has מלאה צבאה 'that her warfare is ended'. The prophet is to tell Zion that the time of her struggle is coming to an end; now she is to receive her salvation. Aquila renders צבאה with ἡ στρατεία αὐτῆς.[1] The Targum version of Isa. 40.2 is interesting: 'prophesy concerning her, that she is about to be filled with the people of her exiles, that her transgressions have been forgiven'. Here the return of the exiles corresponds to the ending of her warfare and the forgiveness of Zion's sins to 'that her iniquity is pardoned'. The warfare is therefore the afflictions which Zion has had to endure before the end time, when the exiles return to Zion and sin has been pardoned. We note the next line in the Hebrew: 'for she has received at the Lord's hand double for all her sins'. If Paul had before him a Greek text of Isa. 40.2 corresponding to that which meets us in Aquila's version, he might well have seen this passage as a prophecy of the afflictions which were to befall the Messiah before the coming of the end time, afflictions which, as we have seen, were to be reproduced in the lives of his disciples. Paul's warfare was to be a prolongation, in the period before the end, of the warfare which Zion had to undergo before her redemption.

Paul goes on in v. 4 to write of 'power to destroy the strongholds', ὀχυρωμάτων. This may be an echo of another messianic passage of scripture which was a favourite with early Christians, and which moreover has a link with Isa. 40.2. This is Zech. 9.12. But it is an obscure passage, which the LXX has misunderstood and mistranslated. Nor is the MT free from suspicion. The MT has:

שובו לבצרון אסירי התקוה

Return to your stronghold, O prisoners of hope.

The word stronghold translates בצרון. But this is a *hapax legomenon* in the Hebrew bible. It is supposed to be derived from the root III בצר meaning 'to be impossible, inaccessible'. O. Procksch in Kittel's *Biblia Hebraica* suggests reading וישבו לך בת־ציון, 'and they shall dwell in thee, daughter of Zion'. This emendation is no doubt inspired by the LXX translation. It offers καθήσεσθε ἐν ὀχυρώματι, δέσμιοι τῆς συναγωγῆς. This is literally 'you shall dwell in the fortress, prisoners of the synagogue'. It must have read וישב. But instead of the MT תקוה it read מקוה, which can mean 'a gathering'. The consequence is that it gives us a meaning which would be startlingly appropriate in Paul's eyes. Unbelieving Jews, who should inherit the hope of Israel, insist on remaining in their fortress of unbelief. This fortress in the course of his warfare Paul is determined to destroy by means of God's power. The link with Isa. 40.2 is provided by the second half of Zech. 9.12:

today I declare that I will restore to you double.

This reminds us of Isa. 40.2c

for she has received at the Lord's hand double for all her sins.

The Targum on Isa. 40.2c almost makes this point: 'for that she has received the cup of consolations from before the Lord, as if she had been smitten twice for all her sins'. Perhaps these two scripture passages provide us with some insight into the background of Paul's theology.

There is however in all probability a much broader scriptural background to 2 Cor. 10.2-6 than that which we have indicated so far. Some commentators have observed that behind this passage there seems to be the story of the building of the tower of Babel in Genesis 11. Thus F.F. Bruce suggests that the passage may be 'a spiritual interpretation of the tower of Babel'.[2] He points out that Philo has treated the same theme. The reference occurs in *De Conf. Ling.* Philo is fully aware of the difficulties presented by the Babel narrative and by its resemblance to Greek myths. He leaves the task of defending the literal sense to others, and proceeds directly to allegorizing the narrative (1-14). Building edifices with bricks is generally equated with materialism and sensuality (62-63). In 114 the tower is identified with any system that opposes Philo's own philosophy, e.g. atheism or determinism, or belief in mere chance. The builders of the city are later identifed with either polytheists or hedonists (144). What destroys the tower is reason. He ends by conceding that the confusion of tongues may indeed by a description of the origin of the Greek and the barbarian languages. But, he insists, we must also offer an allegorical interpretation (190-91).

In a recent article A.J. Malherbe has looked at this 2 Corinthians passage in the light of the interpretation of Genesis 11 given in *De Conf. Ling.*[3] He thinks that Paul uses ὕψωμα to mean 'a rampart' and ὕψωμα ἐπαιρομένου is 'a raised rampart'. After considerable discussion of Philo's treatment of the Babel story he concludes: 'Thus, while Paul shares some details with *De Confusione Linguarum* 128-31, he differs from it not only in the functions of the fortifications, but also in the fact that the issues at stake are cognitive and volitional rather than sophistical' (p. 147). Malherbe then goes on to suggest that Paul was more influenced by some traditions of pagan literature in which Odysseus is made the exemplar of versatility. He quotes from Antisthenes and Seneca to show that the wise man was described as possessing an impregnable fortress (pp. 153-55, 165). He distinguishes three stages in Paul's warfare, demolishing fortifications, taking captives, and punishing resistance (p. 166). He concludes:

> The reasonings (λογισμοί) of his opponents are the fortifications which protect their thoughts (πᾶν νόημα) against the knowledge of God (γνῶσις τοῦ θεοῦ) . . . His humble life, in which God's power is manifest, is the armament with which he attacks his opponents' (pp. 171-72).

This is a weighty article. It confirms H.D. Betz's thesis in his book already referred to.[4] However, before concluding that Paul was directly influenced by Greek literature, one should consider the evidence from the Jewish tradition. As far as concerns Philo's treatment of the theme in *De Confusione Linguarum*, there is no very striking resemblance to Paul. Both writers regard the fortress as any thought-system or argument which they oppose. One can certainly conclude that in Paul's day there was in Judaism a tradition of allegorizing the Babel story, probably rooted in the synagogue homiletic tradition, and that this tradition was known to Paul and followed by him. There is plenty of evidence for this in later rabbinic exegesis. To begin with the Targums: in the Neofiti MS of the Targum of Palestine we have an extensive piece of *haggada* on the Babel story.[5] Men originally spoke 'the language of the sanctuary', because it was by means of this language that the world was created. The builders of the tower intended to place an idol at the top and to put into its hands a sword, so that the idol could organize an army against God: 'for they despised the holy language by which the world was created at the beginning; while their hearts erred afterwards from the Word of him who spake and the world was, at the beginning'. In reading such a passage one realizes how relatively easy it was for a writer such as the author of the Fourth Gospel to apply this language to Jesus Christ. The Targums of Onkelos and Pseudo-Jonathan reproduce this piece of *haggada* also.[6]

In *Tractate Sanhedrin* of the Babylonian Talmud we learn that according to R. Shila the builders wanted to reach the heavens and split them with axes so that the waters should gush forth.[7] Rabbi Jeremiah b. Eleazar said that they divided into three parties: one wanted to ascend and dwell in the heavens; the second wanted to ascend and serve idols; the third wanted to ascend and wage war with God. In the *Midrash on the Psalms* we find a note on Gen. 11.4 'Come let us build ourselves a city (עיר)' to the effect that in Aramaic the word can mean a watcher or angel. They conclude that the builders wanted to make themselves a god.[8]

It is possible however that the word points in another direction as well. The word is used in the LXX of Prov. 21.22. The MT is:

עיר גברים עלה חכם
וירד עז מבטחה

A wise man scales the city of the mighty
and brings down the stronghold in which they trust.

The LXX translation is:

πόλεις ὀχύρας ἐνέβη σοφός,
καὶ καθεῖλεν τὸ ὀχύρωμα ἐφ᾽ ᾧ
ἐπεποίθεισαν οἱ ἀσεβεῖς.

There is some evidence that rabbinic tradition applied this verse to Moses: 'This wise man is Moses, of whom it is said, *And Moses went up to God*'.[9] Another source amplifies this by saying that Moses scaled the city of the mighty and brought down the Torah despite the opposition of the angels.[10] We cannot altogether dismiss the suggestion that Paul had Prov. 21.22 in mind in view of his treatment of Deut. 30.12-14 in Rom. 10.6-8,[11] and also his disciple's treatment of Ps. 68.18 in Eph. 4.8-10.[12] In both of these passages a scriptural text interpreted in Jewish tradition of Moses bringing down the Torah from Sinai is interpreted by a NT writer as a type of Christ bringing salvation from heaven. The Proverbs text might have been interpreted by Paul in terms of Christ bringing salvation in spite of the opposition of 'the rulers of this world'. That same opposition is encountered by Paul and his fellow-apostles in the course of the *militia Christi*.

Some remarks by commentators may well be considered here. Heidland thinks that Paul may have the Babel story in mind:[13] 'He wants to demonstrate the competence of his spiritual weapons by means of this figure, but also the apparent strength of the edifice of this philosophical teaching'. Bauernfeind emphasizes that in this warfare of Paul's the 'meekness and gentleness of Christ' (πραΰτες καὶ ἐπιεικεία, 10.1) set the example—an excellent point.[14] Hauck, Schulz, and Preisker claim that these qualities are regarded as having been shown by Christ during his earthly career, not merely now by the risen and exalted Lord.[15] Windisch writes of Paul's 'prophetisch-apostolische Lehre'. Paul's aim is the overthrow of the evil spiritual powers. Windisch remarks that the messianic character of Paul's war waged on behalf of Christ becomes very clear in this passage. Paul has in mind both this campaign against his opponents and his missionary calling. Obviously all opposition has not yet been overcome.

We must now examine the rest of Paul's vocabulary in this passage, to see whether it can throw further light on the background of his thought. The word λογισμός also introduces us into a scriptural milieu. We find it used in Ps. 33(32).10. The MT is

יהוה הפיר עצת־גוים
הניא מחשבות עמים

The Lord brings the counsel of the nations to naught; he frustrates the plans of the peoples.

The LXX offers:

κύριος διασκεδάζει βουλὰς ἐθνῶν,
ἀθετεῖ δὲ λογισμοὺς λαῶν,
καὶ ἀθετεῖ βουλὰς ἀρχόντων.

Is the third line perhaps a gloss on the second? If Paul read this in either the LXX version or one corresponding to that of Symmachus, he would have seen it as a statement of the way in which God frustrates the evil designs of the elemental powers; Paul would have meant of course that God frustrates them by means of the cross; cf. 1 Cor. 1.19; 3.19-20. Equally relevant is Isa. 65.2. This is a verse actually quoted by Paul in Rom. 10.21:

> I spread out my hands all day to a rebellious people.

The second half of the verse runs:

> who walk in a way that is not good,
> following their own devices.

The MT of Isa. 65.2b is:

> ההלכים הדרך לא טוב
> אחר מחשבותיהם

The LXX renders it with:

> οἱ οὐκ ἐπορεύθησαν ὁδῷ ἀληθινῇ,
> ἀλλ᾽ ὀπίσω τῶν ἁμαρτιῶν αὐτῶν.

But Aquila has given a correct translation of the MT with τῶν λογισμῶν αὐτῶν. These two passages would suggest to Paul a picture of God struggling with a people who would not obey him, a people whom Paul would regard as being the victims of the influence of the hostile elemental powers. In his own situation it suggests that his opponents had a strong Judaistic tendency in their teaching, although it is more likely that they were Jewish Christians than Jews as such. In Paul's day the distinction would not be as clear as it is to us. Heidland says of λογισμούς in v. 4 that Paul has some sort of philosophical terminology in mind, some sort of an ideology that excludes God and exalts self.[16] This seems to be going too far. The indications are rather that Paul's opponents are described as exalting themselves against the knowledge of God, not because they denied God outright, but because they did not rightly know him as revealed in Jesus Christ, and supremely in the cross. Barrett is surely nearer the mark when he explains both λογισμούς and πᾶν νόημα as meaning designs dependent purely on man, or an idol created by man. Héring defines πᾶν νόημα as 'la culture intellectuelle de l'époque'. We would qualify this by suggesting it is rather the intellectual culture of the epoch as mediated by some tradition in Judaism, probably in the form of Jewish Christianity.

The word ὕψωμα in v. 5 has caused a great deal of debate among scholars. Windisch believes that here the word must mean 'strong fortress', though he admits that in Rom. 8.39, the only other place in the NT where it occurs, it has an astrological meaning. Straub[17] holds that Paul is referring to siege-technique. He asks whether ὕψωμα belongs to the same figure. If so, Chrysostom was right when he said that the words meant πύργωμα, a lofty tower. Bertram[18] agrees that in Rom. 8.39 it must have an astronomical reference, a meaning for which there is ample attestation in Hellenistic Greek. In this passage he thinks it means 'the overweening human attitude of spirit', i.e. intellectual superiority or pride. Paul, he adds, uses the vocabulary of the *militia Christi*, but it is a spiritual battle. Allo believes that here Paul means by ὕψωμα a fortress or fortifications. Héring says it refers to all forms of pride, both human and demonic. Barrett comes to much the same conclusion when he says it means 'highmindedness', not in the sense of magnanimity, but of lofty pride.

There is one scripture passage that might throw light on Paul's meaning here. It is Ps. 74(73).3. The MT is:

הרימה פעמיך למשאות נצח
כל־הרע אויב בקדש.

This the RSV translates:

Direct thy steps to the perpetual ruins;
the enemy has destroyed everything in the sanctuary.

The Greek translators obviously had difficulties with this verse. The LXX offers:

ἔπαρον τὰς χεῖράς σου ἐπὶ τὰς ὑπερηφανίας αὐτῶν εἰς τέλος,
ὅσα ἐπονηρεύσατο ὁ ἐχθρὸς ἐν τοῖς ἁγίοις σου.

Presumably the translator understood the word משאות to be derived from the root שוא 'to be worthless', not from I שאה 'to be desolate'. Or he may have connected it with II שאון, which can mean 'impious mob'. He uses ὑπερηφανία for MT שאון in Ps. 74(73).23, where the RSV translates 'the uproar of thy adversaries'. The Vulgate renders it the same way here also: 'superbia inimicorum'. The LXX translator probably thought that God lifting up his hands was less anthropomorphic than God lifting up his feet.[19] Symmachus produces quite a different rendering, though he makes the same mistake about the word משאות. He offers: τὸ ὕψωμα τῶν ποδῶν σου ἠφανίσθη εἰς νῖκος 'the height of thy feet has disappeared into victory'. What he thought that meant it is difficult to say. At any rate, if Paul read this psalm in a text corresponding to Symmachus's version, he would have seen here an appeal against the ὕψωμα or overweening pride of Israel's enemies. And Israel's enemies were God's.

From all the evidence we can gather we must conclude that the word ὕψωμα can be used in the following senses:

(a) 'heave-offering', as sometimes in the LXX.
(b) 'zenith' or 'high position in the heavens' or 'a being in a high position in the heavens'.
(c) 'a high structure on earth'.
(d) 'overweening pride'.

Bertram[20] points out that Philo, emphasizing the superiority of the ten commandments, says that they were composed in the ὕψωμα τοῦ ἀέρος, which we might paraphrase in modern terms with 'in the depths of space' (*De Praem. et Poen.* 2). Bertram adds that ὕψωμα is the sphere into which Christ has broken by means of his exaltation. He concludes that here it means the arrogant human claim to possess the Spirit, which Paul contrasts with the true confession of God. Moulton and Milligan suggest only two meanings, an astrological one and 'high place' (on earth). Grimm–Thayer conclude that here it must mean 'an elevated structure, a rampart'.[21] If we review the four alternatives cited above, we can eliminate (a) at once. It would make no sense here. Though (d) is espoused by several scholars, it seems to have very little lexicographical backing. The sole clear example is that quoted above from Symmachus, and that is really not so clear because we do not know what he means. It is even possible that if Paul had this translation before him he would have understood it as a reference to an elemental power and not to human pride. Let us then suppose for a moment that (c) is correct: Paul is determined to destroy every high fortress that is exalted, or exalts itself, agains the knowledge of God in Christ. He is using metaphorical language; he means literally—what? Either a system of thought or an exalted being. In fact he probably means both, for the exalted being is regarded as using the system of thought to enslave others. I would therefore conclude that (b) is the most probable of the four possible meanings of this word. It has the great advantage that it is certainly the meaning the word bears in the only other context in which Paul uses it, Rom. 8.39. As we have seen, it would fit in with much of the scriptural evidence. Paul regards himself as ranged in battle in the name of Christ against the elemental powers whom Christ has in principle overcome by his cross and resurrection, but whom the Christian, who is 'in Christ', must himself overcome in his own life in the power of God-in-Christ.

As we review this remarkable passage, a picture emerges of Paul engaged in a warfare in which Christ himself supremely engaged during his career on earth. This warfare was amply witnessed to in scripture, most notably perhaps in the Babel story, which is an allegorical foreshadowing of the warfare that is to come. It took place at the end of the days, reached its climax at the cross and resurrection, and now, during the period in which the new age and the old age overlap, it is still being waged by Paul and his fellow-apostles in the name and strength of Christ. The enemies are the world powers who put Christ to death. They use as their tools unbelieving Jews who are still prisoners of the Torah, and idol-worshipping Gentiles who are enslaved to their own gods. So far little has been said about the part which all Christians must play in this warfare, because no doubt in this particular passage Paul is passionately concerned to defend himself against those who have been attacking him personally. But when we turn, as we do now, to a series of other passages in the Corinthian epistles, we shall see that all Christians have a part to play in this warfare. The *militia Christi* is not Paul's sole prerogative.[22]

II

We begin with a passage from 2 Corinthians that has caused much debate among commentators. It is 2.14:

τῷ δὲ θεῷ χάρις τῷ πάντοτε θριαμβεύοντι ἡμᾶς ἐν τῷ Χριστῷ καὶ τὴν ὀσμὴν τῆς γνώσεως αὐτοῦ φανεροῦντι δι' ἡμῶν ἐν παντὶ τόπῳ.

But thanks be to God, who in Christ always leads us in triumph, and through us spreads the fragrance of the knowledge of him everywhere.

The RSV has had to commit itself on the vexed question of the meaning of θριαμβεύοντι, as any translation must. Moffatt, for example, takes the opposite view with his rendering 'he makes my life a constant pageant of triumph in Christ'.[23] We have to decide what θριαμβεύοντι means if we are to understand what place this passage holds in Paul's theology of *militia Christi*. We will divide all the commentators whom we quote into three categories: (a) those who render θριαμβεύοντι so as to make Paul (and his fellow-workers) a participant in the glory of the triumph; (b) those who understand it a meaning that Paul and his allies are victims of God's triumph; (c) those who have any other interpretation to offer.

R.H. Strachan translates 'makes my life a constant pageant of triumph for Christ'. Since he is writing a Moffatt commentary, he naturally begins from James Moffatt's translation. But he seems to accept it as correct, and he quotes, as do many other writers, Col. 2.15 θριαμβεύσας αὐτοὺς ἐν αὐτῷ. This is in itself an extremely obscure passage, but on the whole it seems to suggest Christ (or God in Christ) triumphing over the powers.[24] Perhaps because of this, Strachan hedges to some extent, for he adds 'At the same time, the idea of defeat is not absent from Paul's mind'. This seems inconsistent: Paul cannot mean at one and the same time that he is participating in the glory of the triumph *and* that he is a victim of the triumph. Straub also refuses to allow that θριαμβεύσαντι can mean 'lead as captive' (p. 28). It must mean 'cause to triumph', he says, though he does add 'obwohl Belege fehlen'. Héring is much more explicit: 'non comme un vaincu naturellement, mais comme un général victorieux'. F.F. Bruce draws a contrast between 2 Cor. 2.14 and Col. 2.15: 'the apostles are joyful participants in their commander's triumphal procession, not (like the disarmed principalities and powers of Col. 2.15) the unwilling captives driven before the car'. This argument is more convincing if one accepts the Pauline authorship of Colossians. Bruce also suggests that the reference to the fragrance of the knowledge of Christ in the second half of the verse may be an extension of the figure of the triumph, 'an allusion to the perfumes sprinkled along the triumphal way'. As we shall be seeing, the evidence for this as a regular practice is doubtful. Bruce adds that the triumph was a time of joy for the victors but meant death at the end for the captives. Barrett likewise cannot bring himself to believe that Paul is a prisoner in the triumph. Paul, he holds, must think of himself as the victorious general, a view which he strangely attributes to Allo. But Barrett admits that θριαμβεύοντι cannot be translated 'causes us to triumph'. He, like Bruce, thinks that the incense carried before the victor plays a part in the figure.

Before we turn to those who regard Paul as the victim of the triumph, we should make one point clear: θριαμβεύοντι cannot mean 'causes us to triumph'. There is simply no evidence that the verb can be used in what Héring calls 'a Hiph'il sense'. So those who wish to make Paul a participant in the glory of the triumph must find some other rendering for θριαμβεύοντι.

On the side of regarding Paul as the victim of the triumph is the majority of modern commentators. Plummer writes, 'The victorious commander is God, and the Apostles are—not his subordinate generals, but his captives, whom he takes with him and displays to all the world'. He takes the view that the reference to the fragrance of the gospel extends the figure to cover the incense borne before the victor. Goudge likewise holds that 'St. Paul is God's captive . . . and . . . (God) leads him from province to province of the empire as the great witness to his mercy'. He compares 1 Tim. 1.15-16, 'that Christ may manifest in me the full extent of his long-suffering'. Lietzmann, accepting this sense, points out that the Peshitto translates the word as 'he who makes us his spectacle'. This in fact connects it closely with 1 Cor. 4.9. It must mean, he says, 'leads us in triumph' not 'causes us to triumph'. Allo accepts the same sense, though he points out that the same verb can mean 'to make public'. Delling defends the meaning 'leads us in triumph';[25] he compare Col. 2.15 and comments that there 'der Kreuzesweg Jesu ist—paradoxerweise—der Triumphweg Gottes'. So in 2 Cor. 2.15 Paul represents himself as one of the prisoners in the triumph. But he regards it as a grace. There is an interchange between δουλεία and ἐλευθερία. Denis renders the phrase as 'Dieu . . . qui fait de nous son triomphe'.[26] (p. 426). Of the triumph in which Paul is the prisoner, he says, 'It is a question of the tribulations permitted by God, who continually humiliates the Apostle, uniting him with Christ's sufferings' (p. 427, my tr.). The pleasing odour is the evangelizing activity of the apostles (p. 430). He links the two figures together: 'God triumphs in his captives; by the perfumes burnt in the course of the cortège he manifests the knowledge of Christ by means of the captives themselves'. But if it is doubtful whether the burning of incense was a regular custom at triumphs, this rather complicated link collapses. Bultmann says that Paul looks on himself as someone whom God in Christ has conquered and now exhibits as his trophy. He also thinks that Paul is referring to incense offered at a triumph. He is aware that the only evidence for this comes from Appian's account of the triumph of Scipio Africanus after his conquest of Carthage. But Bultmann does not shrink from the assumption that Paul had this actual instance in mind. The incense symbolizes God's presence rather than Christ's sacrifice, as Denis suggests.

L. Williamson has devoted an important article to the question of the interpretation of this phrase.[27] He distinguishes four senses that have been given to the phrase by commentators: (1) to cause to triumph, (2) to triumph over (win a victory over), (3) to lead in triumph as a victorious general leads his troops, (4) to lead as captives in a triumphal procession. He asserts, as do all who have studied the lexicography, that sense (1) is impossible. It must mean 'celebrate a victory' not 'gain a victory'. When followed by a direct personal object, *thriambeuein* means 'to lead as a conquered enemy in a victory parade' (pp. 317-19). He dismisses the sense 'divulge, make public' as occurring far too late to be relevant here. Even the meaning 'expose to ridicule' is too late for Paul's day (p. 322). The life-situation for the figure must be the entry of a military hero into Rome. Paul's usage elsewhere is not inconsistent with this, he claims. Paul is a δοῦλος, both of God and of Christ. He had been God's enemy. Very remarkably, Williamson refers to all the main passages from 1 and 2 Corinthians that we have been examining (p. 324). He concludes (p. 326) that Paul accepts the paradox of being both a slave exposed to public ridicule and 'a joyful participant in Christ's victory celebration'. Admirable though Williamson's conclusions are in every other respect, I doubt if this last point can be successfully maintained: Paul's joy here seems to arise from the wide proclamation of the gospel. Paul is exhibited as the victim of the triumph *in Christ*. Paul may even be implying that Christ is also the victim, but if we say so we must remember Delling's dictum: 'Jesus' way of the cross is—paradoxically—the triumphal way of God'.

Collange (pp. 22f.) says that Paul is the prisoner, not the conqueror. The phrase describes the life of the apostle exposed to every sort of tribulation. He believes that the reference in Col. 2.15 is part of a hymn which may originally have existed independently of its present context. He also very acutely points out that the verb φανεροῦντι in the second half of the verse is a parallel to θριαμβεύοντι, and in 2 Cor. 4.10 φανεροῦν is used of the manifestation of the life of Jesus by means of the apostles carrying around the νέκρωσις of Jesus in their bodies. He rejects the suggestion that the incense is offered as part of the triumphal entourage. In all regions incense is a symbol of God's presence. That is what it means here. Very recently P. Marshall has published an article confirming the view of the majority of scholars.[28] He emphasizes that the notion of social shame is inseparable from the situation of prisoners led in a triumph (pp. 317-18). If Paul could accept that God led him as a slave he could go on to say that God leads him in triumph as a vanquished enemy (p. 312). He thinks that God is exhibiting Paul as an example of social shame, and that this is what ἀπέδειξεν means in 1 Cor. 4.9 (p. 315). He concludes (p. 316) 'God will continue on his triumphal way though Paul appears only as a figure of shame in the procession'.

Finally we must give some attention to an article by R.B. Egan which proposes a translation that avoids both of these opposed interpretations.[29] He agrees that the meaning 'make to triumph' is untenable (p. 36). But he also rejects the meaning that God defeated Paul, on the grounds that Paul's conversion was instantaneous, whereas θριαμβεύοντι implies an on-going process (p. 37). However on the next page he uses the presence of the word πάντοτε to argue that a triumph did not go on all the time; hence the reference cannot be to a Roman triumph. Nor will he accept the sense 'triumphed over' for θριαμβεύσας αὐτούς in Col. 2.15, on the grounds that the ἀρχαί and the ἐξουσίαι were created beings. Why should God triumph over his own handiwork? It would seem that the answer is obvious: Paul regarded them as rebellious powers, fallen angels. Egan then brings a good deal of evidence to show that θριαμβεύειν can mean 'make public'; e.g. a papyrus of 14 BC has πρὸς τὸ μὴ ἐκθριαμβισθῆναι τὸ πρᾶγμα meaning 'so that the matter should not be noised abroad' (p. 41). He can show that some of the early commentators interpreted 2 Cor. 2.14a in this sense. He therefore renders it 'But thanks be to God who is always making us known in Christ and revealing through us the odor (*sic*) of his knowledge in every place' (p. 50). He would interpret the verb in Col. 2.15 as meaning 'uncovering the powers', powers whom he regards as friendly elements (p. 56). He never explains however why Christ (or God) should want to uncover these friendly powers, or how the cross effected this. He concludes that the basic meaning is that God makes Paul known in Christ (p. 62). This is a weighty article. But Egan has not produced any example of θριαμβεύειν meaning making a person known as a direct object. I do not think that Egan's objections to applying the metaphor of the triumph to the apostolic life are very convincing, especially in view of 1 Cor. 4.9. One might just as well object that spectacles did not go on all the time, but no one would deny that there Paul is referring to the apostolic life. In the context of 2 Cor. 2 Paul has been writing of his anxiety about the situation in Corinth. It is certainly a context of *Anfechtung*. Paul wants to show that God can actually trimph by means of all Paul's afflictions. The figure of Paul as the captive led in God's triumph would fit this very well.

Two other commentators have something to say about Paul's use of ὀσμή here. Billerbeck points out that à propos the Hadrianic martyrs it is said in *Genesis Rabba* that God smelled the pleasing odour of the three young men in the fiery furnace. The figure of the pleasing odour could therefore be used of the death of the martyrs. This would certainly accord with Paul's figure of the triumph. T.W. Manson contributed an article to a symposium edited by N. Sevenster and W.C. Van Unnik in which, among other passages, he gives some attention to Paul's use of ὀσμή here, though he has nothing to add about θριαμβεύοντι.[30] He writes:

> The followers of Christ, and in particular the Apostle himself, are participants in the spiritual activity which is focussed in Christ ... the work of God in Christ is reconciliation; but this process of reconciliation still goes on and the followers of Christ are made partakers in it (p. 156).

He then quotes a number of passages from rabbinic literature in which the Torah is spoken of in much the same way as Paul speaks about the preaching of the gospel here. Manson comments:

> The Law, in these passages, is thought of as something good in itself, which brings life to the right people, whether it be the Chosen Race, or the righteous, or the disinterested student; and death to all others, Gentiles, or unrighteous, or self-seeking students. In our passage in II Cor. Paul speaks of the carriers of the gospel in the same way. To those who make the right response, the response of faith, they are a סם חיים (a life-giving drug); to those who are not they are a סם המות (deadly poison) (pp. 158-59).

Later he writes: 'The followers of Christ become themselves in some measure partakers of this remedial power that is in him (Christ); they are Χριστοῦ εὐωδία' (p. 161). This article is useful as emphasizing both the extent to which the apostolic ministry is regarded by Paul as actually exercising the powers of Christ himself, and as showing that this activity belongs ultimately to all Christians. It suggests perhaps that Paul's use of the figure of the pleasing odour

here has not got much overtone of sacrifice. It is indeed the
indication of the strenuous and precarious life of the apostles, but
this life is not something that prevails with God as we might expect a
sacrifice to do, because the sacrifice has already been made by Christ
once for all upon the cross. Paul is concerned with the making
contemporary of the once-for-all event. In any case, Paul and his
fellow-workers are not surrogates for an absent Christ. They are 'in
Christ' and that is why he can write of them as he does.

We must now attempt to estimate the significance of this verse for
our understanding of the *militia Christi*. We may well conclude that
the thought of the apostles being paraded in public which Paul
presents in 1 Cor. 4.9 has been rather expanded by the time he comes
to write 2 Corinthians. The difficulties which he has experienced
with the Corinthians have shown him that it is God's will that his
servants should be humiliated and degraded in his service, and that
this is God's way of winning his victories and bringing about his
purposes. Certainly the thought of 2 Cor. 2.14 fits in admirably with
the thought of 1 Cor. 4.9-13. The triumph of God over his servants
applies to Paul's fellow-workers quite as much as to Paul himself.
They are the apostolic group who are appointed for this destiny in
the end time. As Collange remarks (p. 27), the apostles' mission must
be regarded as 'a last and eschatological act'.

Next we should observe that God leads Paul and his companions
in triumph in Christ. It is therefore quite possible that Paul regards
Christ as being in some sense equally the victim of the triumph. This
does not mean that Christ is, so to speak, always on the cross, or not
yet risen. But in as much as Paul and his friends are reproducing in
their lives the redemptive sufferings of Christ because they are 'in'
the risen Christ, it cannot be inappropriate to conclude that as long
as the apostles are the victims in God's triumph, so is Christ. But of
course we must add that the cross and resurrection as one saving
event constitute the victory. Hence the triumph of God in the
precarious life of the apostles is the victory of God in which Paul and
his friends in some sense share now, even though they are still
suffering. As Collange has well pointed out, it is exactly the situation
of 2 Cor. 4.10-12: by means of carrying about in their bodies the
'deadness' of Jesus, the apostles are also manifesting his life. And
lastly we may point out that this passage in 2 Cor. 2.14 affords the
link we need between the *militia Christi* and the apostolic function of
reproducing the sufferings of Christ in the life of the Church. Paul is

the man who fights Christ's battle. But he fights it in Christ's way, which is why he can portray himself as a captive in God's triumphal procession.

With this exposition of 2 Cor. 2.14 behind us, we can now turn back to a verse which we passed over in our exposition of 1 Cor. 4.9-13 in Chapter 2. It is 1 Cor. 4.9. We will understand it better as a result of our study of the *militia Christi*.

> δοκῶ γάρ, ὁ θεὸς ἡμᾶς τοὺς ἀποστόλους ἐσχάτους ἀπέδειξεν ὡς ἐπιθανατίους, ὅτι θέατρον ἐγενήθημεν τῷ κόσμῳ καὶ ἀγγέλοις καὶ ἀνθρώποις.

> For I think that God has exhibited us apostles as last of all, like men sentenced to death; because we have become a spectacle to the world, to angels, and to men.

Although we shall be taking issue with the RSV's rendering of ἀπέδειξεν as 'exhibited', it has clearly brought out the meaning of the last phrase: 'the world' comprises angels and men; it is not a third term parallel with the other two. We shall take the various phrases in this important verse in order, and then examine another related verse which comes later on in the same epistle. Paul says that God ἐσχάτους ἀπέδειξεν. Weiss argues that this means 'lowest, basest', and says that there is a paradoxical contrast between the apostles, who should be first in estimation since they are to judge the tribes of Israel (Matt. 19.28b), and the actual way in which they are regarded as the lowest of the low. There are grave objections to this: in the first place, it is most unlike the tenor of the rest of Paul's argument that he should claim a first place for the apostles in the kingdom. He never suggests any such sentiment as 'despite the scornful treatment we receive, we ought to be the first', or even 'we will ultimately be the first'.[31] Next, a reference to Matt. 19.28b implies that by 'the apostles' Paul means the Twelve. But this is very far from being the case. It is much more likely that ἐσχάτους implies precisely eschatology. The apostles (in Paul's sense) are living in the last days; cf. 10.11; 15.45.

The word ἀπέδειξεν has caused some discussion among commentators. The RSV translation 'exhibited' has been adopted by few scholars, although it certainly maintains the figure of the arena. A rich man would 'exhibit' a spectacle in the arena, which would often involve men fighting with animals, or gladiators fighting with each other. This rendering is supported by Weiss and by Barrett and also by Grimm-Thayer *sub* ἀποδείκνυμι. But if the verb is used in this sense it should be in the middle voice. Besides, if Paul meant that God was exhibiting him and his fellow-workers, he would not have used the aorist. The process was going on while Paul was writing; the aorist suggests an act in the past. We must therefore accept one of the two other possible meanings of ἀπέδειξεν in the active, either 'proclaimed' or 'appointed'. Robertson and Plummer decide for 'proclaimed' on the basis of the only other passage in which Paul uses the verb, 2 Thess. 2.4. The man of sin is described as ἀποδείκνυντα ἑαυτὸν ὅτι ἔστιν θεός, 'proclaiming himself that he is God'. This makes excellent sense in the context. Perhaps a more striking effect would be gained if one could translate it 'appointing himself so that he is God', but the syntax would hardly allow this. The RSV translates 'proclaiming himself to be God'. In the context of 1 Cor. 4.9, however, the translation 'God has proclaimed us' suffers from the second objection which we brought against the rendering 'exhibited': it should not be in the aorist. The process is continuing; compare πάντοτε θριαμβεύοντι in 2 Cor. 2.14 discussed above. We should therefore definitely adopt the translation 'appointed'. This is found in the LXX of Susanna 5: καὶ ἀπεδείχθησαν δύο πρεσβύτεροι; it also occurs in the LXX of Dan. 2.48.[32] Nebuchadnezzar appointed Daniel as ruler over the wise men of Babylon.[33] Moulton and Milligan give several instances of ἀποδείκνυμι meaning 'appoint'. This translation also makes the best sense in the context: God has appointed Paul and his companions as apostles, and that is why they are engaged in the cosmic struggle.

ἐπιθανατίους must be taken from the world of the arena. The word is first found in the LXX of Bel and the Dragon 31-32, where it is said that the lions in the lions' den are daily supplied with a ration τῶν ἐπιθανατίων σώματα δύο, 'two individuals from among those condemned to death'. It occurs in Dionysius of Halicarnassus about 20 BC, and then in Paul. The next instance is in Aelian in the second century of our era. Pobee remarks here that the word must refer to the arena.[34]

θέατρον: many commentators quote the Stoic maxim, best presented perhaps by Seneca, that the wise man in conflict with the force of circumstances is a spectacle pleasing to the gods. Similarly Epictetus says that men and gods rejoice at the spectacle of the true philosopher struggling with misfortune (see Lietzmann and Kittel *infra*). Straub holds that the word must refer to gladiatorial shows and not to legitimate drama.[35] Kittel well compares Heb. 10.33, where part of the sufferings of those addressed has consisted in 'being publicly exposed to abuse and affliction', ὀνειδισμοῖς τε καὶ θλίψεσιν θεατριζόμενοι.[36] He does not deny the possibility of Stoic influence, but points to a number of other considerations. There may be a parallel with the position of Job, whose sufferings were witnessed by ἀγγέλοις[37] and by men (his three friends). Also by worldly standards the θέατρον in the case of Paul and his companions is nothing to be proud of. And finally, the spectacle is not as simply related to God as in Seneca and Epictetus. God is the author of the apostle's weakness. The reference to Job is very doubtful; it hardly seems to make sense in the context. But the other two points are well made.

ἀγγέλοις: why should the conflict of Paul and his fellow-apostles be a spectacle to angels? Various parallels have been adduced: in the Slavonic Enoch the punishment of the rebellious angels is to be a spectacle for the elect.[38] But this is the wrong way round. More relevant is Eph. 3.10, cited by Goudge. There the task of the Church is to make known 'the manifold wisdom of God' to 'the principalities and powers in the heavenly places'. These ἀρχαὶ καὶ ἐξουσίαι are ambiguous in status; they may be hostile. The author of Ephesians may be celebrating the victory of God in Christ over the powers; cf. Col. 2.15. As Kittel remarks (p. 43), the reference to angels in 1 Pet. 1.12 is not as relevant, since there the angels wish to witness the triumph of Christ, as they do probably in 1 Tim. 3.16. The reference in Ignatius (*Trallians* 9.1) is even less to the point (quoted by Héring). The whole career of Jesus up to his death is described as having taken place 'in the sight of things in heaven (ἐπουρανίων) and things on earth and things under the earth'.[39] This is simply an assertion of the cosmic dimension to Jesus' career. It is true of course that Paul is here also asserting the cosmic nature of his conflict, but there is no suggestion in Ignatius of a conflict. I conclude that the reference to angels underlines the fact that Paul and his friends are engaged in a warfare which has cosmic dimensions, and in which superhuman forces are engaged. If we refer back to 2 Cor. 2.14 we see that the triumph is made known through the proclamation of the gospel. In Eph. 3.19 it is through the proclamation of the gospel that God's wisdom is made known to the powers. So here the angels are interested in Paul's conflict because the outcome of the cosmic struggle affects them, especially if they are hostile angels. Pobee well points out that in Jewish tradition the fate of the martyrs can be portrayed as part of a cosmic battle.[40]

This conclusion is confirmed by the study of another verse from the same epistle, 1 Cor. 15.32:

εἰ κατὰ ἄνθρωπον ἐθηριομάχησα ἐν ᾽Εφέσῳ,
τί μοι τὸ ὄφελος; εἰ νεκροὶ οὐκ ἐγείρονται,
φάγωμεν καὶ πίωμεν,
αὔριον γὰρ ἀποθνήσκομεν.

What do I gain if, humanly speaking, I fought with beasts at Ephesus? If the dead are not raised, 'Let us eat and drink, for tomorrow we die'.

This verse has been very much a *crux interpretum* ever since it was penned. We might begin by considering the phrase κατὰ ἄνθρωπον. In Paul's letters it usually refers to some point of view which he rejects because it has nothing to do with Christian faith. It seems to me that Barrett gives the best explanation: 'If it was on purely human terms that I fought at Ephesus, what good does that do to me?' This must mean 'I could have given in at Ephesus and avoided all the suffering and conflict that I endured, if I had had no hope beyond the grave'. In other words, Paul risked his life in some struggle in Ephesus; if he had had no hope of the resurrection, there would have been no point in this. He might just as well have avoided the conflict and enjoyed an easy life. His fight was therefore on a point of principle. It was part of the *militia Christi*.

Commentators from the first have been undecided as to whether this fighting with beasts at Ephesus is to be taken literally or not. Plenty of scholars in the past have taken it literally, but I do not know any moderns who do so.[41] Even among those who take it figuratively there is a distinction to be made. There is a small group of scholars, among whom are Weiss and Héring, who take it to mean that there never was any event in Ephesus that could have been described as fighting with beasts, since Paul is expressing an unfulfilled condition: 'If I had fought with beasts in Ephesus, what good would that have done me—on the supposition that Christ is not risen?' This seems to me to be far-fetched, even if the syntax will bear this interpretation. Once grant that the beasts are to be understood figuratively, and there is no point in putting it all into the realm of mere supposition. Paul's point is far more effective if he claims that something happened in Ephesus which could be described as fighting with wild beasts.

Who then were the wild beasts? Men primarily and not angels in the first place. Pompey at Pharsalus is reported by Appian to have exclaimed οἵοις θηρίοις μαχόμεθα 'what brutes we are fighting with!'[42] Robertson–Plummer quote Origen's comment on the verse: ἔστι καὶ θήρια νοητά 'there are also wild beasts in the realm of the mind'. This is perhaps going too far: Paul does not merely mean that he had intellectual opponents to encounter. Allo believes that the reference must be to Jews, a view which we shall see repeated later on. We have already referred to Barrett's convincing explanation of κατὰ ἄνθρωπον. He refers us as well to Ignatius Rom. 5.1, where Ignatius describes the guards who have escorted him from Syria to Asia Minor as 'ten leopards', and he claims that 'from Syria to Rome I am fighting with wild beasts', ἀπὸ Συρίας μεχρὶ Ῥώμης θηριομαχῶ.[43] This is a most telling parallel. Barrett in addition has a cross-reference to 1 Cor. 4.9, the very verse that set us off on the trail that has led to 15.32.

About ten years ago R.E. Osborne published an article in which he refers to the remains of a painting which has been discovered on the wall of the amphitheatre at Corinth.[44] It apparently depicts a *bestiarius* lying under a bull, being licked by a lion. He suggests that Paul is claiming in effect that he is an experienced *bestiarius* in the spiritual arena. Osborne also draws attention to the Qumran interpretation of Hab. 2.17: 'the destruction of the beasts will terrify you',[45] where 'the beasts' are interpreted as those who observe the law. Is Paul perhaps referring to the strict party among Christian Jews, or even to the Pharisaic party among Jews, under the title 'wild beasts'? This is interesting, but we should not forget that in Paul's view behind the activity of those who opposed lay the influence of hostile powers. It is a cosmic war that he is waging. Malherbe has a slightly different suggestion to make.[46] He emphasizes, as H.D. Betz has done, the marked similarity between Paul's style in the Corinthian correspondence and the style of the diatribe. The Cynics were masters of the diatribe; Hercules was one of their heroes and Hercules is the legendary founder of Tarsus, Paul's native city. Hercules frequently fought with beasts, and some writers allegorize this to mean that he fought with his natural passions and subdued them. So θηριομαχεῖν could mean the struggle against hedonism. The Epicureans were frequently accused of hedonism and in particular they are charged with living only for eating and drinking. Paul's adversaries in Ephesus therefore were perhaps hedonists of some sort. If one accepted this argument one might cite Phil. 3.19 in confirmation of it, and go on to suggest that they were antinomians.

However, interesting though Malherbe's theory is, I do not think it quite fits the evidence. Paul quotes Isa. 22.13 not primarily in order to condemn hedonism, but to argue that if one does not believe in the resurrection one might as well give way to hedonism. This conclusion is supported by two small pieces of evidence from the Jewish tradition of exegesis of Isa. 22.13. In *Ta'anith* 11a,[47] this text is used as a description of how an Israelite should not behave when Israel is in trouble. He should not dissociate himself from Israel in order to look after his own safety and comfort. Here then it is not used against hedonism as such. Secondly, the Targum on Isa. 22.13 shows that the text was thought of in connection with the doctrine of the resurrection from the dead. The Targum renders Isa. 22.13 in a quite straightforward manner, but the next verse in the Targum contains the sentence: 'This sin shall not be forgiven you until the second death'. This seems to imply that the sentiment 'Let us eat and drink, for tomorrow we die' was attributed to those who denied the resurrection. That is no doubt why Paul uses it here. Paul therefore is not likely to have hedonists in mind in this context.

We conclude that in 1 Cor. 15.32 Paul is referring to the conflict which he endured at Ephesus with opponents, possibly Jewish opponents. Since he believes he is engaged in a cosmic war, he probably saw behind those opponents the influence of hostile angels. There are one or two instances in the Psalms of θήρια being used by the LXX translator of the psalmist's enemies. The clearest instance is Ps. 74(73).19, which in the LXX runs:

μὴ παραδῷς τοῖς θηρίοις τὴν ψυχὴν ἐξομολογουμένην σε
do not deliver to the wild beasts the soul that praiseth thee.[48]

In the book of Daniel the warring nations, Israel's oppressors, are depicted as wild beasts, θήρια in the Greek.[49] So the lion-fight at Ephesus is an episode in the *militia Christi*.[50] Once more we can quote Pobee in defence of these conclusions. He believes that the use of ἐθηριομάχησα here links Paul's struggle to the course of the cosmic war, because in apocalyptic literature the enemies of God were often portrayed as θήρια, wild beasts.[51]

Our next text is, like 1 Cor. 4.9, one which occurs in the middle of a passage we have already considered. But the verse in question we deliberately left for later treatment. It is 2 Cor. 6.7:

ἐν λόγῳ ἀληθείας· ἐν δυνάμει θεοῦ, διὰ τῶν ὅπλων τῆς δικαιοσύνης
τῶν δεξιῶν καὶ ἀριστερῶν

by . . . truthful speech, and the power of God; with the weapons of
righteousness for the right hand and the left.

We reproduce the RSV, but do not thereby endorse its translation of
ἐν λόγῳ ἀληθείας. Schmiedel maintains that δικαιοσύνης here does
not mean righteousness by faith: Paul is waging a war against
iniquity. We shall be questioning this conclusion presently. Héring
suggests that holding the weapons in the right hand and the left only
means that Paul is well-armed. We must not here associate the right
hand with goodness and the left hand with evil. It could mean simply
offensive and defensive armour: the sword would be held in the right
hand, the shield would hang on the left arm. Several editors maintain
that 'the word of truth' means the preaching of the gospel, and surely
they are right.[52] We have seen in our study of the *militia Christi* that
the preaching of the gospel plays an essential part in it. The RSV
rendering 'truthful speech' is very feeble. Goudge compares with
v. 7b Isa. 59.17a, where it is said of God 'he put on righteousness as a
breastplate'. We shall be considering the significance of this
presently; it certainly suggests that δικαιοσύνη here is not just a
moral quality, the opposite of iniquity. Goudge also compares 2 Cor.
5.21, where Paul describes God as having made Christ to be sin that
we might become the righteousness of God in him. This too suggests
that δικαιοσύνη in 2 Cor. 6.7 is God's saving righteousness which
those who are 'in Christ' receive. Court has an interesting suggestion
to make about 'for the right hand and for the left'.[53] Paul's weapons
of righteousness on the right hand and on the left may mean 'virtues
and blessings' on the one hand as listed in vv. 6-7a and 'sufferings' on
the other hand as listed in vv. 4b and 5 (p. 224). This may well be
right; as we have seen, the *militia Christi* is waged by means of the
apostles' experiences, both blessings and sufferings.

In fact however it is possible to trace quite an extensive scriptural
background to this phrase διὰ τῶν ὅπλων τῆς δικαιοσύνης, one
which throws considerable light on Paul's meaning here. In Gen.
15.1 God appears to Abraham in a vision and says:

fear not, Abraham, I am your shield;
your reward shall be very great.

The phrase 'I am your shield' in the MT is אנכי מגן לך; LXX renders
this with ἐγὼ ὑπερασπίζω σε, but Symmachus has ὑπερμάχομαι

καθάπερ ὅπλον.[54] Now Genesis 15 is an important passage for Paul because it is here that he finds scriptural support for the belief that righteousness by faith began with Abraham. In Gal. 3.6 and Rom. 4.3 he quotes Gen. 15.6 to this effect. If therefore we may suppose that Paul had in his Greek version the same translation as appears in Symmachus' text, the phrase he uses in 2 Cor. 6.7 will have great significance. The God who justifies the sinner, the God of righteousness by faith, is described as Abraham's weapon. Paul's weapons of righteousness therefore are intimately connected with righteousness by faith. The life of faith is the life defined here in terms of *militia Christi*.

The Targums are interesting in this connection. Both the Targum of Palestine and Pseudo-Jonathan here insert a piece of *haggada*. Pseudo-Jonathan represents Abraham at this point as concerned lest his conquest of the kings narrated in Genesis 14 may have used up all his store of righteousness with God: 'Woe to me, because I have received the reward of my appointments in this world, and have no portion in the world to come'. But the Word (*pithgama*) replies: 'My Memra will be thy shield'.[55] The Targum of Palestine has a slightly different version: 'or it may be that righteousness was found in me at the former times, that they fell before me; but at the second time it may not be found, and the Heavenly Name will be profaned in me'. God replies: 'Fear not, Abraham, though they should gather together and come against thee with many legions, My Word shall be thy reward and thy shield in this world, and a protector over thee all the days of the world to come'.[56] Here we find the word, the power of God, and the arms of righteousness, precisely what we find in 2 Cor. 6.7. It looks as if that verse in 2 Corinthians had behind it a meditation on Abraham in Gen. 15.1-6. The righteousness in this verse is certainly the righteousness that is by faith, not merely a moral quality.

Paul uses the language of the Christian's armour more than once. In 1 Thess. 5.4-8 we find Christians described as 'sons of light'. They must put on 'the breastplate of faith and love, and for a helmet the hope of salvation'. In Rom. 13.12 Paul writes: 'Let us cast off the works of darkness and put on the armour of light (τὰ ὅπλα τοῦ φωτός)'. All this language is no doubt inspired by Isa. 59.17, as Goudge has reminded us:

> He put on righteousness as a breastplate,
> and a helmet of salvation upon his head.

This is a favourite chapter with NT writers: Isa. 59.20-21 is quoted in Rom. 11.26-27. In the passage we have in mind God bestirs himself to come to the help of his elect who are oppressed by the sins of Israel. The Targum of Isaiah 59.17ab runs: 'And he shall reveal himself to work deeds of righteousness for his people; strength and salvation shall he bring with his Memra for him that fear him to do them'. Thus the language of God's armour is associated with God acting for the salvation of the faithful. Paul transfers it to the ministry of the apostolic group, because they are 'in Christ', who is the supreme revelation of God in action. But, as we have seen, he can also apply the figure to Christians as a whole. Once more we realize that the apostolic warfare is not to be confined to the apostles, but to be passed on to each newly founded Christian community.[57]

III

Throughout the Gospels we gain the impression that Jesus regards himself as engaged in a campaign against the powers of evil. We think of such texts as Mark 1.24; 5.7; Luke 10.18; John 12.31. But there is one particular passage in the Synoptic Gospels where the *militia Christi* motif seems to be expressed more clearly than elsewhere. This is Mark 3.27 (par. Matt. 12.29) and Luke 11.21-22. Matthew here follows Mark almost verbatim, so we need only quote Mark and Luke. Mark 3.27 runs:

ἀλλ᾽ οὐ δύναται οὐδεὶς εἰς τὴν οἰκίαν τοῦ ἰσχυροῦ εἰσελθὼν τὰ σκεύη αὐτοῦ διαρπάσαι ἐὰν μὴ πρῶτον τὸν ἰσχυρὸν δήσῃ, καὶ τότε τὴν οἰκίαν αὐτοῦ διαρπάσει

But no one can enter a strong man's house and plunder his goods, unless he first binds the strong man; then indeed he may plunder his house.

This is expressed in terms of a householder being attacked by a burglar. Luke expresses it in terms of a ruler attacking a castle:

ὅταν ὁ ἰσχυρὸς καθωπλισμένος φυλάσσῃ τὴν ἑαυτοῦ αὐλήν, ἐν εἰρήνῃ ἐστὶν τὰ ὑπάρχοντα αὐτοῦ, ἐπὰν δὲ ἰσχυρότερος αὐτοῦ ἐπελθὼν νικήσῃ αὐτόν, τὴν πανοπλίαν αὐτοῦ αἴρει, ἐφ᾽ ᾗ ἐπεποίθει, καὶ τὰ σκῦλα αὐτοῦ διαδίδωσιν.

When a strong man, fully armed, guards his own palace, his goods are in peace; but when one stronger than he assails him and overcomes him, he takes away his armour in which he trusted, and divides his spoil.

Commentators agree that this parable indicates Jesus' awareness of his fight against Satan. Gould remarks: 'this victory over Satan is part of (Jesus') self-consciousness'. Rawlinson writes: 'Mark suggests Our Lord as the binder of Satan', and he very pertinently gives a cross-reference to 2 Cor. 10.5. Swete harks back to Isa. 49.24-25, which we must examine presently. He sees three stages in the process of victory: 'a personal victory . . . the disarming of the defeated οἰκοδεσπότης . . . the spoiling . . . and distribution of his ill-gotten gains'. Lagrange holds that the σκεύη must be men. One can see how such a parable taken literally could give rise to the later ransom theory of the atonement, whereby Christ has robbed Satan of his prey, the souls of men. Vincent Taylor gives two interesting OT cross-references, Isa. 24.22f., and 53.12ab. He comments: 'the idea of the binding of the evil powers is an eschatological conception'. Branscomb, discussing Jesus' miracles in connection with this verse, remarks that Jesus saw his miracles as signs of the breaking down of the rule of Satan. Sherman Johnson quotes *T. Levi* 28.12 'And Beliar shall be bound by him', i.e. by the Messiah. Bultmann writes; 'The saying could originally have meant the victory of Jesus over the demons had demonstrated that God had already overthrown the devil's reign'.[59] He believes that the logion is authentic, for he writes: 'It will only be in a very few cases that one of the logia can be ascribed to Jesus with any confidence: such sayings as arise from the exaltation of an eschatological mood, like Mark 3.27 (Satan is already overcome) . . . So here if anywhere we can find what is characteristic of the preaching of Jesus'.[60] Klostermann believes that the σκεύη are the demons. The conqueror is God acting through Jesus. E. Schweizer writes: 'The very fact that this parable is a summons to faith demonstrates that it is a genuine saying of Jesus'. Haenchen makes an interesting point: in Mark's Gospel generally the demons, unlike men, recognize Jesus as the Son of God. But in 1 Cor. 2.8 the demonic powers, according to Paul, failed to recognize him. I would suggest that it might be more accurate to say that the powers in 1 Cor. 2.8 failed to recognize in Christ crucified the revelation of God.[61]

Commentators on the Luke passage make very similar remarks. Lagrange thinks that the battle is regarded as taking place in heaven.[62] He says that αὐλή means a prince's palace. Plummer believes that the ἰσχυρότερος is Christ, and he very relevantly compares Col. 2.15.[63] Klostermann wonders whether perhaps τὰ ὑπάρχοντα may not be the souls held in thrall by Satan. We may add that Paul like Luke thinks in terms of military action rather than of civic disturbance. G. Kittel notes that making Satan prisoner was a messianic function.[64] He offers an interesting comparison with Eph. 4.8 ᾐχμαλώτευσεν αἰχμαλωσίαν. There the author interprets Ps. 68.18 so as to make it refer to Christ's victory in the resurrection. Kittel holds that the prisoners are the evil spirits.

The primary scriptural reference of this Synoptic passage must be to Isa. 49.24-25:

> Can the prey be taken from the mighty,
> or the captives of a tyrant[65] be released?
> ... Surely the captives of the mighty shall be taken
> and the prey of the tyrant be rescued,
> for I will contend with those who contend with you,
> and I will save your children.

The LXX has verbal echoes both in the Synoptic passages and in Paul:

> μὴ λήμψεταί τις παρὰ γίγαντος σκῦλα;
> καὶ ἔαν αἰχμαλωτεύσῃ τις ἀδίκως σωθήσεται;
> ... ἐάν τις αἰχμαλωτεύσῃ γίγαντα, λήμψεται σκῦλα·
> λαμβάνων δὲ παρ' ἰσχύοντος σωθήσεται.

It is worth noting that in the LXX of the second verse we have the idea of the strong man being made prisoner. In all three Synoptic writers the logion comes in a context in which Jesus is accused of being inspired by demonic powers. This is certainly what the Gospel writers understand by the logion, and there can be no doubt but that this is what Jesus meant by it: the power of God manifested in his own healings is showing itself stronger than Satan. The intertestamental literature is full of accounts of conflicts between the forces of God and the forces of evil; this must be the sense in which Jesus understood Isa. 49.24-25.

There are however two more passages in Isaiah which may be relevant to this logion. The first is Isa. 53.12a:

MT: לכן אחלק לו ברבים
ואת־עצומים יחלק שלל

LXX: διὰ τοῦτο αὐτὸς κληρονομήσει πολλοὺς καὶ τῶν ἰσχυρῶν
μεριεῖ σκῦλα.

RSV: Therefore I will divide him a portion with the great, and
he shall divide the spoil with the strong.

The chief interest of this passage is that it identifies the subject of 49.24-26 with the servant of the Lord. It is interesting to observe that in the *Sifre to Numbers* this verse is applied to Phinehas, à propos Num. 25.13.[66] In a previous work I have claimed that there is a considerable piece of *haggada* connected with Numbers 25 lying behind Col. 2.14-15.[67] In the *Sifre* context the comment is made that Phinehas's atoning priesthood is not confined to that one event described in Numbers, but will continue for ever 'until the dead are raised'. In a similar vein we find Isa. 53.12a applied to Moses in *Sotah* 14a in the Babylonian Talmud;[68] the editor of this Tractate suggests that this is anti-Christian polemic. There was therefore a tradition in Judaism that Isa. 53.12a could be applied to a saviour figure. In early Christian exegesis it was applied to Christ as victor over the powers of evil.

The third passage is Isa. 24.21-22:

> On that day the Lord will punish
> the host of heaven, in heaven,
> and the kings of the earth, on the earth.
> They will be gathered together as prisoners in a pit;
> they will be shut up in a prison,
> and after many days they will be punished.

The Hebrew for 'in a prison' is על-מסגר, which the LXX translates with εἰς δεσμωτήριον. But the word 'in a pit' is rendered εἰς ὀχύρωμα. Here the ὀχύρωμα is the place in which the enemies of God are imprisoned. But the Targum brings the stronghold into the first verse, for it paraphrases v. 21 thus: 'And it shall come to pass at that time, that the Lord shall punish the mighty hosts that dwell in the stronghold'.[69] This establishes a tenuous link with 2 Cor. 10.4.

The concept of God punishing the rebellious angels is of course founded on this passage, Isa. 24.21-22. There is plenty of evidence that this belief continued right through into the Christian era. See *Midrash on the Psalms* 82.3; 104.1; 145.1; *Pesikta Rabbati* 42.9. Two authorities believe that in this passage the angels punished are probably the angels of the nations. See K.G. Kuhn, *op. cit.*, p. 698, and J. Bonsirven, *Textes Rabbiniques etc.* 9, section 86.[70]

But a much more definite link between the concept of imprisoning the forces of evil which occurs in 2 Cor. 10.5 and contemporary Jewish literature can be found in the Hodayoth of the Qumran community. 1QH 3.18 is translated as follows by Mansoor:[71]

> And they shall shut the gates of the pit upon her who conceives
> injustice,
> And the bars of eternity upon all the spirits of naught.

Delcor suggests that the female who conceives iniquity is some sort of female demon,[72] pehaps Lilith, and Mansoor agrees. What is even more interesting however is that Delcor goes on to conclude that those who do the imprisoning here are the messianic community of Qumran. Here then is a very good parallel (*mutatis mutandis*) to Paul's claim on behalf of the messianic community of the early Church that he is imprisoning the forces of evil.

One more question might be examined: in Luke's version of the logion we can distinguish three stages in the conflict, as has already been pointed out: the conquest, the disarming, the division of the spoil. Paul's account of his warfare in 2 Cor. 10.3-6 is closer to Luke's version than to that of the other two Synoptists. Can we trace any equivalence between Luke's description of the warfare and Paul's? It is just possible that we can. Paul writes first about the overthrowing of the strong places, then about the bringing into captivity of every thought, and finally about the punishment of disobedience. There are marked differences of course, but it may be that Paul knew a version of the logion that was close to that which Luke had before him.

We conclude therefore that there is a connection between Paul's *militia Christi* and the logion which we have been considering in the Synoptic Gospels. Jesus saw himself as waging a campaign on behalf of God against the evil one, and he describes the campaign in this metaphor, itself drawn from scripture. Paul is conscious of carrying on the same campaign in the strength of the cross of Christ, and hence uses language that has echoes of the words which Jesus used. But Paul is doing so after the great event of the cross and resurrection. Once again we conclude that there are connections to be traced between the teaching of Jesus and the thought of Paul.

As we look back over this chapter as a whole, we can hardly fail to leave it without some reference to that book in the NT in which the *militia Christi* is most dramatically set forth, the Revelation of St. John the Divine. Here we find essentially the same conflict as that in which Paul is engaged, the war between the beast, itself inspired by Satan, and the Lamb, symbol of the slaughtered and risen Christ. Moreover John the Divine preserves carefully that element of paradox which we have seen to be so essential to Paul's understanding of the cross. The beast wins his victories by means of brute force and ruthless killing. The Lamb wins the ultimate victory by dying, a dying which is made contemporary by the deaths of the martyrs in every generation. John's technique of proclamation is totally different from Paul's; John uses symbols where Paul uses the language of the diatribe. But the message of both writers is essentially the same.

Chapter 7

FUNDAMENTAL QUESTIONS

Not long after I had begun the research for what has now become this book, I asked myself several basic questions about the material with which I was concerned, questions which seemed to me to arise from the passages that had engaged my attention. My hope was that at the end of the research I might be able to give some sort of an answer to them. I believe that I have succeeded in doing this, and the previous six chapters contain the essence of these answers. But it is desirable that both the questions and the answers sould be set out clearly, and also that the answers which scholars and commentators have given, in one form or another, should be considered. This chapter will therefore be devoted to this task. It should serve to clarify and move forward the argument of the book as a whole.

I find that there are five fundamental questions to be answered. I will deal with them in order. Some of them raise issues that have not yet been considered.

1. *How did the paradox of the cross originate?*

Before we face this question, we must deal with an objection. It might be said that there is no mystery about the origin of Paul's doctrine of the cross; it is there already in Jesus' teaching. All Paul was doing was transposing this teaching into the circumstances of his day.

That there is some truth in this objection must be admitted. We have claimed that Paul's description of the persecutions accompanying the apostolic life find their counterpart in some elements in Jesus' teaching as recorded in the Sermon on the Mount. It is also true that in some places in the Synoptic Gospels we can find references to sufferings which disciples will have to undergo for Christ's sake.

There are of course the eschatological afflictions which are part of the apocalyptic discourse in Mark 13.5-23 and parallels. There is Jesus' logion reported in Mark 8.34 about the necessity of taking up one's cross and following Jesus (the parallels are Matt. 16.24; Luke 9.23). Above all there is Mark 10.35-45 (par. Matt. 20.20-28), where Jesus tells the disciples that they are to drink the cup that he drinks and to be baptized with his baptism.

The eschatological afflictions are hardly relevant to the question. They were an acknowledged part of the eschatological programme, and cannot in themselves account for Paul's language. But the two Marcan passages are closer to Paul's thought and deserve some attention. In Mark 8.34 Jesus says:

> If any man would come after me, let him deny himself and take up his cross and follow me.

If this is in all respects an authentic logion, it comes quite close to Paul's concept of being crucified with Christ. Vincent Taylor, who defends the authenticity of the saying, comments: 'The idea is metaphorical, but not mystical as in Gal. ii.20', thereby preserving a difference. Montefiore thinks the detail of taking up the cross is colouring supplied by the early Church.[1] Nineham agrees: 'Probably the present forumulation of the saying is the work of the early Church'.[2] E. Best seems to hold the same view; he points out that the teaching here is similar to that in 1 Corinthians 1 and 2. He seems to assume that the language represents Mark's interpretation of Jesus' teaching, for he writes: 'While the concept of imitation is not absent from Mark's idea of discipleship, the idea he puts forward is much more profound'[3] — more profound, we must suppose, because nearer Paul's. If the logion is wholly authentic then it does supply a foundation for Paul's doctrine. If, as seems more likely, the mention of the cross is the contribution of the early Church, then we may say that something like Paul's doctrine was familiar to other early Christians.

In Mark 10.35-45 Jesus countered the request of the sons of Zebedee for privileged treatment in the kingdom by saying first that the privilege was not his to confer, and then asking whether they could drink his cup and be baptized with his baptism. Here is a difficult case to decide: from one point of view the language looks like that of the early Church: one could descry a reference to the two gospel sacraments. On the other hand the figure of drinking the cup at least has deep roots in the OT, and would be by no means inappropriate on Jesus' lips. Montefiore on this question quotes A. Loisy extensively and obviously agrees with him that most of the logion is the creation of the early Church.[4] Bultmann regards it as 'secondary';[5] but Vincent Taylor defends its authenticity. He calls it 'an original and creative utterance' and suggests that Rom. 6.3 may be 'a development and application of the saying'. Nineham thinks that there are two quite distinct answers here to the request of the disciples. The first occurs in 10.38-39, the reference to baptism and the cup; the second is 10.40: it is not within Jesus' power to decide this question. The second reply he considers authentic. Of the first he writes that it is 'more likely to have originated with early Christians reflecting on Christ's life and death as a whole'.

We may conclude that there is certainly some foundation for Paul's doctrine of the paradox of the cross in the teaching of Jesus, though how much it is difficult to say. The more one believes that these passages were influenced by the creative powers of the early Church, the more one is driven to ask where the idea came from that Christians should actually reproduce Christ's sufferings. At least it is clear from this study that Paul's doctrine was not peculiar to Paul in the early Church. There are traces of it in Mark. However I do not believe that these passages solve our question, 'What is the origin of Paul's doctrine of the paradox of the cross?'. We do not find in them that identification with Christ's sufferings which we find in Paul. Christians are not so intimately connected with Christ's sufferings and death as they are in Paul's thought. Also the paradox of the cross is not there as it is in Paul. At least it is not present in the teaching of Jesus. It is hard to see how it could have been, unless we attribute to him a superhuman knowledge which assorts ill with his full humanity. And thirdly, the element of redemptive suffering on the part of Christians is not to be found in the Synoptic Gospels. But this, we have maintained, is an essential part of Paul's teaching about the cross. The question therefore may remain; we may legitimately seek for an answer.

Anyone who asks this question must begin by a study of Güttgemann's valuable book already referred to several times in this work. Güttgemanns finds the answer in A. Schlatter's contention that what lies behind both the intention of Jesus and the theology of Paul is the desire to obey God's will.[6] Schlatter maintained that Paul was preaching Jesus' gospel in the sense that both Jesus and Paul recognized the contemporary action of God and the requirement to obey it. The combination of God's act and man's act in Jesus is what Paul called sonship (p. 378); so what is in common between Jesus' message and Paul's is God's act, God's will. There is therefore an equivalence in Jesus' life to everything in Paul's message. But this proclamation of the will of God had nothing casual or occasional about it. It took place in the end time. The message of both Jesus and Paul is thus thoroughly eschatological. The difference between the two is that Jesus said the great event was just about to come, whereas Paul preaches that the life, death, and resurrection of Jesus has inaugurated the end time (pp. 388-89). So Güttgemanns in effect concludes that the answer to the question, 'Whence did Paul get the conception of the suffering apostle?', is 'From eschatological belief which goes back to the historical Jesus'. We might put it in other words by saying that Paul's doctrine of the paradox of the cross, the vocation to suffering of the apostolic ministers, and the need for each newly founded Christian community to live this apostolic life, come from the realization of the earliest Christians that they were living in the end time, that the new age had in a sense begun, and that the teaching which the earthly Jesus had given must be expressed in terms of this changed situation. Paul was the profoundest theologian of the earliest community. More of his writings have been preserved than those of any other writer of the NT period. That is why his doctrine of the paradox of the cross is so important for us, not because he invented a doctrine of suffering that was inspired by some exotic influence.

We may refer to two very recent scholars whose views seem to coincide with what we have just written. The first is A.T. Lincoln. In his book already referred to, he is discussing the tension between the heavenly πολίτευμα and the earthly reality, and he writes: 'Paul's Christian apocalyptic is defined both by the future and by the recent past and is about what happens when the age to come has been made available through Christ's resurrection and how that life does not remain centred in heaven but works itself out on earth in the present period of history'.[7] Paul was facing opponents who behaved as if the cross could be relegated to the past and heaven could be stormed now. He has to show them that it is the very arrival of the new age which requires the sufferings of Christ to be reproduced in the Church until the *parousia*. As long as the ages overlapped (1 Cor. 10.11), the cross would be relevant. The other scholar to whom I would refer is Jane Schaberg. In a very recent article she has suggested that Jesus may have seen the picture of the Danielic Son of Man as representing the vocation of himself and his disciples.[8] They would have corresponded to the 'holy ones' in the prophecy of Dan. 7.18, 22, 27. She writes:

> This corporate dimension would fade as the notion of sharing in (Jesus') fate replaces the notion of sharing in the fate of the holy ones...but not fade completely, since the early community's sufferings (at the hands of the Jews and of Gentiles) was seen in the light of his (Christ's) (p. 216).

She also raises the possibility that this connection was not made by Jesus but by the early community. It is indeed interesting that once again the Danielic Son of Man should be brought into connection with Jesus' own conception of his vocation. The wheel has in a sense come full circle. But this sort of explanation would fit in very well with what we have discovered about the relation of Jesus' message to Paul's. If Schaberg's theory is correct, it hardly seems probable that the application of the Danielic Son of Man to Jesus should only have originated in the early Church.

We can however claim to have confirmed Güttgemanns' solution to the problem by our study of the scriptural background to Paul's interpretation of Jesus' sufferings and death. In the Psalms and in other parts of scripture Paul believed that he could find references to the Messiah. But at the same time he found references to a group of people. Sometimes it is merely that the first person plural is found instead of the first person singular. Sometimes the group is called 'the righteous' or 'thy holy ones'. At any rate Paul found quite sufficient references in what he believed were messianic passages in scripture to encourage him to conclude that not only was Christ referred to in such passages, but also his faithful followers, whom Paul identified with the apostolic community, as he understood it.

It is not enough therefore simply to say as Güttgemanns does that what inspired Paul's theology of suffering was eschatology. Jesus had inaugurated the new age. This very statement has two important implications. First, eschatology implies salvation history. The end time is the end of an era. But this implies a knowledge of Israel's history as understood by Paul and all early Christians. Hence reference to scripture, where the course of salvation history is recorded, is unavoidable. The meaning of eschatology for Paul must bring us back to Paul's interpretation of scripture.

Secondly, eschatology means that Jesus brought in the new age. But that age is new compared with what? One cannot merely say 'the new age is come', without presuming some knowledge of the old age, and of what the change from the one to the other actually means. If Schlatter is right in saying that both Jesus and Paul proclaimed the action of God, we may very well ask, what action? It is not enough to claim that Paul saw Jesus as the inaugurator of the new age therefore he believed that the lives of the apostles should reproduce Jesus' life. The connection consisting in obedience to God's will must be brought out, as indeed Schlatter did bring it out. If the pattern that lies behind the whole divine dispensation is, from man's point of view, obedience to the will of God, the obedience of God's faithful servants under the old dispensation, the obedience of the Son during his earthly life, the obedience of the apostolic community in the new age, then the element of the Church cannot be ignored and it ✓ becomes clear that the life of messianic suffering to which the apostolic community is called must be passed on to the Church and maintained from age to age. So the element of scripture and the element of the Church and (somehow) its ministry are necessary parts of the whole dispensation.

This may throw some light on the question on the relation between Christ's life and sufferings and that of Christians in Paul's thought. Merely to call it 'mystical' is not adequate, at least not if that means that the concept was borrowed from the mystery religions.[9] In Paul's thought the Messiah was always accompanied by the faithful; sometimes he spoke on their behalf. When the prophecies written in scripture were fulfilled, the presence of the faithful was as much part of the fulfilment as was the action, or passion, of Christ himself. Hence there could be no question of the experiences of the apostolic group being a sort of appendix to the Christ event. They were part of the Christ event itself.

Later on in his work Güttgemanns seems to come to very much the same conclusion.[10] He quotes 2 Cor. 6.2f. as proof that the salvation event and apostolic authority are closely connected. The apostle's word coincides with the word of God, so that the two are identical, and Christ's presence is mediated by the apostle's preaching. He writes that we must speak 'von der eschatologischen *Präsenz der Zeit des Gekreuzigten* in der apostolischen Verkündigung' (p. 322, italics Güttgemanns'). In our examination of 2 Cor. 5.20–6.2 on p. 56 above, we insisted that Paul could only apply the words of

Isa. 49.8 to himself and to the Corinthian church because the words had already been fulfilled in Christ. In other words, a careful consideration of the scriptural background to this passage confirms the conviction that in Paul's thought Christ and believers in Christ (notably the apostolic group) were part of one and the same event.

A. Schulz in an article published in 1963 claimed that the Hebrew concept of corporate personality explains this interchange which we find in Paul's work between Christ, the apostles, and the Church[11] (p. 268). He begins by asking whether we are justified in classifying Paul's *Leidenstheologie* under *imitatio Christi*. He holds that both the sacramental and the eschatological aspects must be regarded as experiential rather than exemplary (p. 265). Kuss, he says, maintains that baptism in Paul initiates the Christian into a life of reproducing Christ's sufferings and death that can be described as *imitatio Christi*. But Schulz points out that many 'Leidenstheologie' texts, including 2 Cor. 4.10-12; Gal. 6.17; Phil. 3.10f., lack any baptismal reference. Such a reference would fit into Paul's thought well enough, but the connection does not seem to be made (p. 266). Schulz agrees that the sufferings have an apostolic significance: 'Die "Christusleiden" sind nicht die dem Kyrios als Person eigenen pathemata'. There is no suggestion of an ethic of asceticism. All Christians are called to this sort of life (p. 267). The places where Paul uses 'imitation' language are all parenetic, whereas the 'Leidenstheologie' passages are more religious (p. 269). Generally speaking we may say that these are true and valuable conclusions. But it is dangerous to draw too sharp a line between 'imitation passages' and 'suffering passages'. One of the most remarkable 'suffering passages', 1 Cor. 4.9-13, is plainly written in order to persuade the Corinthians to follow the example of the apostles and enter the area of conflict. Again, no doubt from the point of view of the history of religion the passages in the Psalms and elsewhere that contain descriptions of the individual alternating with the group are based on the Hebrew conception of corporate personality. But this explains why they were written, not why Paul interpreted them as he did. Paul saw in them a prophecy both of the suffering of Christ and of the suffering of the faithful, because he had inherited a tradition in Judaism which interpreted such passages messianically and because an application to the experience of the apostles, justified by the language of scripture, made sense in his own situation.

To return to Güttgemanns: he makes an excellent point when he claims (p. 251) that the identity between the earthly Jesus and the risen Lord is not a bodily one, because (a) Paul claims to have seen Jesus but he did not see his body, (b) Christ is manifest in Paul's sufferings; but this is not a bodily manifestation of Christ. In true Pauline thought, he believes, the σῶμα of the regenerate Christian is not a σῶμα τῆς ταπεινώσεως[12] (Phil. 3.21). That phrase, he conjectures, is not Paul's but belongs to a formula known to the Philippians (p. 245). On the basis of this distinction Güttgemanns would not seek to identify the sufferings of the apostle with those of the community; in his exposition of his theology of suffering Paul does not use the σῶμα Χριστοῦ concept (p. 323). But a few pages later (p. 327) Güttgemanns admits that the apostolic sufferings can become the sufferings of the community, and he cites Gal. 4.12. It seems to me that Güttgemanns has reached the right conclusion for the wrong reasons. It is quite true that Paul does not use σῶμα Χριστοῦ language in connection with his theology of suffering. But this may be because Christians are *called to be* the body of Christ. This is what they are corporately to become. But suffering for Christ is a present condition, a present reality: if you are a Christian your sufferings represent the sufferings of Christ. Since it is quite plain that Paul intends that the Church corporately should carry on the task of representing Christ's sufferings, what is needed is not proof that Christians must suffer, but a reason why Paul does not use σῶμα Χριστοῦ language in connection with that suffering. Perhaps we could draw an analogy with the other great basic description of the Church, the Church as the people of God. This is not something the Christians must strive to become, it is what baptism makes them to be. So perhaps it is with the suffering of the people of God. It is an unavoidable destiny; the question is, are they alert so to use it as to become the body of Christ?

The year after Güttgemanns published his book an important study by H.D. Betz on the imitation of Christ appeared.[13] In it there is an illuminating discussion of what it means for Paul to imitate the sufferings and death of Christ. Betz insists that the imitation is an imitation of the incarnation, passion, and death of Jesus, not of the details of his life (p. 161). The words οὐχ ἑαυτῷ ἤρεσεν ('did not please himself') in Rom. 15.3 refer to the incarnation event and nothing else. This seems to be excluding too much. After all, five verses later Paul says that Jesus came to be a servant of the Jewish people. This was a life-long process; it was not something that was accomplished in a week. Again, in Phil. 2.7 Christ is described as 'taking the form of a servant'.[14] This too was a life-long vocation. Betz goes on to say that nineteenth-century exegesis took the example of the Christ-hymn in Phil. 2.6-11 as an ideal of Jesus' life. Lohmeyer later insisted that the meaning was incarnational; the example was set by the act of the incarnation. The great objection to this is that the incarnation of a divine being is not something which we can imitate. This was Käsemann's argument against Lohmeyer. Käsemann himself thinks that there is a semi-Gnostic myth in the background, but the Christian content consists in the stress on obedience. The pre-existent being was obedient, and this we can imitate.[15]

Güttgemanns had in fact argued along very similar lines when discussing 2 Cor. 10.1 (p. 139). He actually claims that here Paul means that his own πραΰτης and ἐπιείκεια ('meekness and gentleness') are a manifestation of Christ's. This seems a most strained interpretation of the text. Why should Paul not be permitted to refer to the meekness and gentleness of Christ during his earthly life? In fact Güttgemanns does not completely eliminate such a reference to the historical Jesus. The Corinthians, he says, wanted to shed the earthly Jesus (p. 140). Paul insists that the earthly Jesus is identical with the exalted Lord, and is manifested in Paul's own ministry. But Güttgemanns adds that these qualities were manifested in Christ's obedience.

Certainly this emphasis on obedience, which we have found to be so central in the accounts of both Güttgemanns and Betz, is absolutely crucial. But we might still put in a pleas for the place which the character of the earthly Jesus has to play in this scheme of things. Neither gentleness not meekness nor obedience can be adequately manifested in one action only, even if that action is drawn out along the week of the passion. It is much more likely that Paul thought of the meek, gentle, and obedient *character* of the earthly Jesus as manifested throughout his career, though coming to a climax of course in the cross. We can here relevantly refer to the picture of the righteous man recorded in Wisdom 2.10-20, a passage which might well have influenced Paul. The ungodly here complain that the righteous man opposes their works and reproaches them for their transgressions of the law. He styles himself the child of God (παῖδα κυρίου) and boasts that God is his Father. So they decide to put him to the test:

for if the righteous man is God's own son, he will help him,
and will deliver him from the hand of his adversaries.
Let us test him with insult and torture,
that we may find out how gentle he is (τὴν ἐπιείκειαν αὐτοῦ),
and make trial of his forbearance (τὴν ἀνεξικακίαν αὐτοῦ).

Here certainly the supreme trial of the righteous man's gentleness
comes in the ordeal to which he is subjected by the ungodly; but it
would be absurd to deny that his character had not been already
manifested in his life as a whole.

In 1972 H.D. Betz published another interesting study of Paul, in
which he compared Paul's style of writing, and to some extent his
actual arguments, with that of the Cynic tradition.[16] In particular he
compared Paul to Socrates, the hero of the Cynics. Socrates had
argued that he was superior to all contemporary philosophers
because he knew that he knew nothing. He was aware of his own
ignorance in a society replete with philosophers who claimed to be
able to impart extensive knowledge about everything in the world. In
the same way Paul, faced with opponents who claimed great
superiority because of charismatic powers and special revelations,
based his claim on his own weakness. The resemblance is certainly
striking, but it does not account for certain important elements in
Paul's theology of the apostolic ministry. In the first place, Paul's
paradox goes deeper than that of Socrates. Paul is not only weak, he
is also persecuted, despised, treated as the dregs of humanity. This
goes much farther than Socrates' deliberate cultivation of a slovenly
appearance. Next, Paul does not claim to know nothing, as Socrates
did. He claims to know nothing but Christ crucified (1 Cor. 2.2).
Christ crucified is in fact so important an item of knowledge that it
supplies Paul with a complete theology! Above all, there is nothing in
the Socratic tradition to parallel the atoning element in Paul's sense
of vocation. As we shall be arguing below, the apostolic life (which
Betz compares to the Cynic ideal of existence), because it represents
the atoning life of Christ, has a reconciling, expiatory effect. Finally
we might note that there is apparently nothing in the Cynic tradition
equivalent to the strong corporate element of Paul's theology of the
cross. The precarious life of the suffering apostle is to be handed on
to the Church. It seems to me unlikely that Paul had any conscious
intention of imitating or rivalling the Socratic tradition. The
question of the actual form of his writings is a distinct one, to which
we must give some attention later.

We may conclude our answer to the first of the five questions by glancing at what Ahern has to say about the origin of Paul's theology of the cross.[17] In Corinth, he suggests, Paul realized that suffering and affliction provide the most favourable climate for the activity of God's saving power (p. 6). This in turn fits in with the thought of late Judaism, especially as reflected in the *Hodayoth* of Qumran, where the poor (ענוים) are those who are totally dependent on God. We have already pointed out the significance of that word ענוים. This would seem to confirm our suggestion made above.[18] Paul's experience in Corinth enabled him further to articulate his thought on the subject of the cross.

One other suggestion about the origin of Paul's thought comes from Pobee.[19] Christ, he says, died a martyr's death, because of his devotion to the will of God, a point, as we have seen, very rightly emphasized by Güttgemanns following Schlatter. Pobee adds later 'The persecutions he endured authenticated (Paul's) words as a servant of Christ (2 Cor. 11.23), an apostle'. All this is quite true. No doubt the martyr tradition of Judaism was one of the influences that went to make up the early Christian belief about the atoning death of Christ. But this alone was not enough. We must allow for the eschatological element in Paul's belief, rightly brought out by Güttgemanns. In addition we may claim as another important factor Paul's interpretation of scripture.

2. *Does the action of the apostolic community have an atoning value?*

We refer first to our study of 1 Cor. 4.9-13. There we concluded that behind vv. 12-13

λοιδορούμενοι εὐλογοῦμεν, ...
δυσφημούμενοι παρακαλοῦμεν

lay not only a word of Jesus himself but also a reference to Psalm 109, and in particular to v. 3 of that psalm as it appears in the LXX (Ps. 108.4), in which the psalmist complains that in return for his love his enemies slandered him, and that they repaid his good deeds and love with hatred and enmity. This is a clear case of Paul taking up a piece of Jesus' teaching and applying it to the apostles. He must have believed that in the original psalm the Messiah was describing what would happen when he came, that is that he would receive hatred in return for his love. When he did come, not content with returning good for evil, he taught his disciples to do the same. The supreme climax of this action came on the cross, whereby in return for this terrible treatment he won redemption for those who had so maltreated him. Now in the beginning of the new age his disciples are represented by the apostles. The natural conclusion is that the precarious life and sufferings of the apostles are a continuation of the process of redemption, or rather a making it contemporary in each generation. We would need very strong evidence on the other side in order to prove that these sufferings are not regarded as redemptive.[20]

These verses are immediately followed by the occurrence of two remarkable words which Paul applies to himself and his companions, περικαθάρματα and περίψημα. We have shown that the lexicographical evidence is very much in favour of the conclusion that these words have an expiatory significance. Also, if we are right in claiming that there is an echo of Lamentations 3 here, this in its turn may provide a link with Isa. 50.6a, where there is certainly a suggestion of atoning power, since the Servant of the Lord's suffering and death is clearly described as having expiatory power. Even if this link (which admittedly is indirect) is doubted, the mere fact that the Messiah is regarded as foretelling his sufferings in Lamentations itself implies atoning suffering, and these two remarkable words apply that atoning suffering to the life of the apostles.[21]

We came to similar conclusions about 2 Cor. 4.10-14. There the carrying about of the νέκρωσις of Jesus in the apostles' bodies cannot mean anything else than a representation in the life of the apostles of the 'having-been-deadness' of Jesus, not a continuation of his dying, since as we have seen νέκρωσις cannot mean the process of dying, but the fact of his being dead, or of his having been dead. Now this can only imply that the effect of his death, the redemption of those who believe, is to be represented in the apostles' lives. Otherwise νέκρωσις in this context is virtually meaningless.[22]

Undoubtedly this conclusion causes alarm to some scholars, especially perhaps to those of the Lutheran tradition—and we can never forget how much we owe to scholars of this tradition both of good and less good in NT critical research. They are naturally afraid that if we once admit that the sufferings of the apostles have redemptive value, we will be attributing redemptive value to something man can do and will be thereby committing ourselves to a doctrine of salvation by works. One can only protest that this is very far from our belief, or, in my opinion, from the belief of St. Paul. He can only attribute redemptive value to the sufferings of the apostles because he believes that they are in Christ and that God-in-Christ is active in them. After all, most scholars, including especially perhaps Lutheran scholars, would readily admit that in Paul's preaching of the gospel message God is uttering his word. It is not a great step from that to say that in Paul's suffering God in Christ is making contemporary the once-for-all redemptive work of Christ.

Precisely such a tendency to avoid this conclusion is exhibited in two of the scholars whom we have frequently quoted in this work. Thus Güttgemanns denies à propos 2 Cor. 4.10-15 that Paul's life has atoning efficacy.[23] The death of the apostles, he says, is not the ground of the Corinthians' life. He believes that in v. 12 Paul is answering a Gnostic protest: 'We are enjoying heavenly life; you seem to be experiencing degrading death'. However a consideration of the significance of the scripture passage which we have shown to lie behind these verses must surely argue in favour of a redemptive force being represented as active in the lives of the apostles. In Ps. 115.6 (LXX) Paul would have read:

> Precious in the eyes of the Lord
> is the death of his holy ones.

And three verses later the Messiah declares his intention of paying his vows to the Lord in the presence of all his people. A communal reference cannot be avoided here. Paul would see in this psalm a prophecy of the atoning sufferings and death of the Messiah and *and of his holy ones*. The whole point of the psalm quotation is to join the action of the Messiah and his faithful ones together, as the reference to the resurrection in 2 Cor. 4.14 shows.

In the same passage Güttgemanns refers to 2 Cor. 1.4, claiming that there Paul's affliction is not the cause of the Corinthians' salvation. A reading of the subsequent verses however must render this conclusion doubtful. In v. 4 Paul says that God comforts him in all his affliction, so that he may be able to comfort those in any sort of affliction by means of the comfort with which he and his fellow-workers have been comforted by God. In v. 5 he continues the theme: just as Christ's sufferings have been abundantly shared by the apostolic group, so their comfort through Christ abounds. He goes on: 'if we are afflicted, it is for your comfort and salvation', and adds that their comfort will spring from the endurance of the same sufferings as Paul and his companions have met with. It is very difficult to avoid the conclusion that both comfort and sufferings equally derive from Christ and are equally conducive to salvation when shared by all. Paul would not have understood our fear of Pelagianism (*sit venia verbo*). He had no doubt that all came from God in Christ, nor that the sufferings of the Church were genuinely redemptive.

The other scholar who denies an atoning efficacy to the sufferings of the apostolic group is Pobee. He is in fact commenting on Col. 1.24, which he believes to have been written by Paul. There is no idea here, he writes, of 'vicarious atoning efficacy attached to his sufferings'.[24] Pobee has not perhaps chosen his words very carefully. I would entirely agree that there is no idea of *vicarious* suffering in Paul, if by this is meant, as the word conveys, that Paul is suffering instead of someone else, so that if Paul suffers enough the Colossians will not have to suffer at all. There is no such idea, as far as I know, in any of Paul's writings or in the Deutero-Paulines. We have to consider Col. 1.24 in our next chapter when we examine the post-Pauline development. But in the meantime we may very well take the opportunity of dismissing the notion of *vicarious* suffering on the part of the apostles. Their suffering, and that of all Christians, is to be redemptive, not substitutionary.

E. Kamlah in a long article written in 1963 gives an exposition of the meaning of Paul's sufferings which amply confirms the view taken in this book.[25] Referring to 2 Cor. 4.10-12, he says that the meaning of Christ's dying is made apparent in Paul's dying life (p. 226). It follows that all sufferings on behalf of righteousness in obedience to God are Christ's sufferings. It is not a question of Christ's sufferings being related to the sufferings of Christians as universal to particular, but rather Christian suffering is the representation and outworking ('Vorbildung und Aufwirkung') of a fundamental event. Christ's sufferings, he adds, come in between the sufferings of the righteous in the OT and Paul's sufferings. It follows that Paul's sufferings have atoning value (pp. 228-29). And he believes that the phrases in 1 Cor. 4.13 do indicate an atoning action (pp. 229, 257). Suffering, he concludes, is an overcoming of the flesh, a breaking out into the new life of the resurrection (p. 232). This is a clear and convincing statement of the view that the sufferings of the apostolic community, and of Christians in general, have atoning value.

Another point might be made here: in the last chapter we have discussed at considerable length the concept of *militia Christi*, and have found that it is deeply rooted in Paul's thought and also goes back to the thought of Jesus himself. But the spiritual warfare which Paul and his companions wage is not only one of action but also of passion. Suffering is God's special way of bringing about redemption. Hence the warfare often means simply Paul's weakness and vulnerability. But no one will doubt the effectiveness of this spiritual warfare. As we read the passage in 2 Cor. 10.2-6 with which we began our study of *militia Christi*, we cannot fail to be impressed by Paul's determination and confidence that he does overthrow fortresses and bring every rebellious thought into obedience to Christ. Hence the spiritual warfare is itself a process of redemption.

In this context it might be worth comparing the four main passages with which we have been concerned. We shall find that the element of redemption through suffering is either explicit or implicit in all of them. We might set it out thus:

λοιδορούμενοι εὐλογοῦμεν... δυσφημούμενοι παρακαλοῦμεν... περικαθάρματα... περίψημα	πάντοτε τὴν νέκρωσιν τοῦ Ἰησοῦ ἐν τῷ σώματι περιφέροντες, ἵνα καὶ ἡ ζωὴ τοῦ Ἰησοῦ ἐν τῷ σώματι ἡμῶν φανερωθῇ	ἐν ἡμέρᾳ σωτηρίας ... διὰ τῶν ὅπλων τῆς δικαιοσύνης	τοῦ γνῶναι αὐτὸν καὶ τὴν δύναμιν τῆς ἀναστάσεως αὐτοῦ, καὶ [τὴν] κοινωνίαν [τῶν] παθημάτων αὐτοῦ συμμορφιζόμενος τῷ θανάτῳ αὐτοῦ
when reviled, we bless... when slandered, we try to conciliate... refuse ... offscouring (1 Cor. 4.12f.)	always carrying in the body the death of Jesus, so that the life of Jesus may also be manifested in our bodies (2 Cor. 4.10)	the day of salvation ... with the weapons of righteousness (2 Cor. 6.2, 7)	that I may know him and the power of his resurrection, and may share his sufferings, becoming like him in his death (Phil. 3.10)

The presence of the redemptive power of the apostles' suffering is explicit in the first two passages, but it is implicit in the other two. In 2 Cor. 4.2 the word σωτηρία reminds us that the whole ministry, to which Paul has referred in 5.18-20, is a process of salvation; and the reference to the weapons of righteousness brings us, as we have seen, right into the middle of the *militia Christi*, itself a redemptive activity. So also in Phil. 3.10 sharing in Christ's sufferings and becoming conformed to his death have exactly the same significance as has the passage in 2 Cor. 4.10. The atoning value of the apostles' suffering is an essential part of Paul's theology of the cross.

3. *Is the process to be passed on to the Church?*

This question need not detain us very long, since it has been very largely answered by our discussion of the first question. We will begin with a review about our conclusions drawn from the scriptural evidence.

We saw in that tightly packed verse ˙2 Cor. 1.20 the implication that what has been received by the apostolic community must be passed on to the Church. The 'we' of v. 19 refers to the group that first evangelized Corinth, Paul and Silvanus and Timothy. But the Corinthians themselves are those who utter the 'Amen' to God's promises in Christ in the course of Christian worship. The apostles are there for their sake and they must in their turn accept the calling of the apostolic life.[26] Then in our examination of 1 Cor. 4.12-14 we noticed that almost the same phrase as is used in vv. 12-13 describing the apostolic group occurs in Rom. 12.14 as an exhortation, and we observed the interchange whereby what is paraenesis on the lips of Jesus becomes description of the apostolic ministry, and then paraenesis again when it is applied to the Christian community. So there can be no question of the description of the precarious life of Paul and his companions in 1 Cor. 4.9-13 being regarded as a unique event. It must be passed on to the Corinthians.[27] Similarly, in our attempt to trace the full meaning of the words περικαθάρματα and περίψημα in v. 13 we suggested a connection with Lam. 3.45.[28] But this only makes sense on the assumption that the first person plural in that verse is understood by Paul as applying first to Christ and then to the apostles. However, if challenged to say why it was cast in the first person plural, Paul would probably have replied that even under the old dispensation the Christian community was foreshadowed. It is not very likely that he would have believed in a direct reference to the apostolic community as such in scripture. There, he must have held, we meet only the Messiah and the faithful community. The apostolic phase was necessary but temporary. So the fact that scripture refers to the community must imply that in the era of fulfilment the Church is involved.

In our discussion of the phrase 'in an acceptable time' we brought in a relevant comparison with Rom. 15.3, where Ps. 69.9 is quoted. On the whole that psalm is a very individualistic one compared for example with Psalm 44, quoted by Paul in the same epistle. But in the LXX of Ps. 68.33-34 the Greek can be translated thus:

Let the poor see and rejoice,
seek (plural) God and your soul shall live,
because the Lord has paid attention to the poor,
and he has not rejected his prisoners.

As we noted when we were considering it, this psalm is a favourite both with Paul and with the early Church. So in this very significant passage of scripture the sufferings and triumph of the Messiah are associated with the suffering and triumph of God's faithful servants. If one could venture a generalization, from Paul's point of view scripture almost never gives us information about the Messiah without also mentioning his faithful disciples.[29] Then, when we came to consider Paul's use of Psalm 44, we pointed out that this psalm, though written throughout in the first person plural, must have been considered as messianic by Paul. We suggested that the words 'rouse thyself' and 'arise' in vv. 24 and 27 would be taken as referring to Christ's resurrection.[30] In any case the fact that a psalm which vividly describes the sufferings of God's people can be applied to the Church in Rom. 8.36 must carry the implication that the suffering of the apostles is not peculiar to them, but is to be mediated to the Church.

Paul's use of Psalm 118 is another example of the same thing. It must have been regarded by him as primarily a psalm describing the unexpected vindication of the humiliated Messiah, just as it was understood by other writers in the NT. But Paul uses it in 2 Cor. 6.9 as part of a description of the apostolic life; and v. 24 of that psalm runs:

This is the day which the Lord has made,
let us rejoice and be glad in it.

Plainly it is in Paul's eyes a reference to the Church rejoicing in its experience of the new age.[31] A last instance may be cited from Paul's description of the *militia Christi*. Though in 2 Cor. 10.3-6 he gives a very specific description of his own warfare against the powers of evil, in other letters he urges Christians themselves to wage the same warfare.[32] Armed though he believed himself to be with apostolic authority over the communities which he had founded, he was very far from wanting to preserve this authority as a unique prerogative. He wanted to hand it on to the Church.

Those who write on the subject of suffering in Paul's letters are generally agreed that the suffering had to be passed on to the

Church. Thus Ahern writes that 'suffering with Christ' and 'putting to death the deeds of the flesh' are the same thing.[33] But every Christian is called to put to death the deeds of the flesh. He goes on to say that all 2 Corinthians does is to apply this teaching to the painful context of Paul's relations with the Corinthian church. He agrees with our interpretation of 2 Cor. 1.4-5 (see above pp. 141-42). The παθήματα τοῦ Χριστοῦ, he says, are the sufferings of Paul and of the Corinthians (p. 20). Kamlah makes a very similar point when he says that Paul brings to each new community which he founds not only the message of Christ, but also the sufferings of Christ and the grace of Christ, all of which must be found in the community.[34]

Proudfoot in an article already referred to claims that what Jesus suffered in the flesh is of special importance in this context. He writes: 'Paul's own suffering and that of the Corinthians must be interpreted as bearing a special relation to what Jesus suffered in the flesh. But Christ in the flesh and the risen Christ are one; therefore Paul and the Corinthians are related in the same way to the risen life of Christ'.[35] We accept the conclusion but not the argument. Christ in the flesh and the risen Christ are one, but not one as far as concerns Christ's flesh. God condemned sin in Christ's flesh (Rom. 8.3). The flesh is what Christ left behind when he rose from the dead. It is not identical with Christ's body. We may well refer to Güttgemanns' argument detailed on p. 136 above. Christ is manifest in the sufferings of Christians, we may certainly say, but this is not a manifestation of Christ's flesh. Last of all we note a useful comment by Güttgemanns. For Paul, he says, σῶμα is correlative to κύριος; the σῶμα Χριστοῦ indicates the reality of the community in as far as it is obedient to Christ. So the σῶμα Χριστοῦ is where the νέκρωσις is to be manifested.[36] It is not necessary any further to labour the point that the process of suffering and dying is to be handed on to the Church. But the point is an important one to have clarified, since it affects our conclusions about how the Church of today should frame its doctrine of the ministry.

4. *What is the nature of the apostolic office?*

This is a subject which has often in the past been a cause of bitter theological debate. Claims have been made about the apostolic office in the primitive Church that emphasized one form of ministry as having the right to call itself apostolic as against all other forms of ministry. The twelve apostles have been presented as a closed college in whose hands lay all church authority. Jesus has been understood as having authorized a ministry which alone had, and has, true jurisdiction over all Christians, with the intention that such a ministry should be continued as long as the Church should last. Moreover these claims are still being made by responsible church leaders. Only a week or so before these words were written a clergyman of the Church of England appeared on T.V. as the leader of a group within the church who are opposed to the ordination of women to the priesthood. He presented himself as a member of an organization which claimed that its aim was to defend 'the apostolic ministry'. Obviously therefore the conviction that there is an apostolically authorized ministry which can trace its lineage back to the Twelve is still held by many relatively well-informed Christians.

It must be admitted that our study does nothing to support such claims. The apostolic ministry in Paul's writings is not identical with the Twelve. On the contrary, Paul regards as apostles all who join with him in the work of evangelism, Barnabas, Silvanus, Timothy, Titus, and a number of others. They do not seem to have any formal relation to the Twelve. More remarkable still, the apostolic office does not primarily seem to be one of exercising authority over others, though Paul does exercise such authority in his two Corinthian letters. But the essence of the apostolic office seems to consist in suffering. The apostles are subject to the worst that the world can do to them, as was their Master. Far from being figures obviously possessing divine authority that can be recognized by the world, they are despised, ill-treated, mocked. By the mysterious interchange which is at the very centre of Paul's thought about the cross, they thereby bring life to those whom they evangelize.[37] Ebeling is therefore right when he says that the stigmata to which Paul refers in Gal. 6.17 are the marks of apostleship.[38] These are not the reproduction of Jesus' five wounds, as in the case of St Francis, but the consequence of the ill-treatment and hardship which are an essential part of the apostolic office. Their activity can also be described in terms of warfare. They are engaged in the same battle as that in which Jesus took part during his earthly career, in the course of which he won the supreme victory, a victory which is also reflected in the lives of the apostles.[39]

Besides the element of passion, their main activity consists in preaching the gospel. We must not carry away the impression that the apostles suffer simply for the sake of suffering. Their suffering is incurred in the course of their great activity of declaring the good news of what God has done in Christ. Paul can describe the activity of preaching the gospel in a variety of ways: it can be spreading the odour of God's presence (2 Cor. 2.15-16); or pouring oneself out as a libation to God (Phil. 3.17); or as a priest offering the Gentiles to God (Rom. 15.16). It is noteworthy that language which at a later period would naturally be used of the priestly aspects of the Church's ministry, especially of presiding at the eucharist, is used by Paul of preaching the gospel, an activity which today we tend to regard as the duty of all Christians. It only goes to show how different our understanding of ministry is to Paul's. In his day the distinction between clerical and lay had not yet emerged.

This does not mean however that anyone could be an apostle. The apostles were appointed[40] by God; how they were appointed we do not for the most part know. We know how Paul was appointed, but we have no information about the others.[41] However, the fact that Paul describes the apostles as being appointed implies that they were a limited number. The mysterious reference in Rom. 16.7 to two people who were 'outstanding among the apostles' suggests that they could be quite obscure people and that not all apostles were part of Paul's mission. We must also add that preaching the gospel did not end with mere proclamation. As all Paul's letters abundantly witness, it also involved building up the Church, disciplining it (or rather inducing it to discipline itself), and caring for it. Moreover the sufferings which the apostolic office inevitably incurred were not all inflicted by outsiders, opponents of Christianity. As is clearly shown in the Corinthian correspondence, some of the severest afflictions which the apostles had to endure were caused by the behaviour of the Corinthian Christians themselves.

The apostolic office was not one which conferred a prerogative on its holder with which he must not part. On the contrary, the aim of the apostolic group was to enable the communities which they founded to carry on the Christian life themselves, and that meant suffering and proclaiming the gospel just like the apostles themselves (see Phil. 2.16). No doubt the fact that Paul never seems to concern himself with the continuation of the apostolic office is accounted for by his belief that it was essentially an eschatological office. The time was short; the apostles were men (and perhaps women)[42] sent out at the end of the ages to proclaim the final revelation of God in Jesus

Christ and to build communities of believers to be the renewed Israel. The question of apostolic succession did not arise.

Scholars have quite a lot to say about apostleship, though their remarks tend to be occasional. Dupont maintains that Paul saw himself as a prophet as well as an apostle, on the basis of his use of the words οἰκοδομή and καθαίρεσις in 2 Cor. 10.8; 13.10.[43] Dupont finds here an echo of Jer. 1.10. Like Jeremiah, Paul also was called from his mother's womb (Gal. 1.15). It is, however, hard to believe that Paul saw himself as called to be a prophet independently of his calling in Christ. Paul would regard all prophetic vocation in scripture as fulfilled in Christ. And Paul never explicitly claims to be a prophet as he does to be an apostle. It would seem more appropriate to apply Jer. 1.10 to St John the Divine, who was called to prophesy to kings and rulers (see Rev. 10.11). Dupont has also an interesting discussion of Paul's use of ἐξουσία ('right') in 1 Corinthians 9.[44] Paul did not claim a special ἐξουσία as an apostle. He proceeds to give natural reasons for the existence of this ἐξουσία (no soldier has to support himself etc.). But Paul admits that this is an argument on human authority, and he next quotes both scripture and a word of the Lord in his defence (9.8f.). Admittedly the scriptural proof would hardly convince us today, being based on an allegorical interpretation of Deut. 25.4,[45] but it obviously impressed the early Church. See 1 Tim. 5.18. It is significant perhaps that Paul chose not to use this right; he supports himself as an apostle. He does this so as not to cause an obstacle to the gospel of Christ (9.12). Compare 2 Cor. 6.3: 'We put no obstacle in anyone's way, so that no fault may be found with our ministry'. Apostolic authority was given for a purpose. It was not an end in itself.

C.K. Barrett has what is almost a prophetic utterance on apostleship.[46] He writes:

> The primary meaning of apostleship is eschatological; the apostle is a unique link between the end of the Old World and the beginning of the New. This is a lofty position, which is lowered rather than exalted, distorted rather than adorned, when the apostle's office is turned into one of ecclesiastical pre-eminence and administrative authority.

We can sympathize with this, especially when one hears some claim to superior ecclesiastical authority based on an historically indefensible belief in the existence of an apostolic ministry specially commissioned by the earthly Jesus. But there remains a problem of

justifying ministerial office in the contemporary Church, a problem
on which Paul's conception of the ministry has some light to shed, as
we try to demonstrate in our last chapter.

In the light of 2 Cor. 4.7-12 Ahern uses the remarkable phrase
'apostolic suffering'.[47] It is suffering, far more than ecclesiastical
leadership, that takes first place in Paul's thoughts about apostleship.
Stanley claims that 'Paul conceived his apostolic vocation as a
prolongation of Jesus' role as the suffering servant of Yahweh'
(p. 866).[48] This is a view which is not held by most NT scholars
today, though I personally believe it is correct. At least we can say
that Paul understood Jesus in terms of the suffering servant of the
Psalms and of Isaiah. Schulz, in his article already quoted, says that
the sufferings of Paul and his companions certainly have an apostolic
significance.[49] They are not therefore accidental or incidental, but
part of the office.

To revert to Güttgemanns: he believes that Paul's sufferings are
closely connected with the apostolic office.[50] On the basis of εἶτα τοῖς
ἀποστόλοις πᾶσιν ('then to all the apostles') in 1 Cor. 15.7, he
believes that the phrase must apply to a wider circle than the Twelve.
Paul never refers to the Twelve as apostles (p. 83). Later (p. 107)
Güttgemanns makes the profound observation that Paul's activity as
an apostle is a manifestation of Christ, but that this does not apply to
his religious experience. Perhaps we might be forgiven for saying that
in a situation today in which increasingly religious experience is
being offered instead of the gospel, this is a point of fundamental
importance. We should also note Güttgemanns' insistence that
apostolate and proclamation of the gospel are closely bound together
(p. 123). He quotes Käsemann as saying that the apostolate is 'the
earthly manifestation of the gospel'. Why 'earthly'? Surely not in
contrast to the heavenly? Is it just to emphasize, as Paul does in
2 Cor. 4.7, that we have this treasure in earthen vessels? Would it not
be sufficient to say that the apostolate is the manifestation of the
gospel?

H.D. Betz well reminds us of another aspect of the apostolate: it is
service.[51] Paul's life is lived in the service of the Corinthian church.
In this repect of course apostolic ministry is based on the ministry of
Christ himself. A.T. Lincoln writes in this context: 'The main issue
at stake between Paul and his opponents is the nature of apostleship
and its accompanying life-style'.[52] This is a useful reminder. We must
not forget that Paul and his companions were not the only early

Christians who claimed to be apostles. There was also a group of people whom Paul calls 'pseudo-apostles' at work in Corinth (2 Cor. 11.13). But their claim to apostleship was evidently based on their superior powers of speaking, the remarkable revelations which they had been granted, and (perhaps) their relationship with the Jerusalem church. Indeed it was no doubt partly by contrast with these pseudo-apostles that Paul was gradually led to define more clearly his own conception of apostleship.

5. *Is there a link with the citizens of the kingdom?*

Throughout this work we have tried to provide evidence that such a link exists, but it may be useful here to summarize the evidence. We began with a hint, which we did not pursue, that Paul's stress on the foolishness of the preaching in 1 Cor. 1.20f. may be connected with the logion in Matt. 11.25-26 (parallel Luke 10.21-22) where Jesus rejoices that the revelation has been given to 'babes' and hidden from the wise.[53] We followed with a suggestion, much more fully worked out, that Paul's teaching about doing good to those who persecute you, found in 1 Cor. 4.12-13; Rom. 12.14, 17, is based upon Jesus' similar precept in the Sermon on the Mount, and that this in its turn goes back to certain verses in Psalm 109.[54] We followed this with an investigation of the possibility of Paul's 'treasure' language in 2 Cor. 4.7 having been inspired by Jesus' teaching concerning a man's treasure,[55] and we concluded that Paul did know this logion in some form. Then we worked out in some detail the parallels between the description of the apostolic ministry in 2 Cor. 6.4-10 and the description of those who are fit for the kingdom in the Sermon on the Mount.[56] The discussion of the meaning of the word πτωχοί, common to Matt. 5.3, Luke 6.20, and 2 Cor. 6.10, took us far into scriptural exegesis, and in particular into an investigation of the significance of Isa. 61.1f.[57] We found quite a different type of link connecting Paul to Jesus' teaching in the language which Paul uses about dogs in Phil. 3.2f., and we concluded that Paul knew Jesus' logion about throwing the children's food to the dogs, and also the principle he laid down, itself drawn from scripture, 'first to Israel, then to the Gentiles'.[58] Finally we provided ample evidence that the tradition of spiritual warfare which Paul inherited came from Jesus, and that Paul must have known some form of the logion recorded in Mark 3.27; Matt. 12.29; Luke 11.21-22.[59]

Taken altogether, this body of evidence creates a strong conviction in favour of the conclusion that Paul knew a considerable amount of Jesus' teaching, and that he has transposed it so that what Jesus said about the citizens of the kingdom Paul applies to the apostolic group of his day.

'The pretended conviction that Paul knew next to nothing of the teaching of Jesus must be rejected'. So writes D.C. Allison in an article already quoted.[60] But the conviction has been sufficiently widespread to ensure that not many scholars have suggested that there could be any links between Paul's letters and Jesus' teaching such as we have claimed to show exist. Kamlah à propos the hardships endured by Paul as described in 2 Corinthians 11 compares the 'Leidensparanäse' at the end of the Sermon on the Mount.[61] As we have seen, Güttgemanns draws our attention to. Schlatter's account of the relation of Paul to Jesus. Schlatter, he says, had actually claimed that Paul was preaching Jesus' gospel, only in a form suited to the post-Easter era.[62] Dungan has a very interesting discussion of the way in which Paul uses the material known to him from the teaching of Jesus.[63] He emphasizes that Paul is quite ready to modify it and even ignore it if necessary. For example, having referred in 1 Cor. 9.14 to the command that those who preached the gospel should be supported by those to whom they preached, he declares that he is not intending to follow it. Dungan also believes that he has shown to what extent Paul modified the Lord's command about divorce: 'He and his associates simply made a practice of setting this regulation aside whenever they encountered circumstances where to have kept it would have made it a hindrance to the gospel' (p. 141).

In a recent article N. Walther has raised again the question of Paul's relation to the earliest traditions of Jesus.[64] He admits that there is a resemblance between 1 Cor. 4.11-13 and exactly the passages from Matthew and Luke which we have examined in this connection (p. 501). He adds that in such passages the 'Peristasen-katalog' resembles material in the beatitudes, and he conjectures that Paul knows the instructions which Jesus gave to his messengers (p. 509). He asserts, as Dungan does, that Paul could alter the original meaning of the Lord's words in order to suit the circumstances of his day (p. 11). He adds that Jesus' words were important for the 'apostolische Existenz' of the missionaries (p. 514). His conclusion is that there was not an 'ungebrochenen direkten und kompletten

Traditionszusammenhang zwischen Paulus und Jesus' (pp. 517-18), or at least that this has not been proved.

These are cautious conclusions: does Walther mean that there was a broken, indirect, and fragmentary connection between the tradition of Jesus and Paul? To invert his conclusion seems to give us an equally unprovable proposition. What sort of a connection are we looking for? It seems to me to have been amply proved that Paul knew a substantial amount of Jesus' teaching. If Walther means that we are very much in the dark as to the form in which the teaching tradition reached Paul, we must of course agree. As we have seen, attempts to pin-point the teaching known to Paul are speculative, and suggestions about parallels between a block of teaching in any one Synoptic Gospel and any one passage in Paul's letters are highly conjectural. But we must hold to our conclusion that Paul was not largely ignorant of Jesus' teaching.

This discussion does however give rise to a very interesting comparison. We have claimed that Paul reproduced the teaching of Jesus, adapting it to the circumstances of the post-Easter situation. Now to some extent at least this is what all the Synoptic writers did. Of course the question of how far the Synoptic writers modified or added to the teaching of Jesus in order to adapt it to the circumstances of their day is the central problem of NT scholarship, one about which nothing like a scholarly consensus has been achieved. In a work such as this we could not possibly attempt an answer to such a question. It is sufficient for our purpose if we assume that all the Synoptic writers did to some extent modify and even add to Jesus' teaching. All of them to some extent projected the risen Christ onto the figure of the earthly Jesus. We have already given an example of this from Mark 8.34, when we concluded that the reference to the cross was probably the addition of the early community.[65] Nor is it difficult to find examples of this from the First Gospel that would be conceded by the great majority of scholars. Perhaps the addition of Matt. 11.28-30 to 11.25-27 is one such example.[66] Similarly there would be very few modern commentators who would not describe Matt. 18.15-17 as very largely the creation of the early community.

When we turn to the Fourth Gospel, the process has of course gone much farther. Especially where John is giving us the discourses of Jesus, he has broken away from any attempt to reproduce Jesus' words to a much greater extent than any of the Synoptic writers.

This is most marked when Jesus is talking about himself, as he does most of the time. We must attribute this wide license in developing and inventing teaching thought appropriate on the lips of Jesus to the high christology held by the author of the Fourth Gospel. He has very nearly substituted the risen Lord for the Jesus of history, the Second Person of the Trinity for the original Jesus.

When we compare Paul's handling of the Jesus tradition with either of these techniques, that of the Synoptists or that of John, we must be impressed by his moderation and clarity. He does not claim to be telling his readers what the earthly Lord taught. He is giving them that teaching in the light of the presence of the risen Lord. It is because they are 'in Christ' that they can be apostles and disciples. Those who in the time of the earthly Jesus were prospective citizens of the kingdom are now the apostles, whose task it is to pass on the gospel to newly-made Christians in order that they too may begin to live the precarious dying-and-rising life in Christ. In handing on this teaching he does not alter its form much. It is more a question of application in new circumstances than of extensive modification. We have none of that difficulty in guessing what was the original logion of Jesus that we are always encountering in the Fourth Gospel.

No doubt the reason for Paul's moderation as far as concerns the alteration of Jesus' teaching is because he wrote nearer the time of the historical Jesus than did the Synoptists, though this is not so certain in the case of Q. But it was not because he had a low christology. On the contrary, his christology is actually higher than that of any of the Synoptists. Hence it might in theory be possible in some instances to check the way in which the Synoptists have preserved the tradition by means of noting the way in which Paul has preserved it. We instinctively do the opposite, forgetting that Paul is the earlier witness. But before we could do his with any effect we would require a much higher degree of certainty about what Paul has preserved, and about how far the Synoptists have modified their tradition, than we have at present.

We may, however, confidently treat Paul as a witness to some of the traditions of Jesus' teaching. And we may perhaps accept his tradition with all the greater confidence because he is not claiming to give us a picture of the earthly Jesus. His tradition in fact seems in some cases to be more faithful than that of the Synoptists because he is not trying to fit it into the framework of Jesus' life. In the context in which Paul gives it to us it often appears to have gone through the transition from pre-Easter to post-Easter situation with very little change. We should be grateful for Paul's fidelity. His concern is with the relation of the risen Christ to the apostolic community, but this does not prevent him giving us a remarkably faithful witness about the teaching given by Jesus concerning the citizens of the kingdom. While we acknowledge our debt to Paul for this, we should also confess that we are grateful to the early Church for its decision that the Fourth Gospel should put an end to the number of Gospels to be accepted as canonical. By the time that Gospel was written the tradition of Jesus' teaching was in grave danger of running out of control.

Chapter 8

THE DEVELOPMENT OF THE POST-PAULINE TRADITION

In this chapter we trace the development of Paul's theology of suffering in the post-Pauline tradition. That will mean not only examining the Deutero-Pauline epistles Colossians and Ephesians, but also what are sometimes called the Trito-Paulines, the Pastoral Epistles. Since I hold that the Pastorals were written very early in the second century,[1] this brings us to within ten years of the writing of the letters of Ignatius of Antioch. He has much to say about suffering, so it seems appropriate to include him also in our review of how the Pauline tradition developed.

I

One of the most outstanding differences between Colossians–Ephesians and the acknowledged Pauline letters is that the genuine Paul always regards the Christian's resurrection as an event in the future, whereas in Colossians–Ephesians we have already been raised with Christ. See Col. 2.12; 3.1; Eph. 2.6-7. In Ephesians we are already actually seated in the heavenly places. It is difficult to see what else there is that could happen to us. It is not surprising that a few years later we find the author of the Pastorals complaining of those who teach that the resurrection has already taken place (see 2 Tim. 2.18). Koester notes this contrast,[2] and alleges this as an important reason why Colossians cannot be Pauline. He even suggests that Paul's opponents in Philippi may have claimed to be the people who were τὰ ἄνω φρονοῦντες ('setting their minds on things above' Col. 3.2). Lietzmann comes to the same conclusion when, commenting on καὶ ἡμᾶς σὺν ᾽Ιησοῦ ἐγειρεῖ ('will raise us up with Jesus') in 2 Cor. 4.14, he says that this excludes the notion of a resurrection in baptism or a spiritual resurrection already accomplished. If we compare, for example, Rom. 6.4-5 with Col. 2.12, we will see that Paul steadily refers to our resurrection as a future event, whereas for the author of Colossians it has already happened in baptism.

A second marked difference between the genuine Paulines and Colossians–Ephesians is that in these latter epistles the figure used for the relation of Christ to the Church is different: Christ is the head, the Church is the body; see Col. 1.18; 2.19; Eph. 1.22-23; 4.15-16; 5.23-30. This looks like a simplification of Paul's very difficult doctrine of the whole Church being called to become the body of Christ. The doctrine in Colossians–Ephesians also means that the Church can be more easily distinguished from Christ than is the case in Paul's genuine letters. This is brought out more clearly in Col. 2.11:

ἐν ᾧ καὶ περιετμήθητε περιτομῇ ἀχειροποιήτῳ, ἐν τῇ ἀπεκδύσει τοῦ σώματος τῆς σαρκός, ἐν τῇ περιτομῇ τοῦ Χριστοῦ·

In him also you were circumcised with a circumcision made without hands, by putting off the body of flesh in the circumcision of Christ.

The reference is to baptism, as the following verse shows. It looks as if the author held that in baptism Christians put off the body of flesh (a unique phrase in the NT) and put on the body of Christ. If so, 'the body of Christ' represents some ontological change. But the danger of complete monism is avoided by the distinction between the body and the head. The body for example can grow (Col. 2.19; Eph. 4.13-16). This would obviously be quite inappropriate to predicate of the head. We will have more to say about this presently.

The treatment of the apostles in these two letters is also markedly different from what we find in the genuine Paulines. In both epistles Paul is *the* apostle, though it would appear that Paul's position in Colossians is higher than in Ephesians. In Ephesians Paul is the apostle of the Gentiles (3.1, 6, 8), but the author looks back to the apostles generally as the founders of the church, together with the prophets. Who the prophets are, is a disputed question. It is not impossible that they are the OT prophets, in which case the author of Ephesians is here being entirely true to his master. For that matter, it is not exactly clear who the apostles are, except that Paul is one of them. They are not characterized as the Twelve. Nielsen has recently argued that in Colossians Paul holds an absolutely unique position.[3]

He claims that in the epistle Paul's status is greatly exalted. He is the only apostle. He is the apostle not only to the Gentiles but to the entire world. Nielsen even suggests that in 1.24 Paul is regarded as alone completing Christ's atoning work in a way which nobody else could (pp. 112-13). This seems to me to be improbable. The author of Colossians, as Nielsen admits, knew his master's mind and works well. He must therefore have known Paul's doctrine of the apostolic ministry of suffering. In our next section we discuss the difficult passage Col. 1.24-26 more fully; but we must interpret it in the light of the passages we have been considering in this book. To regard Paul as alone of all mankind carrying on the redemptive suffering of Christ would be quite alien to Paul's thought. It is worth while pointing out at the same time that neither Ephesians nor the Pastorals regard Paul as the apostle to the whole world. In both works he is presented as the apostle to the Gentiles; see Eph. 3.1, 6, 8; 1 Tim. 2.7; 2 Tim. 4.17.

The author of Ephesians, though he certainly takes some of his material from Colossians, has his own view of the apostles. They are the foundation, together with the prophets. Whoever precisely may be indicated by 'the apostles and prophets', it is clear that they are already figures of the past. There is no suggestion that the author's contemporaries were carrying on an apostolic ministry; see Eph. 2.1-20; 3.6; 4.11. It is not clear whether when either Colossians or Ephesians was written an ordained ministry already existed. Thus, as far as the development of Paul's thought is concerned, these two epistles seem to stand half way between the genuine Paulines and the Pastorals. The Pauline doctrine of the apostolic ministry seems to have disappeared, but its place has not yet been taken by the ordained ministry, as it has in the Pastorals.

One feature we have noted in the Paulines which reappears in Colossians-Ephesians is the *militia Christi*. It is of course very fully exemplified in Eph. 6.14-17, where it applies to all Christians. But the theme of Christ's conquest of the powers on the cross also appears in Col. 2.13-15. This is an extremely obscure passage. In a former work I have claimed to find behind this a midrash on Num. 25.1-5,[4] the incident of Israel's joining in the worship of the Baal of Peor and also the next incident, related in Num. 25.6-9, Phinehas's act of retribution. I claim that the author of Colossians[5] was acquainted with the targumic tradition connected with these passages. I argue that here Christ is represented as overcoming the elemental powers on the cross and triumphing over them (presumably in the resurrection). They are hostile powers whom God in Christ had to overcome. There is nothing in this that is incompatible with Paul's own thought. In fact in the only two places where Paul seems to be using similar figures, 1 Cor. 4.9 and 2 Cor. 2.14, it is Paul and his companions who appear among the conquered captives. But we could hardly expect the author of Colossians, who must have had an immense respect for the martyred Paul, to reproduce that element. We have already noted that the author of Ephesians has a precisely similar doctrine.[6] See Eph. 4.11, where the captives are probably the evil powers. It is remarkable that both authors should use the medium of a midrash on scripture to set forth their doctrine of Christ's victory over the hostile powers.

II

We must now consider one passage in Colossians which is closely connected with our subject. It is one which has caused much debate among scholars, so we must reproduce it in full. Col. 1.24-26 runs:

> νῦν χαίρω ἐν τοῖς παθήμασιν ὑπὲρ ὑμῶν, καὶ ἀνταναπληρῶ τὰ ὑστερήματα τῶν θλίψεων τοῦ Χριστοῦ ἐν τῇ σαρκί μου ὑπὲρ τοῦ σώματος αὐτοῦ, ὅ ἐστιν ἡ ἐκκλησία, ἧς ἐγενόμην ἐγὼ διάκονος κατὰ τὴν οἰκονομίαν τοῦ θεοῦ τὴν δοθεῖσάν μοι εἰς ὑμᾶς πληρῶσαι τὸν λόγον τοῦ θεοῦ, τὸ μυστήριον τὸ ἀποκεκρυμμένον ἀπὸ τῶν αἰώνων καὶ ἀπὸ τῶν γενεῶν—νῦν δὲ ἐφανερώθη τοῖς ἁγίοις αὐτοῦ.

> Now I rejoice in my sufferings for your sake, and in my flesh I complete what is lacking in Christ's afflictions for the sake of his body, the church, of which I became a minister according to the divine office which was given to me for you, to make the word of God fully known, the mystery hidden for ages and generations but now made manifest to his saints.

The problem about this passage is that it seems to attribute to Paul a power of redemptive suffering equal to Christ's and also that it seems to suggest some inadequacy in Christ's act of redemption that has to be made up by Paul. Another question is raised by the phrase ἀπὸ τῶν αἰώνων καὶ ἀπὸ τῶν γενεῶν in v. 26. If this means 'from angels and men', as it is rendered in the RSV margin, then we may well institute a comparison with 1 Cor. 4.9. These are two quite distinct questions and we will deal with them separately.

We will take first the question of the meaning of ἀνταναπληρῶ τὰ ὑστερήματα τῶν θλίψεων τοῦ Χριστοῦ. Lightfoot paraphrases 'Christ the sinless Master (has) left something for Paul the unworthy servant to suffer'.[7] He compares 2 Cor. 1.5, where Christ's sufferings 'overflow' onto the apostle (but this is precisely the opposite sense to what we have here!). He makes a distinction between Christ's 'satisfactory' sufferings and Paul's sufferings which 'continue the work which Christ began'. This is a distinction which seems invented for the sake of avoiding a conclusion that Lightfoot dislikes rather than one which arises naturally from the context. Abbott employs a similar device:[8] 'the plural is used because the afflictions are not regarded as a unity from which there is a definite shortcoming... But the notion that Christ suffers affliction in his people is nowhere found in the NT'. He believes that the phrase indicates Paul's own afflictions. He points out, as do other editors, that the phrase αἱ θλίψεις τοῦ Χριστοῦ is found nowhere else in the NT. He suggests that Christ's sufferings are regarded as 'the type of all those that are endured by his followers on behalf of the Church'. Such explanations strike one as something of an evasion of the issue. The claim that in the NT Christ is not regarded as suffering in his followers is surely rendered doubtful by all that has gone before in this present work.

Dibelius and Greeven believe that the question of the afflictions can be solved by means of eschatology.[9] Perhaps, they suggest, a certain amount of suffering must be endured before the *parousia*. The gap between Christ's own suffering and the *parousia* is filled by the σῶμα Χριστοῦ. This would surely be strange doctrine in an epistle where the *parousia* seems to have faded very much into the background. Moule rejects the idea that there could be anything incomplete about Christ's sufferings;[10] he also dismisses the notion that Paul by his sufferings could make Christ's suffering available to Christians. The phrase could mean that every Christian must bear his share in Christ's sufferings; or else that there is a quota of sufferings which 'the corporate Christ', the messianic community, is destined to undergo before God's purposes are completed. He inclines towards this latter view. The second interpretation which he rejects is very like that which we have defended in this work. Ahern remarks discouragingly that 'no compelling view has emerged from the centuries-old study of the text.[11] He adds 'As a minister of the gospel Paul has received a commission to fulfil this need (sc. to fill up

what is lacking in the sufferings of Christ) by preaching (v. 25
πληρῶσαι τὸν λόγον) and by suffering'. Ahern considers that Paul is
here speaking for every Christian: such suffering is not peculiar to
Paul himself. Proudfoot agrees that the ὑστερήματα are not just
Paul's to fill up; nor is there any deficiency in Christ's sufferings.[12]
The writer is referring to the Church's afflictions. The relationship,
he adds, is not mystical nor metaphysical. It is a participation in
Christ, not just an imitation of Christ. Kamlah holds that the text
refers to a specific amount of suffering that must be undergone
before the end.[13] But this, he says, is incompatible with the
traditional early Christian demand that one should rejoice in one's
sufferings.

Güttgemanns, who, it will be remembered, denied that Paul's
sufferings had an atoning value, says that our text might suggest an
atoning process, and considers this as an indication of the inauthen-
ticity of Colossians.[14] Lohse considered that the difficulty could be
explained by the belief that a certain amount of affliction was to be
expected in the messianic age:[15] 'The concept of a definite measure
for the last days determines the phrase'. He suggests that in the
second generation the apostolic task or office was closely connected
with suffering, since it so often led to martyrdom: 'The sufferings of
the apostle belong to the unique dignity of the office'.

Houlden writes: 'Paul is not addressing himself to the problem
whether Christ's sufferings and death made a perfect atonement for
the sins of the whole world, and emerging with a dangerously loose
answer . . . It is the pattern of Christ's own saving work into which
the believer has been incorporated . . . It is not Christ's sufferings
which are being completed, but Christ's sufferings *in Paul*'.[16]
R.P. Martin in a work written in 1972[17] suggests that 'the sufferings
of Paul were evidently an embarrassment to the Asian congregations'.
Paul did not identify his sufferings with the atoning sufferings of
Christ, he says, and he writes of 'the tally of Messianic sufferings'.

In his commentary on Colossians published two years later Martin
echoes the same view.[18] He writes of the messianic sufferings that
must precede the end. E. Schweizer comments that this verse goes
farther than anything which Paul wrote.[19] He does not think that
Christ is understood to be still suffering in his Church. The text
means 'the sufferings endured by the community for the sake of
Christ', or 'in Christ'. He rejects the idea of 'a precisely predetermined
measure of sufferings'. He writes: 'The apostle represents Christ in

the world, and he brings Christ's work to fulfilment.' Gnilka has a very full treatment of the text.[20] It is not, he says, a question of Jesus' historical sufferings. In the Deutero-Paulines Paul's function as apostle to the Gentiles is underlined. In all the epistles the apostle is a representative of Christ. If Christ speaks through him, the sufferings of Christ must be manifest in him: 'The suffering apostle takes the place of the exalted Christ, who is no longer subject to suffering'. Pobee follows the conventional line when he insists both that 'there is a full score of sins to be completed before the end of the world'[21], and that there is no idea here of 'vicarious atoning efficacy attached to Paul's sufferings'.

The problem presented by this passage from Colossians can be succinctly presented thus:

> How is it that Paul says the following?
> > If one member suffers all the members suffer;
> > we are the body of Christ and members individually.
> > He and his companions reproduce in their lives the
> sufferings of Christ.
> > But he does not say that the Church's sufferings are
> Christ's sufferings.
> Whereas the author of the Epistle to the Colossians
> > holds a simple doctrine of the Church as the body of
> which Christ is the head, and
> > has no hesitation in claiming that what is lacking in
> Christ's sufferings is filled up by Paul in his body on behalf of
> > the Church, which is Christ's body.

Perhaps the solution may lie in some such consideration as this: the ecclesiology of the author of Colossians was more realized than that of Paul. We *are* risen. He could say this because his doctrine of the Church as the body of which Christ is the head enabled the Church to distance itself from Christ in a way that Paul's doctrine did not. Paul's doctrine was always in danger of identifying the Church with Christ. This was not Paul's intention, both because he was no Monist and because the *parousia* had not yet arrived. In his thought the Church was called to be the body of Christ. It had just the same status as that of the individual Christian, who can be described as being in the process of being redeemed in this life (cf. 1 Cor. 1.18 τοῖς . . . σῳζομένοις ἡμῖν), but who still looks for his redemption in the future. This is why Paul does not say that the sufferings of the body are Christ's sufferings, just as he does not say that we are already risen. The eschatological tension has become relaxed in Colossians–Ephesians as it has not in the genuine Paulines. How far Paul or his disciple was right is a question which we must consider in our last chapter.

What no doubt accounts for this change in doctrine between Paul and his disciples[22] is the growing realization in the early Church that the *parousia* would not take place as immediately as Paul and his contemporaries had expected. Paul believed that at the *parousia* Christ and the Church would be truly united. Since the author of Colossians claims that in some sense we are risen already, and since it is obvious that this does not mean an identity between Christ and the Church, he can afford to describe that union in more realized terms.

But what does this actually mean? It is all very well to say that we have been raised and are now sitting with Christ in the heavenly places, but what difference does this make to daily living? Is there in practice any difference between Paul's 'not yet' and the realized eschatology of Colossians–Ephesians? It looks as if the simpler doctrine of the Church espoused by Paul's disciples can help here. The body can grow, as the head cannot. In fact Ephesians complicates matters by also using the metaphor of a building, which nevertheless grows like an organism (see Eph. 4.11-16). Perhaps our 'sitting in the heavenly places' and having our lives 'hid with Christ in God' meant for the authors of Colossians–Ephesians a less close relationship than that which Paul believed would take place at the *parousia*. It would follow then that since the Church as the body of which Christ is the head meant a less direct relationship than that described by Paul, the sufferings of the body could be represented as filling up what was lacking in the sufferings of Christ without the implication that Christ actually suffered in the process. Though Christ be the head, the sufferings of the body need not be the sufferings of the head. The body grows, the head does not. That which is lacking belongs to the sum of the afflictions which the body must suffer in the human mode, which is the Church's life, but not in the divine mode, which has already been accomplished. It might offer a parallel to the doctrine of Christ's sacrifice in Hebrews. That sacrifice Christ has already accomplished once and for all, but that does not mean that there are no sacrifices which Christians must make, though no doubt they are made 'through Christ'; see Heb. 13.15-16. The whole aim of Colossians–Ephesians seems to be to state what it means to believe that we are saved through Christ by God, while still remaining under obligation to struggle and attain, *in the light of the fact that the imminent arrival of the parousia need no longer be taken into account*. We should expect an approximation towards a Johannine theology of realized eschatology, and that is no doubt precisely what we have. Just as the christology of Col. 1.15-19 forms a bridge between Paul's christology and John's, so also with the eschatology of Colossians–Ephesians.

We might set out the contrast between Paul and his disciples thus:

Paul	*Colossians–Ephesians*
The Church is called to be the body of Christ	Christ is the head of which the Church is the body
Our sufferings are in Christ but are not the body's sufferings	Our sufferings are the body's sufferings
The Christian's resurrection is yet to come	Christians are risen in Christ
The *parousia* is imminent	The *parousia* is largely ignored[23]
Apostolic office is now being exercised for the benefit of the Church	Apostles are a feature of the past

We conclude therefore that as far as concerns the relation of the Church to Christ and the apostolic office, Paul's thought has been developed in Colossians–Ephesians to fit the circumstances of the next generation. The disciple has taken a step beyond the master. A leading feature of this new situation is that the imminence of the *parousia* has receded, and that therefore it need not influence theological thought as much as it did in the time of Paul. We must now turn our attention to the other problem which we noted in Col. 1.24-26. Does the author of Colossians say in 1.24 that the mystery was hidden from angels and men?[24]

Most commentators take ἀπὸ τῶν αἰώνων καὶ ἀπὸ τῶν γενεῶν in a purely temporal sense. Thus Lightfoot remarks: 'An αἰών is made up of many γενεαί', and he compares the LXX of Isa. 51.9, which has γενεὰ αἰῶνος as a rendering of the MT דֹּרוֹת עוֹלָמִים 'the generations of long ago'.[25] Lightfoot explains the apparent pleonasm thus: 'Not only was this mystery unknown in remote periods of antiquity but even in recent generations'. This strikes one as an unconvincing explanation. Why should anyone expect the mystery to be revealed in recent generations as contrasted with remote antiquity? Neither Paul nor the author of Colossians had any idea of an evolutionary development of revelation. According to Judaeo-Christian exegetical tradition, Abraham knew as much as Isaiah. T.K. Abbott follows suit, and so does C.F.D. Moule. Sasse also takes this view.[26] He claims that the sense of αἰών as a personality is foreign to the NT. The only possible exception to this is Eph. 2.2. If αἰών is taken as referring to personal beings, he adds, it is a mythological introduction of syncretism, something which later developed into Gnosticism. This seems an unjustifiably violent reaction against the suggestion that the phrase in question might mean 'from angels and men'. Büchsel in his article does not try to distinguish the meaning of γενεά from that of αἰών.[27] Lohse specifically rejects the notion that the mystery is hidden from the *aeons*, and so does Schweizer. And Gnilka agrees that the αἰῶνες must be understood in a temporal sense and not as personal powers.

Houlden on the other hand writes: '*aiones* could be a term for angelic powers ruling the world of time and space. *Generations* would then mean the inhabitants of the earth'. He well compares Col. 1.16, where Christ is described as the agent of creation for everything both in the heavens and on earth. On the whole Houlden inclines to this view. R.P. Martin accepts as a possible alternative translation a reference to 'the aeons or spiritual rulers of the world-order in a mythological sense, as in I Cor. 2.7f'.[28] Dibelius–Greeven go to the opposite extreme to those who reject the rendering 'from angels and men'. They write: 'Die αἰῶνες und γενεαί sind dann die ἄρχοντες τοῦ αἰῶνος τούτου aus I Cor. 2.7f'. But, though it is clear that in some contexts αἰῶνες can mean 'angelic powers', is there any evidence that γενεαί can mean this also? The phrase in question surely means either 'from ages and generations' or 'from angels and men'. There are no reasonable alternatives to these two translations.

Before making up our minds on this question we should observe that, whatever the meaning here, it does not bear the same sense as 1 Cor. 2.6-10. There the reason why the mystery was hidden from 'the rulers of this age' was that the rulers were rebellious angels, fallen powers, whose failure to recognize God in Christ was a moral failure: they could not conceive it possible that God should act as he did in the cross.[29] The author of Colossians is at most claiming that the mystery was formerly hidden from angels and men, but has now in the new age been revealed. As for the question whether αἰῶνες could mean 'angels' in Col. 1.24, we may say at once that Paul uses αἰών, whether in the singular or plural, only in a temporal sense. This is also true of Ephesians, with the striking exception of Eph. 2.2, where κατὰ τὸν αἰῶνα τοῦ κόσμου τούτου ('according to the *aeon* of the world') is parallel to κατὰ τὸν ἄρχοντα τῆς ἐξουσίας τοῦ ἀέρος ('according to the ruler of the power of the air'). It may well be that in Ephesians, whereas *aeon* in the plural meant 'ages', *aeon* in the singular could mean 'a demonic power'. It should be added that the author of Ephesians in paraphrasing Col. 1.26 writes τοῦ μυστηρίου τοῦ ἀποκεκρυμμένου ἀπὸ τῶν αἰώνων ἐν τῷ θεῷ(3.9) ('the mystery hidden from the *aeons* in God'). Theoretically this could mean 'hidden from the the elemental powers', but in 1.21; 2.7; 3.11; 3.21 he uses *aeon* in the plural in an unmistakably temporal sense. This last, 3.21, is worth reproducing, εἰς πάσας τὰς γενεὰς τοῦ αἰῶνος τῶν αἰώνων 'to all generations for ever and ever'. It is interesting however that the author of Ephesians does not reproduce the words of Col. 1.26, ἀπὸ τῶν αἰώνων καὶ ἀπὸ τῶν γενεῶν. It may be that in Ephesians the use of αἰῶνες was in process of change from being a word which could only be used in a temporal sense to being a designation of a superhuman being.

It would be rash to pronounce a definite verdict on this question. The evidence seems very evenly balanced. On the one hand the lexicographical evidence is on the whole against the probability that ἀπὸ τῶν αἰώνων in Col. 1.26 means 'from the angels'; on the other, if the two words αἰῶνες and γενεαί here both have a temporal significance, the author of Colossians is being pleonastic and to that extent pedestrian. But he does use pleonasms: in 1.3-12 for example we can point to καρποφορούμενον καὶ αὐξανόμενον in v. 6, ἠκούσατε καὶ ἐπέγνωτε in the same verse, προσευχόμενοι καὶ αἰτούμενοι in v. 9, and also ἐν πάσῃ σοφίᾳ καὶ συνέσει; and καρποφοροῦντες καὶ αὐξανόμενοι in v. 10, as well as εἰς πάσαν ὑπομονὴν καὶ μακροθυμίαν in v. 11. If therefore we do take the phrase in 1.26 in a purely temporal sense, we do not need Lightfoot's nice distinction between αἰῶνες and γενεαί.

Nevertheless there is sufficient force in the arguments on the other side to make it worth our while to consider the significance of the phrase 'from angels and men' in the context of Col. 1.24-26. If we do understand it in this sense, we must confess that the author of

Colossians is being faithful to his master here as far as his theology is concerned. The mystery has been hidden from angels and men because only with the event of the cross could the mystery be known by anyone. Now it is revealed to the saints. This is quite in line with 1 Cor. 4.9-13: the paradoxical nature of God's revelation in the cross can now be known by angels and men, even though it was hidden from them formerly. But of course faith is needed in order to recognize what is happening, so Paul would have held just as firmly that the mystery is only revealed to the saints (cf. 1. Cor. 1.24; 2 Cor. 2.15). We traced in 1 Cor. 4.9 an echo of the *militia Christi*, and, if the phrase in Col. 1.26 means 'from angels and men', exactly the same overtone is present. We have already seen that the theme of the overthrow of the powers of darkness is very much present in Colossians. Here therefore it may be concluded that angels as well as men will be interested in the revelation of the mystery, since their fate also depends on the outcome of the struggle.

We see therefore in Colossians–Ephesians a fairly successful attempt by two of Paul's disciples to adapt the tradition of their master to the conditions of their own day. Some things have been lost: it was impossible that the expectation of an imminent *parousia* should continue to be so influential on Christian thought in the second generation, and to stress the element of realized eschatology was undoubtedly the right way to deal with this. More serious is the loss of the sense of the apostolic commission of the community as a whole and the virtual confinement of Paul's theology of suffering to the single instance of Paul himself. But the conviction that Christians are living in the new age is as vivid as ever, and Paul's tradition of scripture exegesis has by no means been forgotten. These two authors were dealing with situations which were somewhat different to those which Paul faced. We may surely conclude that they dealt with their circumstances according to the genuine Pauline tradition.

III

When we turn to the Pastoral Epistles we find ourselves in a very different atmosphere to that of the other Deutero-Paulines. Indeed Trummer has actually suggested that they be classed as Trito-Paulines, on the analogy of describing Isaiah 56–66 as Trito-Isaiah.[30] We are not dealing with a disciple of Paul's who understands his master's thought and only wishes to apply it to the circumstances of his day. The author of the Pastorals was an admirer of Paul's, but not a disciple in the way in which the authors of the two Deutero-Paulines were. He was no profound theologian; he freely uses material from a variety of sources. He does not indulge in much theological argument with his opponents. He prefers abuse.

We are not surprised therefore to find that the depths of Pauline theology are not reflected in the Pastorals. Thus Paul's difficult doctrine of the Church as called to become the body of Christ, which was (as we have seen) modified by the authors of the Deutero-Paulines, makes no appearance at all in the Pastorals. On the other hand there is plenty of language in the Pastorals about the inevitability of suffering for the Christian. Timothy, who is probably to be regarded as representing the church leaders of the author's day, is told that he must be prepared to suffer hardship for the sake of the gospel (2 Tim. 1.8; 2.3; 4.5). Paul himself has suffered (2 Tim. 3.11) and continues to suffer (2 Tim. 1.12; 3.9). All Christians must be prepared for suffering (2 Tim. 2.10-12). In 1 Tim. 6.13 Jesus Christ is held up as an example to Timothy because he 'witnessed the good confession' before Pontius Pilate. Most strangely, there is no explicit reference to the cross or to the sufferings of Christ in the Pastorals, one of the strongest reasons for holding that they are not Pauline. But in this passage at least the example of Christ is given to Timothy in order to encourage him to 'maintain the noble contest of the faith' (1 Tim. 6.12).[31] Again in 2 Tim. 3.12, à propos Paul's sufferings in the past, we are told that 'all who wish to live piously in Jesus Christ will be persecuted'.

We conclude that the author was well aware both of the frequency of language about suffering in the Pauline letters, and also of the difficulties involved in being a Christian in his own contemporary situation. He expressed all this as well as he could in terms of his own rather shallow theology.

There is no hint in the Pastorals of the apostolic ministry as understood by Paul. There is in effect only one apostle, the martyred Paul, and from him all apostolic authority descends. The author was probably anxious to claim that he himself possessed that devolved authority, for he represents Paul as arranging for his work to be carried on by his two great disciples Timothy and Titus. They are depicted as exercising authority in the churches of Ephesus and Crete respectively. Timothy is described as having been ordained by

Paul himself (1 Tim. 4.14; 2 Tim. 1.6). Titus is instructed to appoint presbyters in every town in Crete (Titus 1.5). For Paul's own authority see 1 Tim. 2.6; 2 Tim. 1.11. One could therefore reasonably conclude that some sort of doctrine of apostolic succession has emerged by this time, though the author himself is only concerned to trace it back to Paul.

A regular ordained ministry has by this time been established. It comprises at least two orders, presbyter-bishops and deacons. I think it probable that the author of the Pastorals was aware that monoepiscopacy had emerged in some communities.[32] The distinction between clergy and laity is now accepted. The consequence is that a great deal that Paul put on the shoulders of the local community as a whole has now been taken over by the clergy, e.g. discipline (see 1 Tim. 5.19) and preservation of the gospel: witness the frequent exhortations to Timothy to 'preserve the deposit', and to hand it on to selected persons (1 Tim. 1.8; 3.9; 6.14, 20; 2 Tim. 1.12-14; 2.2; 3.14; Titus 1.9). Thus we can see just beginning in the Pastorals that process whereby, in the Western Church at least, the clerical order monopolized all authority and all teaching functions in the Church, leaving to the laity, in theory at least, a purely passive role. This is quite contrary to the spirit of Pauline ecclesiology.

It is not easy to decide whether there really is any clear concept of the *militia Christi* in the Pastorals. As we have already observed, we must not be misled by English phrases such as 'fight the good fight'. The author is only using the figure of an athletic contest, itself borrowed from Paul. It is true that in 1 Tim. 1.18 Timothy is urged to 'wage the good warfare', and in 2 Tim. 2.4 the author uses the figure of a soldier on active service. In 2 Tim. 4.17 he writes of Paul as having been rescued from the lion's mouth. He may here be echoing 1 Cor. 15.32, or even following Ps 23.21.[33] Thus there is probably a faint reproduction of Paul's vivid language about *militia Christi*. One might claim the ὤφθη ἀγγέλοις (Christ 'was seen by angels') in the christological hymn in 1 Tim. 3.16 refers to Christ's triumph over the hostile powers through his resurrection. But it is by no means clear and in any case this looks very like a hymn taken by the author from some source available to him. We do not know how far he consciously accepted the theology implicit in it.

We have claimed that one of the sources of Paul's belief that the sufferings of Christ were to be reproduced in the lives of the apostles was his interpretation of passages in scripture where the same language is applied to the one and the many. The author of the Pastorals is by no means devoid of ability to handle the scriptures in a way that illustrates his theology. We have in fact an instance of this in 2 Tim. 2.19, where a number of scriptural references occur to throw light on the relation of Christ to the Church. So this tradition of Pauline exposition had not been lost by the time the Pastorals were written. But we should point out that in 2 Tim. 2.19 the author of the Pastorals is very much dependent on Paul's own handling of scripture.[34]

The *parousia* is by no means ignored in the Pastorals. Relatively speaking, it occupies more attention than it does in the Deutero-Paulines. But some of the references are misleading, since they are written from Paul's point of view but actually refer to the author's own day. Thus in 1 Tim. 4.1 and 2 Tim. 3.1 the statement that 'in the last days' various evils will arise is only a way of referring to the opponents in the author's day. He does not seriously consider the possibility that the age is to end, since, as we have seen, Timothy is instructed to hand on the deposit of faith to trustworthy persons, a command which was certainly intended to apply to the author's own time. Other references to the *parousia* occur in 1 Tim. 6.15; 2 Tim. 2.12; 4.1, 8. In these last two places it is not quite clear whether τὴν ἐπιφάνειαν αὐτοῦ ('Christ's appearance') refers to the incarnation or to the *parousia*. I follow those who believe it refers to the *parousia*. Titus 2.13 speaks of 'our blessed hope, the appearing of the glory of our great God and Saviour Jesus Christ'. Thus the *parousia* certainly figures in our author's theology. It is an event to be looked forward to. But it is just an event, the last event. It is not, as it is in Paul, the event whose imminence casts its shadow upon contemporary events. Nor do we find in the Pastorals the profound conviction that we find in Paul, the conviction that the new age has dawned, with all the important implications of this which we have noted above.

As far as concerns the elements in Paul's thought in which we are specially interested, we may say of the author of the Pastorals what we must say of his work as a whole: he did his best to reproduce the true Pauline tradition as he understood it. But his echoes of Paul are feeble and muffled both by his own inadequate grasp of Paul's thought and by the space of time that elapsed between Paul's day and his own.

IV

Ignatius of Antioch would seem at first sight to be closer to the genuine Pauline tradition than are the Pastoral Epistles. His letters are full of references to suffering; he refers quite frequently to the apostles. We might begin by examining his use of one particular Pauline word, περίψημα. In *Eph.* 8.1 he describes himself as περίψημα ὑμῶν; and in 18.1 he writes: περίψημα τὸ ἐμὸν πνεῦμα τοῦ σταυροῦ. Of 8.1 Kleist comments: 'All that Ignatius seems to mean is " I devote my life to you".... or perhaps "I am your lowliest servant"'.[35] But Paulsen renders it with 'Ein Sühnopfer bin ich für euch'.[36] He remarks that the phrase 'fits in well with the style of ancient letter-writing', but he thinks that the theology of martyrdom which runs all through the letters makes it more likely that the translation which he gives is the right one. Kleist translates 18.1 with 'I offer my life's breath for the sake of the cross'. Paulsen suggests that this is a commentary on 1 Cor. 1.20, presumably much the same sentiment as John Newton's

> When I survey the wondrous cross
>> where the young Prince of glory died,
> my richest gain I count but loss,
>> and pour contempt on all my pride.

Ignatius also uses the word ἀντίψυχον ('ransom') of himself; cf. Mark 10.45; 1 Tim. 2.6. In *Eph.* 21.1 he says ἀντίψυχον ὑμῶν ἐγώ, which Lightfoot translates 'I am devoted to you'. In *Polycarp* 2.3 Ignatius writes κατὰ πάντα σου ἀντίψυχον ἐγὼ καὶ τὰ δεσμά μου ἃ ἠγάπησας; and in 6.1 ἀντίψυχον ἐγὼ τῶν ὑποτασσομένων [τῷ] ἐπισκόπῳ, πρεσβυτέροις, διακόνοις. Then there is *Smyrnaeans* 10.2 ἀντίψυχον ὑμῶν τὸ πνεῦμά μου καὶ τὰ δεσμά μου. Kleist translates this last passage with 'a ransom for you are my life and my chains', and *Polycarp* 2.3 with 'For your sake I sacrifice myself, chains and all, which are your delight'. Paulsen points out that early Christians used to kiss the martyr's chains. In *Polycarp* 6.1 Kleist offers 'ransom' again, and Paulsen 'Lösgeld'. One cannot help asking how far this language of περίψημα and ἀντίψυχον is becoming more conventionalized in Ignatius. Behind it all however lies Ignatius's vivid consciousness of the value of his martyrdom. The difference from Paul's usage is this: Paul describes the apostles as περίψημα and περικαθάρματα simply because they are exercising the apostolic office and living the apostolic life. Ignatius uses similar language of himself because he is to be martyred. Both writers closely associate their sufferings with Christ's, and only because of this do they suggest that their sufferings have atoning value.

In *Eph.* 12.1-2 we have a very remarkable passage in which Ignatius is surely referring to 1 Cor. 4.9-13. It runs thus:

ἐγὼ κατάκριτος, ὑμεῖς ἠλεημένοι· ἐγὼ ὑπὸ κίνδυνον, ὑμεῖς ἐστηριγμένοι. πάροδός ἐστε τῶν εἰς θεὸν ἀναιρουμένων, Παύλου συμμύσται τοῦ ἡγιασμένου, τοῦ μεμαρτυρημένου, ἀξιομακαρίστου, οὗ γένοιτό μοι ὑπὸ τὰ ἴχνη εὑρεθῆναι, ὅταν θεοῦ ἐπιτύχω.

Lightfoot translates this as follows:

> I am a convict, ye have received mercy; I am in peril, ye are established. Ye are the high road of those that are on their way to God. Ye are associates in the mysteries with Paul, who was sanctified, who obtained a good report, who is worthy of all felicitation; in whose footsteps I would fain be found treading, when I shall attain unto God.

There are several problems connected with this passage. The contrast, though it certainly recalls that found in 1 Cor. 4.9-13, is in fact quite different. Ignatius contrasts himself as a convict with the Ephesians, who have 'received mercy', presumably from God—it can hardly be from the Roman authorities. The second clause is much more like the original in Paul, but it has none of the irony of the Pauline passage: Ignatius is not trying to shame the Ephesians into (literally) joining him in the arena. Then comes another problem: why are the Ephesians described as 'fellow-mystics with Paul'? Does he simply mean that, because Paul founded their church and wrote letters to them, they have shared in his experiences? The word translated 'obtained a good report' has a strong overtone of martyrdom in it. It may be an echo of Heb. 11.2, 5, 39. Through it all runs Ignatius's conviction that his personal way of salvation can only be through martyrdom. But he does not demand this of anyone else. It is almost as if—*per impossibile*—Ignatius is suggesting that he has been justly condemned to death by the Roman authorities. It reminds one of Dante's argument that Pontius Pilate in condemning Christ's humanity to death was acting according to perfect justice, since in his humanity Christ represented all mankind, and mankind deserved to die for Adam's sin.[37] Now Paul followed very much the same course as did Ignatius fifty years later. He was condemned by the Roman authorities and died as a martyr. But Paul according to Ignatius is 'sanctified'. Is this because he died as a martyr? Does Ignatius hold that certain people can only attain salvation through martyrdom? Paulsen's comments are illuminating; he notes how clearly Ignatius distinguishes his situation from that of the church. For Ignatius, he says, the goal is unity with God, by him to be obtained only through martyrdom. And Paulsen suggests that Ignatius has subordinated Paul's ideas to his own theology, a very just remark.

There are two other references in Ignatius which seem to be closer to the true line of Pauline thought. In *Magnesians* 5.2 he writes:

> δι' Ἰησοῦ Χριστοῦ, δι' οὗ ἐὰν μὴ αὐθαιρέτως ἔχωμεν τὸ
> ἀποθανεῖν εἰς τὸ αὐτοῦ πάθος, τὸ ζῆν αὐτοῦ οὐκ ἔστιν ἐν ἡμῖν.

Lightfoot offers: 'through Jesus Christ, through whom unless of our own free choice we accept to die unto his passion, his life is not in us'. The second passage is *Philadelphians* 3.3: εἴ τις ἐν ἀλλοτρίᾳ γνώμῃ περιπατεῖ, οὗτος τῷ πάθει οὐ συγκατατίθεται. Lightfoot translates 'If any man walketh in strange doctrine, he hath no fellowship with the passion'. In both these passages it seems to be implied that all Christians are in some sense called to share in Christ's passion. In *Magn.* 5.2 Kleist renders τὸ ἀποθανεῖν εἰς τὸ αὐτοῦ πάθος with 'to die in order to share his passion', which might make it a reference to martyrdom: 'to die physically in order to share his passion'. Undoubtedly Ignatius has grasped something of Paul's theology of suffering, but it is constantly overshadowed by his own theology of martyrdom. See also *Romans* 6.3, where Igantius uses the striking phrase 'Allow me to be an imitator of the passion of my God'.

There are occasional hints of the *militia Christi* in Ignatius. In *Polycarp* 6.2 he writes:

> Please the captain in whose army ye serve, from whom also ye will receive your pay. Let none of you be found a deserter. Let your baptism abide with you as your shield; your faith as your helmet; your love as your spear; your patience as your body-armour (Lightfoot).

This would seem to be inspired by Eph. 6.13-17 (in the NT, not in Ignatius). Elsewhere in his letters Ignatius echoes the canonical Ephesians.[38] This is not however a very profound treatment of the theme; nothing is said of the adversary. Paulsen comments that Ignatius's circumstances were such that he would naturally use the language of the Roman army. In any case, he adds, the figure was traditional.

More significant perhaps are Ignatius's echoes of 1 Cor. 15.32, Paul's famous reference to fighting with beasts at Ephesus. In *Rom.* 5.1 he writes, presumably of his guards ἀπὸ Συρίας μέχρι Ῥώμης θηριομαχῶ 'from Syria as far as Rome I am engaged in a continual fight with wild beasts'. In *Trallians* 10 he returns to the theme:

> If, as some who are atheists (that is, unbelievers) say, his (Christ's) suffering was mere appearance (though they themselves are mere appearance), why am I in chains? And why do I hope to fight with wild beasts? In that case my dying is in vain. Yes, and I am a liar in the Lord's eyes (ἄρα οὖν καὶ καταψεύδομαι τοῦ κυρίου).[39]

In *Smyrnaeans* 4.1 Ignatius describes heretical opponents thus: 'I warn you beforehand against the wild beasts in human shape (τῶν θηρίων τῶν ἀνθρωπομόρφων)'. See also *Eph.* 7.1. In *Smyr.* 4.2 he uses the same argument as in *Trallians* 10: if the Lord's passion was in appearance only, then Ignatius's chains are mere appearance. If that were the case, why should he give himself up to death? He adds 'only in the name of Jesus Christ so as to suffer with him' (my tr.). But this is a reference to his own approaching martyrdom. It looks as if Ignatius understood Paul literally in 1 Cor. 15.32, and compares his own approaching ordeal in the arena to that from which Paul presumably escaped. The more literally Ignatius takes the figure, the less significance is there for the *militia Christi* concept. Behind the beasts there do not seem to lurk any spiritual enemies.

Of course this is not to deny that Ignatius believes in the power of evil. A glance at *Eph.* 19 must refute any such suggestion. This is the passage in which Ignatius declares that the ruler of the *aeon* 'failed to observe the virginal conception and child-bearing of Mary', and that by means of these events 'the old kingdom' was destroyed and the overthrow of death planned. Compare also *Eph.* 13; *Trall.* 8.1; *Philad.* 6.2. But Ignatius does not associate the overthrow of the powers of darkness with his own struggle, as Paul does.

Ignatius has plenty to say about the apostles. In *Magn.* 6.1 he imagines the whole Christian community in Magnesia gathered together with its bishop, its presbyters, and its deacons; and he compares the bishop to God and the presbytery to 'the college of the apostles'. This certainly suggests that by this time the apostles were remote, sacred figures. Paulsen well points out that this use of συνέδριον τῶν ἀποστόλων implies both that Ignatius thought of the original apostles as having comprised a limited college, and also that the presbyters in the Magnesian church of his day comprised a limited college. Ignatius's greeting to the Trallian church is remarkable: ἣν καὶ ἀσπάζομαι ἐν τῷ πληρώματι ἐν ἀποστολικῷ χαρακτῆρι 'which church I also salute in the divine plenitude after the apostolic fashion' (Lightfoot). Kleist, ever eager to discover signs of apostolic succession, suggests that the phrase may mean 'holding to the apostolic tradition'. But Paulsen rightly says that Ignatius is not here claiming apostolic authority, which elsewhere, as we shall see, he specifically disclaims, but that he is following the example of the way in which the apostles greeted the churches in their letters.

Next we must look at two passages in which Ignatius makes this disclaimer. The first shortly follows the greeting in *Trall.* 3.3:

[ἀλλ᾽ οὐχ ἵκανον ἐαυτὸν] εἰς τοῦτο ᾠήθην ἵνα ὢν κατάκριτος ὡς ἀπόστολος ὑμῖν διατάσσωμαι[41]

but I did not think myself competent for this, that being a convict I should order you as an apostle (Lightfoot).

The other passage is *Rom.* 4.3:

οὐχ ὡς Πέτρος καὶ Παῦλος διατάσσομαι ὑμῖν· ἐκεῖνοι ἀπόστολοι, ἐγὼ κατάκριτος· ἐκεῖνοι ἐλεύθεροι, ἐγὼ δὲ μέχρι νῦν δοῦλος. ἀλλ᾽ ἐὰν πάθω, ἀπελεύθερος Ἰησοῦ Χριστοῦ, καὶ ἀναστήσομαι ἐν αὐτῷ ἐλεύθερος.

I do not order you like Peter and Paul. They were your apostles; I am a convict; they are free, but I am a slave up to this moment. However if I suffer I am the freedman of Jesus Christ and will rise in him a free man (my tr.).

As Paulsen points out, in both these passages Ignatius clearly disclaims apostolic authority. Apostles are figures in the past, and their authority cannot be claimed by church leaders of a later age. Paulsen believes that Ignatius's slavery only consists in his being a prisoner. But we have the same strange anomaly here as we met in *Eph.* 12.1-2. Ignatius contrasts himself as a convict with the apostles who are free. But he must have known that both Peter and Paul had been at one time convicted prisoners. Was their freedom only obtained with their martyrdom? This is not the contrast that Paul makes; all the paradox has gone out of it. When Paul describes himself as the offscouring of the world, as a man doomed to death, he does not mean that this condition has been imposed upon him by the verdict of a Roman magistrate. Ignatius's theology of martyrdom has modified Paul's theology of the cross.

We may consider one more passage in this context. In *Philad.* 5.1 Ignatius describes himself as προσφυγὼν τῷ εὐαγγελίῳ ὡς σαρκὶ Ἰησοῦ καὶ τοῖς ἀποστόλοις ὡς πρεσβυτερίῳ ἐκκλησίας, 'having taken refuge in the gospel as in the flesh of Christ, and in the apostles as in a presbytery of the church' (my tr.). The gospel here, remarks Paulsen, is not a written book but the Christian message of salvation. It is interesting that here the apostles are regarded as a sort of court of appeal.[42] The historical Christ and the apostolic testimony go together. Kleist suggests that it means 'and in the apostles as represented by the presbytery of the church', a tendentious rendering which is not supported by the grammar of the sentence. Ignatius did not write 'the presbytery of the church', but (literally) 'presbytery of church', i.e. a church presbytery. It is illegitimate to introduce here any body of clergy contemporary with Ignatius to which he is referring. He is indeed appealing to apostolic tradition, but not to any contemporary apostolic institution or authority. Paulsen translates, 'als ich bei dem Evangelium als dem Fleisch Jesu und den Aposteln als dem Presbuterium der Kirche Zuflucht suchte', 'since I have taken refuge in the gospel as in the flesh of Jesus and in the apostles as in the presbytery of the Church'. Except that Paulsen has imported two definite articles that are absent from the Greek, this is correct.

Ignatius does not exclude the local Christian community as a whole from a share in responsibility for ordering its own life. In *Polycarp* 6.1 (a passage we have already quoted), after exhorting his readers to be subject to the bishop, the presbyters, and the deacons, he says that they must be ὡς θεοῦ οἰκονόμοι καὶ πάρεδροι καὶ ὑπηρέται, 'as God's stewards and assessors and ministers' (Lightfoot). The whole local church is still regarded as having a ministerial function. It is worth noting also that Ignatius apparently has accepted the tradition of ecclesiology of the Deutero-Paulines rather than that of the authentic Paul, for he writes in *Trall.* 11.2

οὐ δύναται οὖν κεφαλὴ χωρὶς γεννηθῆναι ἄνευ μελῶν, τοῦ θεοῦ ἕνωσιν ἐπαγγελλομένου, ὅς ἐστιν αὐτός.

Now it cannot be that a head should be found without members, seeing that God promiseth union, and this union is himself (Lightfoot).

There is no clear evidence that Ignatius knew Paul's letter to the Romans, but he certainly knew 1 Corinthians and Ephesians, so he must have deliberately chosen the easier form of the doctrine.

It cannot be said that Ignatius has no interest in exploring the scriptural background to his theology, though this is not a major feature of his letters. We can mention three places where he uses scripture to point to a fulfilment of salvation history in the widest sense of the word. The first is *Eph.* 15.1:

> εἷς οὖν διδάσκαλος, ὃς εἶπεν καὶ ἐγένετο· καὶ ἃ σιγῶν δὲ πεποίηκεν ἄξια τοῦ πατρός ἐστιν.

> There is therefore one teacher, who spoke and it came to pass; and all he has done in silence is worthy of the Father (my tr.).

This is an echo of Ps. 33.9:

> For he spoke, and it came to be;
> he commanded, and it stood forth.

The LXX of the first line is ὅτι αὐτὸς εἶπεν καὶ ἐγενήθησαν[43] (Ps. 32.9). The part of the psalm which immediately precedes this verse describes God's creation of the world. Ignatius is here referring to the creation of the world by the Logos. The phrase ἃ σιγῶν πεποίηκεν ('all he did in silence') must indicate the action of the Logos proceeding from the aboriginal silence of eternity when he had been inseparable from the Father. Compare *Magn.* 8.2, where Ignatius writes: 'there is one God who manifested himself in Jesus Christ his Son, who is his Logos proceeding forth from silence'.

The second reference is *Magn.* 10.3:

> ἄτοπόν ἐστιν ᾿Ιησοῦν Χριστὸν λαλεῖν καὶ ᾿Ιουδαΐζειν, ὁ γὰρ χριστιανισμὸς οὐκ εἰς ᾿Ιουδαϊσμὸν ἐπίστευσεν, ἀλλ᾿ ᾿Ιουδαϊσμὸς εἰς χριστιανισμόν, ᾧ πᾶσα γλῶσση πιστεύσασα εἰς θεὸν συνήχθη.

> it is monstrous to talk of Jesus Christ and to practise Judaism. For Christianity did not believe in Judaism, but Judaism in Christianity, wherein every tongue believed and was gathered together unto God (Lightfoot).

This is an echo of Isa. 66.18: 'For I knew their works and their thoughts, and I am coming to gather all nations and tongues, and they shall come and see my glory'. The LXX is

> κἀγὼ τὰ ἔργα αὐτῶν καὶ τὸν λογισμὸν αὐτῶν ἐπίσταμαι· ἔρχομαι συναγαγεῖν πάντα τὰ ἔθνη καὶ τὰς γλώσσας, καὶ ἥξουσιν καὶ ὄψονται τὴν δόξαν μου.[44]

Ignatius takes this passage as a prophecy of the time when all Gentiles will believe in the true God. This has (in principle presumably) now been fulfilled. Jews should have understood this and believed in Christ. Judaism should lead to Christianity and not *vice versa*. The passage in Isaiah 66 is a very universalistic one. Verse 19 runs: 'And from them I will send survivors to the nations . . . and they shall declare my glory among the nations'. Ignatius is here using scripture effectively to make his point.

The third passage is *Smyrn.* 1.2:

> ἀφ᾽ οὗ <Χριστοῦ> καρποῦ ἡμεῖς ἀπὸ τοῦ θεομακαρίστου αὐτοῦ πάθους· ἵνα ἄρῃ σύσσημον εἰς τοὺς αἰῶνας διὰ τῆς ἀναστάσεως εἰς τοὺς ἁγίους καὶ πιστοὺς αὐτοῦ, εἴτε ἐν Ἰουδαίοις εἴτε ἐν ἔθνεσιν.

> (of which fruit are we, that is of his most blessed passion); that he might set up an ensign to all the ages[45] through his resurrection, for his saints and faithful people, whether among Jews or among Gentiles, in one body of his Church.

There are two alternative sources for this quotation, Isa. 5.26 and 49.22. But the context in 5.26 is not at all appropriate: God raises an ensign for foreign nations who are to come and punish Israel for her sins. We therefore prefer to examine 49.22:

> Behold I will lift up my hand to the nations,
> and raise my signal to the peoples;
> and they shall bring your sons in their bosom,
> and your daughters shall be carried on their shoulders'.

The LXX of 49.22ab is

> Ἰδοὺ αἴρω εἰς τὰ ἔθνη τὴν χεῖρά μου,
> καὶ εἰς τὰς νήσους ἀρῶ σύσσημόν μου.[46]

Ignatius takes this passage as a prophecy, fulfilled in the death and resurrection of Jesus Christ, of the time when God will call all nations into the fellowship of his Church. It is quite possible that Ignatius took both the last two quotations from a collection of *testimonia* about the accession of the Gentiles.

Judged by these three passages, Ignatius is a competent rather than a brilliant exegete of scripture, but he does not attain to the virtuosity even of the Deutero-Paulines. A marked feature of his attitude towards the Old Testament is his conviction that the OT prophets were virtually Christians before Christ. Thus in *Magn.* 8.2 he writes:

For the most divine prophets lived according to Jesus Christ (κατὰ Χριστὸν Ἰησοῦν). This is why they were persecuted, being inspired by his grace[47] so that unbelievers should be fully persuaded that there is one God ... (my tr.).

A little later (9.3) he shows his belief in Christ's *descensus ad inferos*:

Of him (Christ) also the prophets being disciples in the Spirit were expecting him as a teacher. And because of this, he, whom they had rightly awaited, came in person and raised them from the dead' (my tr.).

The same thought is expressed more fully in *Philad.* 5.2:

and let us love the prophets, because they too have proclaimed with a view to the gospel (εἰς τὸ ἐυαγγέλιον κατηγγελκέναι), and hoped for him and awaited him. Because they believed in him they were saved in the unity of Jesus Christ. They are saints worthy of love and admiration, having been approved (μεμαρτυρημένοι) by Jesus Christ and numbered together in the gospel of the common hope (my tr.).

The prophets being approved by Christ presumably means that Christ confirmed the truth of their prophecies by fulfilling them. Here the prophets are virtually regarded as Christian saints.

A third reference occurs in *Philad.* 9.1:

He (Christ) is the door of the Father, by which enter Abraham and Isaac and Jacob and the prophets and the apostles and the Church. All these are held within the unity of God (πάντα ταῦτα εἰς ἑνότητα θεοῦ) (my tr.).

We can easily guess why Ignatius speaks of the prophets in this vein. He wishes to claim them for Christianity. But his strong emphasis on the Christian character of the OT prophets makes him less interested in the task of relating Christianity to the OT than Paul was, and he certainly shows none of the ability to apply the Hebrew concept of corporate personality to the explication of Christian theology that Paul did.

In 1982 I published an article in which I compared the 'theology of suffering' of the Pastoral Epistles with that of Ignatius.[48] In it I concluded (p. 696) that Ignatius had 'a full Pauline doctrine of the Christian life as a process of sharing in the passion, death and resurrection of Christ'. Since then a fuller study of Ignatius has convinced me that I was mistaken in this judgment. Ignatius, it is true, is in some sense a successor to Paul in that he, like Paul, links the passion, death, and resurrection of Christ closely to the Christian life. But his theology of suffering, because of his special circumstances, always tends to become a theology of martyrdom, and too often he leaves one with the impression that only the martyr can really reproduce Christ's sufferings. He has no notion at all of the apostolic ministry as carrying on in the new age the rôle of the citizens of the kingdom. The paradox of the cross, which is at the burning centre of Paul's theology, has been to some extent modified and deprived of its challenge in Ignatius. The cross however is much more central to his thought than it is in the theology of the author of the Pastorals. In view of the comparative neglect into which the theology of the cross fell in the period subsequent to Ignatius, we ought rather to admire him for what he retained of Pauline thought than to censure him because he did not retain more.

The apostolic period, in Ignatius's view, is entirely in the past. There is no suggestion that anyone can exercise an apostolic ministry now, though of course the apostolic teaching (as understood in Ignatius's day) has to be retained. In this respect he reminds one of the Pastoral Epistles. In complete contrast to Paul, Ignatius regards the ordained ministry, and one particular form of it which was by no means universally adopted in his day, as essential for the existence of the Church. See *Trall.* 3.1 χωρὶς τούτων ἐκκλησία οὐ καλεῖται, 'without these (the bishop and the presbyters) there is nothing that can be called a church'. Ignatius's extreme emphasis on the importance of the bishop[49] makes it very likely indeed that the office was under attack. Necessary for the continuance of the Church though the ordained ministry undoubtedly was, it is a pity that Ignatius was driven to exalt into so prominent a place in his ecclesiology something which simply did not exist in Paul's day. However the ordained ministry which Ignatius so fervently commends was still in a healthy relation to the local church. There is no sign in Ignatius of a doctrine of apostolic succession such as developed during the course of the second century, nor of an ecclesiology that hands all power and authority to the ordained ministry over against the laity, nor of an attempt to set up some super-authority that would command the obedience of the universal Church.

*****

As we look back over the period of roughly fifty years which we have reviewed under the rubric of the development of the Pauline tradition, certain features stand out. The first, and perhaps the most striking, is that Paul's conception of the apostolic ministry has disappeared. It was not maintained by the Deutero-Pauline writers, and therefore did not survive to appear in either the Pastorals or Ignatius. After Ignatius's day a different theology of apostolic ministry will appear, one which traces a direct line of succession in authority back through the Twelve (plus Paul) to Jesus himself. Secondly, if we judge the last term in this development, Ignatius, by the standard of a Pauline theology, we must say that the cross is still at the centre of Christian thought, though something of its strangeness has been lost. The paradox is fading. Thirdly, and this was to prove of immense significance in later ages, the ordained ministry has appeared on the scene and is playing an increasing part in the life of the Church. Such a development was inevitable and necessary if the Church was to survive and spread in the Roman Empire, but it is a pity that more attention was not paid to the relation of the ministry to the Church, a point on which Paul, even as understood in the second and subsequent centuries, could have provided valuable guidance. Fourthly, the link with the kingdom has been lost. We have seen how in Paul the apostolic ministry is often described in much the same terms as Jesus used to describe the citizens of the kingdom. The loss of the connection meant the loss of a certain degree of eschatological tension which the Church always needs. Its place has been supplied by recurrent adventist expectations, a very unsatisfactory substitute. Finally (and this is more visible in Ignatius than in any of the other post-Pauline documents), the rise of the canonization of the New Testament is beginning to overshadow the Old. This was an absolutely necessary development, one which saved the Church from the danger of a sub-Christian doctrine of God. It is this fact perhaps more than any other that makes it impossible for Christians living in any period later than the middle of the second century to put themselves in the place of the apostolic Church.

Chapter 9

THEOLOGICAL ISSUES AND CONCLUSIONS

In this chapter we attempt to face some of the theological issues raised by the material we have been dealing with in this book. Such an attempt should not need justification, for very few scholars study the New Testament out of mere interest in its contents. Nearly all are themselves trained in theology and profess some form of Christian commitment. Most people therefore who will have read through this book to this point will be asking themselves: what bearing have the conclusions come to above on our modern understanding of Christian faith and practice? It would seem inadequate for instance to try to expound what Paul believed about the apostolic ministry without giving some attention to the question of how we view the apostolic ministry today. Similarly, throughout this work we have stressed the importance for Paul of the eschatological dimension, and we have shown how much the failure of the *parousia* to appear influenced the thought of Paul's successors. We ought therefore to ask ourselves what we today make of this eschatological dimension.

Our material falls into three parts: we first consider the form of Paul's description of the apostolic ministry, the *Gattung*. We tackle in fact the very first question which originated the present quest: why in describing the activity of the ministry does Paul so often express himself by means of paradoxes? This might seem at first sight to be a literary rather than a theological question. But we hope to show that it has a theological aspect. Next we consider the question of eschatology, which also comprises the problem of *Frühkatholizismus*, the emergence in the early Church of the features and institutions which later came to be described as catholic. Finally we ask what conclusions we may draw from our study about the theology of the Church and of the ordained ministry.

I

Anyone who writes on the subject of Paul's literary form in 1 and 2 Corinthians must begin from the basic study undertaken by Bultmann as long ago as 1910.[1] He points out that the philosophers who used the diatribe form were often tilting against accepted notions and therefore freely used paradox (p. 27). One could say much the same thing of Paul, in that his theology of the cross implied a startlingly new conception of God. We have already noted the Stoic predilection for the theme of the wise man's battle (p. 29); for this sort of philosopher ordinary life was death (p. 30). Again a certain parallel with Paul's message appears. Epictetus, says Bultmann, begins by saying 'This may seem absurd', but then proceeds to resolve the paradox so that the absurdity disappears (p. 46). Here is a contrast with Paul; the paradox of the cross never disappears. The more one examines it the more astonishing it seems. Another difference, pointed out by Bultmann, is that in the philosophers, though citations from other philosophers and from poets are frequent, they are never used in order to support an argument. They are used purely for adornment (pp. 46, 95-96). But Paul's use of scripture has in the great majority of cases the purpose of supporting his argument.[2] Bultmann points to Paul's use of rhetorical questions as a link with the diatribe style (p. 86), but such a feature is too common in biblical literature to count for very much. Consider how often Deutero-Isaiah uses rhetorical questions, or for that matter Jesus himself. Bultmann very rightly notes that all the characteristics of the diatribe which he detects in Paul can also be detected in the epistle of James (p. 107). But this suggests that Paul borrowed his diatribe style from the literature of contemporary Hellenistic Judaism rather than directly from pagan philosophers. After all, one could find many of the features of the diatribe in Philo. He had certainly gone to school with the Greeks in a way which Paul had not. It is from writings such as his perhaps that Paul learned his diatribe style.[3]

Bultmann's work has made it clear that in the most impassioned passages of his letters Paul is very close to oral address. Behind much of his letters we may certainly detect the language of homilies which he has personally delivered. In such addresses his theology must be manifested; since the paradox of the cross was at the centre of his theology, it is not surprising that when he was to some extent speaking from the heart he should express himself in paradoxes.

Perhaps such passages show us something of what Paul meant by his speaking ἐν πνεύματι (in the Spirit); or at least if ἐν πνεύματι must be strictly confined to glossolalia, we see something of what Paul meant by prophesying. See 1 Cor. 14.6-19.

Then, sixty years later, H.D. Betz produced his important book on Paul and the Socratic tradition, already referred to more than once.[4] He maintains that Paul was consciously influenced by the Cynic tradition of philosophy. He suggests for example that Paul in his description of the *militia Christi* in 2 Cor. 10.4-6 is definitely thinking of his Sophistic opponents (p. 68). In view of the extensive scriptural background which we have uncovered it would seem more probable that this Cynic influence was mediated to Paul by Hellenistic Judaism.[5] Betz makes much of the parallel between Socrates and Paul found in Socrates' claim to be a better philosopher than his contemporaries because he knew that he knew nothing. But, as we have already pointed out, Paul does not claim this. Nor does Paul's boast that when he was weakest he was strongest because God's power was manifest in him really remind us of Socrates. As Betz himself remarks (p. 96), 'Das paulinische καυχᾶσθαι (boasting) ist ein καυχᾶσθαι ἐν κυρίῳ (boasting in the Lord)'. There is indeed irony in Paul: we meet it in 1 Cor. 4.9-13; but it is not the same as the Socratic εἰρωνεία, which consisted in the fact that his ignorance made him wiser than others. Paul's irony consists in the contrast between the disinterested attitude of the Corinthians and his own deep involvement. The Socratic irony lies in the contrast between sincere ignorance and spurious knowledge, Paul's lies between moral neutrality and total commitment.

Betz makes an admirable point when he says (p. 137) that according to Paul the essence of divine power does not lie in some superhuman quality but in the divine love manifested in humanity. Paul's opponents believed that the evidence of the presence of God was afforded by remarkable healings, the revelation of mysteries, a process by which one ceased to be a mere man and became a θεῖος ἀνήρ ('a divine man'), one who has escaped from the world of flesh and lives in the world of spirit (p. 139). Paul claims that salvation (*Heil*) is experienced not by transcending humanity but by a process of humanizing (p. 140).

Illuminating and learned though Betz's study certainly is, it does not quite convince one that Paul was directly influenced by the Socratic tradition. Paul obstinately refrains from quoting any of the

Cynic philosophers! I conclude that anything which Paul gained
from this tradition he gained from such Hellenistic Jewish writings
as Philo, and the sources that lie behind the epistle of James, the
author of which no one could accuse of not being well acquainted
with Jewish tradition. After all, if one is intending to write in literary
Greek, as Paul had to do and was well able to do, one could not avoid
assimilating some of the techniques involved in writing literary
Greek, especially if what one was writing was of an argumentative,
quasi-philosophical nature.

Before we reach our final judgment on this topic, we may refer to
what one or two other scholars have to say on the subject. Allo,
commenting on 2 Cor. 4.8-10, writes 'Les versets 8-10 sont
(instinctivement) rhythmés'. He goes on to say that the passage is
'related to the external contradictions to which the apostle is
exposed'. This is an interesting comment, verging towards the
conclusion that we have been adumbrating, that Paul's use of
paradox is largely influenced by the paradoxical nature of his subject;
the literary form is in fact theologically conditioned. As we have
noted,[6] Collange and Fiedler want to apply the technical term
περιστάσεις to Paul's catalogues of sufferings. The word has been
imported, unhappily I think, from the vocabulary of Cynic
philosophy. Its use rather prejudges the issue as to the background of
Paul's thought. We might refer also to our conclusion on p. 74 above
about Mealand's scholarly article. He does not in fact seem to differ
from us very much, since he seems to attribute the resemblance in
Paul's style to contemporary Cynic and Stoic writing more to the use
of a common medium than to direct imitation.

We conclude therefore that the reason why Paul uses the literary
form of a series of paradoxes in 1 and 2 Corinthians is primarily
because he was struggling to express for the first time in literary
Greek the paradox of the cross, and that therefore such a form of
expression naturally suited both his subject and his own emotional,
fiery temperament. One could perhaps find a number of analogies
both in the NT itself and beyond it. Scholars have often pointed out
how similar is the list of qualities desirable in a general drawn up by
Onosander, a Greek writer of about AD 50, to the list of qualities
desirable in a bishop drawn up by the author of the Pastorals.[7] But
we do not have to infer that the author of the Pastorals was
deliberately imitating Onosander. I have myself drawn a comparison
between 1QH15 and John 17.[8] Both authors are presenting the

prayer of the leader of a religious community: though their theology is different, style and even contents are certainly comparable. To move to a much more modern example, may we not say that Kierkegaard in his fierce criticism of the Hegelian system often uses the technical terms and even the thought-forms of the system he is attacking in order to expound his ideas? So there is no question of Paul having deliberately chosen the diatribe *Gattung* for his arguments with the Corinthians. His theme was paradoxical and so easily expressed itself in paradoxes. What he was attempting to do was sufficiently close to what the authors of contemporary diatribes were attempting to do as to make the similarity of form, though not of content, apparent through the common medium, which consisted of good, lively Hellenistic Greek.

II

The issue with which we are to deal in this section is one to which we have occasionally referred throughout the book. It can be stated very simply: Paul, as we have emphasized at every turn, was deeply influenced in his theology by the conviction that the cross and resurrection of Jesus Christ had inaugurated the new age, which was shortly to be consummated by the *parousia*. But the *parousia* did not take place and has not yet taken place nearly two thousand years later. How far then can Pauline theology be relevant for us? In other words, we are dealing with the problem of eschatology. In what sense can Christianity be an eschatological faith today?

In the 1950s Martin Werner wrote an influential book which dealt with precisely this problem.[9] His thesis was that in the course of the first two Christian centuries an eschatological gospel about Jesus Christ as the messianic Saviour became transformed into a sacramental religion centred round an incarnate God. This development he regarded as wrong: faith in the sacraments, and particularly in the eucharist, should not have been allowed to replace faith in the *parousia*, and the primitive attribution to Jesus of the status of an angel should not have been replaced by faith in the Redeemer who is God incarnate. We propose to offer a critique of Werner's book in the light of our investigations set out above.

In order to support his thesis Werner emphasizes very much the eschatological nature of Jesus' own message, largely along the lines set by Albert Schweitzer. He attributes to Jesus belief in an eschatological Son of Man which few scholars today would support (p. 19). Werner is quite justifiably anxious to preserve the strong eschatological element in Paul's thought and is fully aware of the centrality of the cross for Paul. He quotes Franz Overbeck's quip: 'In the post-apostolic period no one understood Paul any longer, and the one person who did understand him, namely Marcion, misunderstood him' (p. 53). This is a brilliant generalization, but like all generalizations it requires modifying in the light of the actual facts. The Deutero-Paulines (which Werner tends to neglect) are not strictly speaking apostolic, but it would be absurd to claim that the author of Colossians did not understand Paul, and unjust to say that the author of Ephesians misunderstood him. We entirely agree with Werner when he writes that the Pastorals are, among other things, an attempt to simplify Paul (p. 54). I think however Werner is unjust to Ignatius; though Ignatius's doctrine of suffering is not exactly that of Paul, it has much in common with Paul's; and Ignatius certainly knew what justification by faith meant.

I think that Werner exaggerates the extent to which Paul had to misinterpret the Old Testament. He claims that Paul used allegory in order to obtain from scripture the sense he wanted (p. 57), but he fails to distinguish allegory from the method which Paul uses much more frequently on scripture, typology. Indeed Paul or his disciple is sometimes helped by the fact that Jewish exegetical tradition had already typologized scripture for him. Jewish exegetes saw Moses where Paul saw Christ.[10] It is not fair to accuse Paul of using essentially the same technique of allegorizing scripture as does the author of the *Epistle of Barnabas* (p. 57). It never seems to have occurred to Werner that there were any elements in the OT to which Paul could have legitimately appealed. But there were. There were those elements in the prophets in which faith in God is demanded without any reference to the Torah. And there was also the general expectation of the prophets that God would ultimately reveal himself for vindication and judgment.

One of Werner's strongest contentions is that the theology, both incarnational and sacramental, of the Fourth Gospel eclipsed the original Pauline doctrine: 'The true cause of the canonisation of the Fourth Gospel was the gradual victorious advance of the new Logos-Christology and the new realistic-sacramental soteriology of the Johannine writing which was closely connected to it' (p. 63). The question of the sacraments we leave aside for the moment. But it is surely a mistake to give the impresssion that Johannine christology was fundamentally opposed to Paul's christology. Paul never clearly stated how precisely he thought Jesus Christ was related to God. But he certainly believed in the pre-existent Christ (a point which Werner concedes, p. 127). Colossians in fact provides a bridge between the two christologies. If Werner had given more attention to the significance of the Deutero-Paulines, he would not have been led into so starkly opposing the Johannine Christ to the Pauline Christ in the way he does. John's Logos-christology was an answer to the challenge of the day: do Christians believe in two gods? Quite apart from the non-arrival of the *parousia*, this question had to be faced and answered if Christians were to have a consistent doctrine of God. In a similar vein Werner accuses the author of the Epistle to the Hebrews of assisting the Church in the task of loosing itself from Paul's primitive gospel. The Epistle, he says, isolates the death of Christ and makes its effect operative in the heavenly sphere (p. 76). But the question which, as far as I can see, is never faced by Werner is this: what should the Church have done in the face of the non-arrival of the *parousia*? Paul had in effect said: 'Christians are living in the new age and are to reproduce the death and life of the Redeemer in their lives. When he returns, as will happen soon, the process will be complete'. He did not return in Paul's generation, nor the next, nor the next. The Church in fact responded to this situation by saying: 'We must go on living the life and dying the death of the Redeemer indefinitely, inspired by the Holy Spirit, who is available to believers, and sustained by the eucharist, which is the *panis viatorum*'. This does not strike me as an unreasonable reaction, nor one that necessarily belied Paul's gospel.

On p. 114 Werner sums up his argument thus: 'At first it was the transformation of the doctrine of redemption, but finally the whole corpus of dogma was transformed from the primitive eschatologically determined faith into a new non-eschatological doctrine of the Catholic Church'. There is a reasonable stopping place or *via media* between these two extremes in the doctrine of the eucharist of the second and third centuries. In that period the eschatological aspect of the eucharist was very prominent. During the celebration of the rite one was in heaven; one was anticipating the joys of paradise. This aspect became obscured later, but while it lasted it testified to the continuing eschatological atmosphere of the Church. After all, the *parousia* had not arrived, so the very earliest faith, based on a belief in the imminence of the *parousia*, was no longer completely tenable.

Werner describes Paul's doctrine of redemption in the following terms (pp. 165-66):

> the redemptive event . . . completed itself in the individual believer as death and resurrection with Christ to a new bodily form of a supernatural-pneumatic kind. This was the mode of being in the new aeon. It was achieved in as far as the eschatological general resurrection of the dead, which commenced with the resurrection of Christ, began already to be effective before the *parousia* in the persons of the faithful, who came into a communion with Christ through baptism.[11]

Even if this were an accurate statement of Paul's soteriology (and its anthropology is hardly consistent with what we have already accepted of Güttgemanns' thesis), it is not clear why the non-arrival of the *parousia* need have modified it so drastically. Paul himself had to some extent to cope with the problem, in as much as believers were dying during his lifetime. This did not cause him to modify his own doctrine. One suspects that the problem was not as agonizing for the early Church as Werner suggests.

A great deal of Werner's argument is of course connected with christology. He maintains that Paul's christology essentially consisted in attributing an angel status to Jesus. It was an angel christology. The mistake of Paul's successors was to abandon this in favour of a doctrine which identified Jesus with the Godhead. It seems to me that Werner is looking at the dilemma both of Paul and of his successors too much through modern spectacles. For us the distinction between angel christology and substance christology is all-important, because that, or something like it, is the development which christology actually followed. But Paul, as the first real theologian of the Church, was a pioneer. He was feeling his way. For him the event of Jesus was unique, one which had somehow to be expressed in intelligible terms. But the only terms he had were those available to a highly educated Jew of the first century. Werner claims (pp. 121-22) that the earliest christology viewed Jesus as an 'angel, a heavenly Son of Man', and that neither the Synoptists nor Paul envisaged Christ as having existed from all eternity nor as going on for ever. As far as Paul is concerned (and this is no doubt true of the Synoptists also) the question of eternity had not yet appeared on the horizon. Paul must not be judged by the standards of later christology. Even so, Werner sometimes makes rather arbitrary judgments, determined as he is to label Paul as one who did not believe in what a much later age would call 'the divinity of Christ'. Thus he argues (p. 122) that because Adam was a created being, so must the Second Adam have been. This does not seem to me to follow: the first Adam is ἐκ γῆς χοϊκός (of the earth earthy). The Second is ἐξ οὐρανοῦ and ἐπουράνιος (of heaven, heavenly). See 1 Cor. 15.47-48. Paul is here speaking of origin. One whose origin is in heaven can hardly be thought of as created. In the same passage Werner claims that 'equality with God' is not attributed to Christ in Phil. 2.6. But what else does τὸ εἶναι ἴσα θεῷ mean? Again, on p. 123 we read: 'while Paul did indeed apply sayings of the Septuagint concerning the *Kyrios* to Christ, there is not one instance of his having done this when the saying referred to God, an exception which cannot be accidental'. All this proves is that Paul did not *identify* Christ with the Father. If he had, he would have involved himself in inextricable theological confusion. In fact Paul believed that he could trace in the OT evidence of the existence of two distinct divine beings, a belief shared by the Deutero-Paulines and the author of the Fourth Gospel.[12] It was left to this last theologian to resolve the dilemma which this belief presented. Paul did not resolve the dilemma himself, but he made its eventual resolution a necessity for the Church.

When Christians became aware of the necessity of making distinctions within the Godhead, they had no pure, guaranteed, ready-made vocabulary to express it. The vocabulary used by scriptural characters in speaking of (or to) angelic beings would be one of the obvious choices. Werner is in effect saying that if Paul had meant that Christ was really God in the later sense, he should have said so using the later vocabulary. But the realization of the full divinity of Christ, like the doctrine of the Trinity, was necessarily a later development. The question is: was this development justified by the events concerning Jesus? Perhaps the fundamental difficulty about Werner's whole approach to the NT is that he is essentially a Socinian, that is, he will not accept anything unless it is clearly expressed in scripture (except that in his case it has to be clearly expressed by Paul or the Synoptists). What he lacks is a satisfactory doctrine of tradition. His theology sadly demonstrates the self-destructive tendency of radical Protestantism. He says in so many words that the doctrine of the Trinity was the direct result of the abandonment of the *parousia* hope (p. 125). This is only true in the very obvious sense that if the *parousia* had arrived there would have been no need for either a doctrine of the Church, or the sacraments, or of anything else. But in fact the *parousia* did not arrive. Surely the Church was therefore right to abandon (or at least modify) the *parousia* hope. If it had not done so it would have been self-deluding. Instead of censuring the Deutero-Paulines, Luke, John, and any other NT writer who does not share the belief in the imminence of the *parousia*, we should applaud them. They were willing to face the facts of history. On p. 94 Werner says of the christology of the Fourth Gospel largely accepted by the later Church: 'the new doctrine assigned a primary constitutive significance to the incarnation of the Logos in contradistinction to his death and resurrection'. This is not fair: we should say 'in addition to his death and resurrection'. In any case the problem left unresolved by Paul had to be tackled, the relation of Jesus Christ to God. The arrival or non-arrival of the *parousia* made in principle no difference to this.

Werner never tells us what he thinks the Church should have done in the face of the non-arrival of the *parousia*. He says quite explicitly that the way in which the Church dealt with the crisis was 'fundamentally false' (p. 298). One suspects that his answer would be that they should have given up in despair. But this does not answer the question, 'why did they not do this?' As we have already stated, the fatal defect in Werner's theology is that he has no doctrine of tradition. Everything, he believes, went fundamentally wrong in the second generation of Christianity. Hence there is no room left for a doctrine of tradition. But the questions with which we are concerned in this chapter are essentially questions of tradition. What are we as Christians today to make of the Christian tradition? When we study the development of the way in which the Church through the ages has dealt with its original message (which is the history of the Church's tradition), what conclusions are we to draw about the way in which the Church should present its message today? There have been, and still are, many false and misleading answers to this question, including the Eastern Orthodox Church's answer 'All tradition is sacred and unchangeable' and the pre-Vatical II Roman Catholic Church's answer 'the pope is tradition'. But the answer of the sort of radical Protestantism represented by Werner, 'the Church went disastrously wrong in the second generation, so there is no tradition' is just as false and misleading. It is a tragedy that a scholar

˙of such ability and learning should have been reduced to defending so very unsatisfactory a theological position.

We have criticized Werner for not paying sufficient attention to the Deutero-Paulines in this question of eschatology. The point is well illustrated by Güttgemanns' refutation of the Percy–Robinson thesis about the Church as the body of Christ. J.A.T. Robinson, it will be remembered, took up the thesis originated by Percy that in Paul's view the Church as it actually exists on earth *is* the risen body of Christ.[13] Güttgemanns rejects the thesis on three grounds: (a) it implies an identity between Christ and Christians, which is just what Paul was opposing; (b) if the thesis is correct, Christians themselves should be already risen; but this is not Paul's view; (c) the thesis objectifies the relation between Christ and Christians so as to make it physical. But in fact Robinson at least could never have sustained his thesis if he had not held the full Pauline authorship of Colossians. This enables him to claim that according to Paul Christians are in some sense risen already, although in fact in Colossians–Ephesians we do not find the doctrine of the body that justifies the close identity between Christ and Christian which Robinson's argument demands. In other words, only by alternating between genuine Paul and the Deutero-Paulines, both accepted as representing Paul's theology, can his thesis be sustained. For the question of the meaning of eschatology the position of the Deutero-Paulines is crucial, as perhaps our last chapter has shown.

We have given considerable attention to Martin Werner's work because he is an outstanding example of one who condemns what the Germans call *Frühkatholizismus*, an issue which is still even in these ecumenical days an important one betwen Catholics and Protestants. The word denotes the develoment of structures and tendencies in the early Church which led ultimately to the full institution of the Catholic Church as it appeared in both East and West by about the year 500. What light does our study throw on this question? How far was *Frühkatholizismus* a development away from Paul's position, a betrayal of Paul's theology? As far as our period is concerned (from Paul to Ignatius of Antioch) we can perhaps distinguish four characteristics of this nascent Catholicism which manifest themselves.

The first is of course the emergence of an ordained, and probably paid, ministry,[14] first clearly evidenced in the Pastorals. However we may deplore the extent to which the ordained ministry tended to monopolize the functions of the community as a whole, no reasonable church historian will deny that the emergence of an ordained ministry was necessary and salutary for the Church. The history of those sections of the Church that have tried to dispense with a ministry altogether is surely a witness to this. Either some sort of a ministry re-emerges in the course of time, or tasks essential for the well-being of the Church, such as discipline and ordering of worship, are ignored or inadequately performed. The fact that later on the ministry became tyrannical and an obstacle to the gospel is not an argument against its very existence: *abusus non tollit usum*. If the theology of the ordained ministry can be kept firmly within a Pauline perspective, its existence should not be regarded as an unfortunate development.

Secondly, during this period we see the emergence of the concept of the catholic Church. Already in the Deutero-Paulines ἐκκλησία is being used of the Church as a whole. Even in the Pastorals it is described as 'the pillar and foundation of the truth'.[15] Ignatius uses the expression ἡ καθολικὴ ἐκκλησία (*Smyrn.* 8.2) in a context where he wishes to distinguished it from sectarian Christianity. Only those for whom the word 'catholic' is as a red rag to a bull will deplore this development. It was in fact an essential stage in the growth of the self-consciousness of the Church. It is a tragedy that at the Reformation the word 'catholic' became a party label. One of the happiest results of the ecumenical atmosphere engendered by Vatican II is that it is now possible for a Christian to profess himself to be both Catholic and Evangelical at the same time.

Thirdly, we find the concept of 'the deposit of faith',[16] notably in the Pastorals, but also present of course in Ignatius. In as far as this meant the obligation to be faithful to the apostolic or original tradition, it was a necessary development. But it could be understood, and frequently was understood in later ages, as a deposit of sacred propositions to be handed on from generation to generation without question or scrutiny. The phrase in Jude also carries the implication that all later developments in defence of the apostolic tradition, such as the doctrine of the Trinity, were actually known to the first apostles, even though for one reason or another they did not mention them. This belief was universally held by Catholics up to, and long after, the rise of critical study of the bible and of antiquity.[17] But we can hardly blame this development on early Catholicism. It is true that this concept developed in the West into what might almost be called an obsession with doctrinal orthodoxy that had appalling consequences. But the Church must be concerned with the purity of its message. A man of the intellectual stature and spiritual maturity of Paul could defend the faith without demanding adherence to set formulae. But later generations, with less genius, and facing multiple problems, fell back on the technique of using theological formulae which soon became sacrosanct. This tendency is not peculiar to Catholicism. Protestants can be just as fervid champions of what they regard as orthodox belief expressed in formulae.

Fourthly, we find the eucharist emerging as the centre of the Church's public devotion and worship. Only by the time of Ignatius is this development clearly visible. What is quite remarkable about both Deutero-Paulines and the Pastorals is the absence of overt reference to the eucharist. When the author of Ephesians wishes to define the unity of the Church he mentions one Lord, one faith, one baptism, but he does not add, as modern catholics devoutly wish he had added, one eucharist and one ministry. And when we read in the Pastorals the requirements for a good minister, his sacramental functions simply do not appear.[18] It seems to me that Werner was to some extent right in claiming that the eucharist took the place of the *parousia* hope, but, contrary to Werner's view, the Church was fully justified in making this readjustment.

We have already pointed out that the eucharist of the first three centuries had a strong eschatological element in it. In a sense therefore when one participated in the eucharist (not just attended it), one was by anticipation taking part in the *parousia*. Far from this being an arbitrary development, it was the right course for the Church to take. If the *parousia* is not going to arrive in the immediate future, then let us make the best of Christ's presence in the Spirit in the Church. The early eucharist kept alive the sense that Christians ought to have of living in the new age, even though the old age is still with us. Only later did the method of celebrating, and of understanding, the eucharist become corrupted. Instead of being the joyful messianic feast it became the solemn sacrifice whereby the priest enabled the passive congregation to get rid of their sins. The dynamic, eschatological element became overlaid with the emphasis on the static presence of Christ in the elements viewed as a sort of objectification of God's presence among his people. The Reformation did very little to remedy this state of affairs, since the Reformers were ill-informed about the worship of the early Church, and in any case were preoccupied with removing any suggestion that in the eucharist the priest offers Christ as a sacrifice, so that their eucharistic liturgies were too often largely negative affairs, the old mass filleted of elements which they regarded as offensive, the missing parts being made up by preaching or penitential exercises. Only in this century, when the vast majority of Western Christians have accepted the fruits of the liturgical movement, have we been able to recapture the primitive eschatological element in the eucharist. Here again, as is the case with that word 'catholic', the ecumenical movement has made it posible for Christians of all traditions in the West to return together to a eucharistic rite the essential outlines of which they can all share.

We conclude therefore that the danger of *Frühkatholizismus* is a bogey, an unreal phantom. All the features of early catholicism are to be welcomed by all Christians: an ordained ministry, the concept of the Catholic Church, the obligation to be faithful to the apostolic tradition, the eucharist as the centre of the Church's worship. Yes, and also some later elements, such as the rise of the monastic orders and the detailed observance of the Church's calendar. But, since all things under the sun are subject to corruption and decay, all these featurs of church life should always be viewed in a Pauline perspective. We are not justified by these things, neither by the possession of a regular ministry, nor by our doctrinal orthodoxy, nor by being able to style ourselves catholics, nor by our unfailing observance of the eucharist. And if we ever substitute any of these things for living faith in Christ, the Holy Spirit will judge us and discipline us, whether we recognize it or not. To say that we must view the elements of catholicity in a Pauline perspective is very much the same thing as saying that we must maintain the eschatological tension in our church life. But that brings us to our next topic.

It used to be widely agreed by scholars that the doctrine of justification by faith lies at the centre of Paul's theology. As we have just demonstrated above, we would be the last to minimize the importance of this doctrine. But it looks today as if eschatology must be given the pride of place in this respect. Throughout our study we have seen how vitally important in Paul's thought is the belief that with the death and resurrection of Christ the new age has dawned, even though this does not mean that the old age has disappeared. It is not of course a bloodless, easily attained eschatology. God has indeed brought in the new age in Christ, but at great cost to himself. To this the cross bears witness, so much so that the Christian in this life can never hope to avoid, or wholly to transcend, the cross. The belief that this was possible was perhaps the main error of Paul's opponents in Corinth. But the great difference between Paul's situation and ours is that whereas in his day it was still possible to believe, as he believed, that the *parousia* was imminent, or at least likely to happen within a generation, for us that belief is impossible. An event that for two thousand years is about to happen very soon is a non-event. What difference does this make to our theology? We have seen how acutely Martin Werner posed this question, and we have also seen good reason to reject his attempt to answer the challenge which this question presents. We must face that challenge now.

We have already underlined the important place which the eucharist can play in coping with this situation. But the eucharist, no matter how adequately celebrated, is very far from being a complete answer to this question. Though worship is certainly at the centre of the life of the Church, it does not exhaust the Church's life. It is very significant that in Communist countries the atheist state would like to confine the Church to being a worshipping community. It encourages neither intellectual contact between Christians and Marxists, nor any social activities on the part of the Church. The Church as a whole will never allow itself to be confined to the sphere of worship. To answer our question fully therefore we must look for something more than a mere reference to the eucharist.

First we would emphasize the provisional nature of the Church which a due regard for eschatology makes clear. Paul writes in 1 Cor. 7.31: 'the form of this world is passing away'. We may not understand this in a literal, temporal sense, but we must accept it in a substantial sense. In this world we are not required to commit ourselves completely to anything except God in Christ. Everything else in the Church's life exists only in order to serve that end. Hence we must be constantly on our guard against the danger of institutionalization. Structures in the Church quickly become sacrosanct. What actually originated only a couple of hundred years ago is soon treated as having existed since the days of the apostles. One of the most remarkable changes in ecclesiological emphasis that have followed the Second Vatican Council has been the renewed emphasis on the Church as the pilgrim people of God, as contrasted with the Church as the body of Christ. Of course both figures are present in Paul's theology, but the second had till recently absorbed most of the attention of the theologians of the Church. We have now begun to realize that the first, the concept of the Church as the pilgrim people of God, is more fundamental than the second. The first is a description of what the Church is; the second denotes what the Church is called to be. A pilgrim people is constantly on the move. It cannot settle permanently anywhere. Sociologists will no doubt point out that this reassertion of the ancient (and very biblical) concept of the Church as the people of God coincides with the gradual dissociation between the Church and the state in Europe, and the realization by Christians of all traditions that they are living in a potentially hostile world. For theologians it remains to point out that this rediscovery of the ancient understanding of the Church is closely connected with our renewed comprehension of the eschatological element in Christianity.

Next we must mention the unexpectedness of God. Anyone who reads Paul's exposition of the meaning of the cross, especially in such passages as 1 Cor. 1.18-31, can hardly fail to see how central to his thought is this divine unexpectedness. He demonstrates it of course by frequent and well-justified references to scripture. The prophets of old well understood this element of unexpectedness in God's dealings with men. Of this unexpectedness the cross is certainly the supreme example. In the cross God has so to speak activated his unexpectedness, his strangeness, not in the sense of alienation, but in the sense that he has outstripped our calculations. In the life of the Church this unexpectedness is often expressed by saying that the Holy Spirit acts as he wills. He cannot be wholly confined within our institutions or within the channels through which we normally expect him to act. This is well understood by all the writers of the NT: 'The wind blows where it wills' (John 3.8). One could freely illustrate this unexpectedness from the history of the Church: the unexpected triumph over the persecuting Roman state early in the fourth century, so that within two generations the persecuted sect had become the state Church.[19] Then there was the unexpected way in which the Church during the Dark Ages in the West became the heir and repository of Graeco-Roman civilization. The Reformation was not a sign of the unexpectedness of God, any more than the Russian revolution was. Both these events were foreseen as inevitable long before they took place. But God's unexpectedness was not exhausted by the Dark Ages. There was the unexpected expansion of the Church beyond Europe from the sixteenth century onwards, connected of course with the imperial expansion of the European nations. There was the strange reversal whereby Europe, the nursing mother (though not the cradle) of Christianity for seventeen centuries, became in the course of fifty years the region where Christianity has been and is being most severely persecuted. This is an instance of God's unexpectedness showing itself in judgment. And finally we might join to this the unexpected way in which the Church has survived and even revived under persecution.

All the time there have been unexpected individuals as well: Martin of Tours, Patrick of Ireland, Francis of Assisi, Catherine of Siena, Julian of Norwich, Joan of Arc, Teresa of Avila, Ignatius Loyola, John Bunyan, William Carey, Guiseppe Roncalli . . . The list is endless. All this unexpectedness is a testimony to the eschatological dimension in the Church's life. In Mark 13.32 Jesus is represented as saying about the *parousia* 'of that day or that hour no one knows'. Even during the period when the *parousia* was expected soon thoughtful Christians were agreed that it would come unexpectedly.[20] That unexpectedness of God is a legacy of the early *parousia* expectation which we cannot afford to ignore.

Perhaps a third way in which the eschatological element expresses itself is in a feature of Christianity which is not entirely to its credit: that is the active, disruptive, social nature of Christianity. Christianity has rarely been content with a quietist role. It is a social, community religion at its very heart, and therefore wherever it takes root it seeks to influence society. This is not always a conscious effort. The early Church in the Roman Empire attempted to opt out of society. This was one of the reasons why it encountered persecution. Eventually it found itself dominating society instead. In modern time in third-world countries where Christianity is a minority religion, it nevertheless has a marked influence on society. In India for example, where Christians are a relatively small minority, the Church has in the past pioneered in education and health care, and in the present is pioneering in care for the disabled and the oppressed. This 'activist' character of Christianity has its dark side. It is probably responsible for the fact that of all the great world religions Christianity has the worst record in the matter of persecuting dissidents. But at its best this is a noble and indispensable aspect of the faith. Because God in Christ has inaugurated the new age, this must have its effect on society. This is the strain in Christianity to which all champions of liberation theology can justifiably appeal. We must ascribe this feature to the influence of eschatology.

Fourthly, the *parousia* was always understood to mean judgment as well as salvation. Indeed the belief that there would eventually be a judgment for all men goes very far back in Jewish history. But we can surely apply this belief to contemporary history as well as to what is to happen at the end of the world. It is true that throughout the history of the Church Christians have claimed that they could discern God's judgment in all sorts of events. Too often the claim has simply provided a convenient method of abusing one's opponents. Arius dies of a painful disease. It is the judgment of God. The Black Death is called a judgment on the wickedness of the English (or European) population. The Lisbon earthquake indicated God's disapproval of contemporary Roman Catholic worhip, etc., etc. But once again *abusus non tollit usum*. It is possible legitimately to discern by faith the judgment of God in the events of history. The papacy in the sixteenth century brought upon itself the disruption and enfeeblement caused by the Reformation. The Church of England by its too close association with the ruling classes brought upon itself the indifference and even contempt with which it is viewed by too many in England today. The Protestants in Ulster, by failing to make any attempt to reconcile the Roman Catholics in their midst to the society which they dominated, brought upon themselves their present troubles. In many countries in Europe the main opposition to the Church consists of a bitter traditional anti-clericalism inspired originally by the dominating tactics of the Roman Catholic Church during the eighteenth and nineteenth centuries. The book of Revelation rightly interpreted gives us a pattern for understanding this process of judgment. If we apprehend its brilliant visions not as predictions of some one situation in the future, but as a paradigm of the world under the judgment of the cross, it will begin to make sense in many different historical contexts. The belief in the *parousia* as a symbol of judgment should be a perpetual reminder of the operation of God's judgment in contemporary history.

Finally let us remind ourselves that in Paul's thought the new age was inaugurated by the cross, as well as by the ensuing resurrection. As long as history continues, the dimension of the cross will never fade from our thought if we are faithful to Paul's guidance. This is an essential part of a truly Christian eschatology. Eschatology is not just a belief that everything will come to an end. It is the belief that the end has been precipitated by the suffering and death of the Son of God. Hence suffering and dying must always be somewhere near the centre of the Church's life, and very often suffering will be found to be the explanation of what the Church is really effecting in the world. Paul has emphasized that the apostolic life was to be marked by suffering and death. Still today there are circumstances in which suffering and dying are the means by which the Church most effectively makes its presence known in the world. We must not forget the many who have died as martyrs at the hands of anti-Church régimes in so many parts of Europe, America, and Asia. In some countries all that church leaders can do by way of witness is to go to prison. In one semi-barbarous state in Europe, Albania, it would seem that the only form of Christian witness left is martyrdom—a situation which St John the Divine may well have foreseen. This predominance of the cross in the Church of the twentieth century very largely accounts for the fact that the Church has survived in such areas as Eastern Europe and Russia at all. It is extraordinarily appropriate that in some areas the Church should have rediscovered its apostolic witness by the very means which Paul believed must characterize the apostolic life in the new age. Endurance, suffering, martyrdom, these are the means by which the Church asserts its authority in the world when the world turns hostile. And these are precisely what Paul himself indicated as the signs of the activity of the faithful in the messianic age.

The eschatological element in Christianity is very far from being exhausted with the fading of the *parousia* hope. On the contrary, as long as Christianity remains true to the tradition of St Paul, it will continue to be an eschatological faith in a genuine sense. In the meantime the element of finality, judgment, and hope provided by the *parousia* expectation in Paul's thought will continue to be for the individual Christian provided by the prospect of his own death,[21] and the recurrent attacks of Adventism to which the Church has always been subject will continue to be a deeply unsatisfactory substitute for either the *parousia* hope of Paul's day or the eschatological dimension in the Church's life in our own day.

III

We have now reached the last topic to be explored in this book, one that may seem of less central importance to those who regard the question of the ordained ministry as a minor one. But since it has divided the Western Church ever since the Reformation, it can

hardly be dismissed as irrelevant or academic. It is the question of
the theology of the ordained ministry. We believe that what Paul says
about the apostolic ministry can be of help here. But first perhaps we
should make some attempt to justify this belief. How far can we use
the conclusions of our researches in Paul as a norm for the doctrine
of the ordained ministry?

Ministry is certainly a prominent theme in the NT, not least in the
Pauline letters, though nowhere in the NT do we find any conscious
attempt to provide us with a theology of the ordained ministry.
Indeed the NT can tell us more about the relation of the ministry to
the Church (a topic strangely ignored by theologians) than it can
about the ordained ministry itself. Let us begin by saying that we
must discount all attempts to legitimize any existing form of the
ordained ministry by claiming for it a dominical command, promise,
or institution. Jesus did not institute an ordained ministry. Whatever
Matt. 16.13-20 means, it does not mean that Jesus actually entrusted
leadership and ministerial office in the Church to Peter, still less that
this should extend to Peter's successors as bishops of Rome. The
notion of 'a Petrine office' in the Church is not found in the NT.
Modern Roman Catholic scholars no longer claim that the doctrine
of the papacy can be read off from the pages of the NT.[22] This
conclusion is just as fatal to any Eastern Orthodox or Anglican
attempt to establish a succession of authority stretching from Jesus
through the apostles down to the first bishops, and so on to the
modern episcopate.

We must also state unequivocally that the distinction between
clergy and laity as understood in the Christian Church since about
the end of the first century was unknown in Paul's day. Hence we
cannot expect to find in the earliest records of Christianity any form
of the ordained ministry which can be regarded as normative on any
other grounds than that of being the first form that appeared. In the
Pastorals we find presbyter-bishops and deacons, but we do not find
them commended as successors to the apostles, or as commissioned
by succession from Christ. They are just there; they are taken for
granted, but no one offers any theological justification for them or
tries to connect the institution of the ordained ministry with the
gospel.

Here perhaps is the important point: Paul cannot directly give us a
theology of the ordained ministry, but can he enable us to connect
the ordained ministry with the gospel? If this can be done, then we

may legitimately use what Paul has to say about ministry as a norm for the functioning and form of the ordained ministry. If the ordained ministry is merely something that happened to crop up by the end of the first century which proved useful in the Church's life thereafter, then all attempts to give it theological justification are vain. But if we can show that in some sense the ordained ministry is integrally connected with the ministry of the Church as a whole, then we need not despair of being able to work out a satisfactory 'doctrine of the ministry' in the modern sense.

Before we proceed to make the attempt, we should comment on the present state of the question. Generally speaking, Catholics rather than Protestants find themselves in an embarrassing position when the topic of the ministry is discussed among informed students of the NT. Protestants on the whole have not very much at stake in the claims which they make about the ministry. Most of them are content to claim that they possess *a* valid, effectual, and scripturally defensible form of ministry, without also claiming that they possess *the* ministry. But Catholics are different in this respect. They claim, and they have always claimed, that they possess *the* valid, regular, normative form of the ministry as approved by God and instituted by Christ. And most Catholics are willing to draw the conclusion that all other forms of the ministry are irregular, defective, possibly invalid, and certainly not really approved by God. The word 'Catholics' here includes Roman Catholics, Eastern Orthodox, and many (perhaps most) Anglicans. The embarrassment to which we refer is the fact that well-informed Catholics are aware that these claims about their ministry cannot be substantiated on biblical and historical grounds. This awareness has only gradually permeated the catholic consciousness. Eastern Orthodox theologians do not seem to be aware of it at all, because they still pursue an ostrich-like policy of ignoring critical scholarship. Roman Catholics have only been permitted to be publicly aware of this situation since about 1950. But now they are increasingly accepting it. Those who read the works of Raymond Brown and Robert Daly in America, and E. Schillebeeckx on the continent of Europe, will realize that these scholars have fully absorbed the message: biblical scholarship does not support the claims made for the catholic ministry even as recently as the documents of Vatican II. Anglo-Catholics have been uneasily aware of the situation ever since about the turn of the century, but only recently have they abandoned the attempt to prove the apostolic succession on biblical and historical grounds. The last effort was the symposium edited by Kenneth Kirk called *The Apostolic Ministry*.[23] Since that date it has become apparent that the arguments used by the scholars who contributed to that symposium have failed to convince the world of biblical scholarship. The catholic doctrine of the ministry is left without a foundation.

There is, however, a spurious defence for the catholic doctrine of the ministry which is often encountered today among catholics aware of the situation, who also know that they cannot fall back on any 'ipse dixit' of ecclesiastical authority, but who are unwilling to modify their doctrine.[24] The defence runs something like this: Jesus appointed the twelve apostles to be the officers of his Church. To the body of the Twelve were added a certain number of individuals, Paul and James the brother of the Lord certainly, and possibly others such as Barnabas. But there was a limited number of the apostles. They in their turn passed their authority on to various individuals in different areas: οἱ προϊστάμενοι in 1 Thess. 5.12; the elders in the church in Jerusalem; Timothy and Titus in the Pauline communities. In Acts we see Paul appointing elders in the churches of Lystra, Iconium, and Pisidian Antioch (Acts 14.21-23). The Pastoral Epistles are usually admitted to be only very doubtfully Pauline, but are used as evidence of what went on in Paul's day. Clement of Rome, who is dated about AD 96, is called in as a witness to a belief in apostolic succession. The reference to ἐπίσκοποι and διάκονοι in Phil. 1.1 is (reasonably enough) cited as evidence that there were ordained ministers in Philippi in Paul's day. Who else could have ordained them but Paul? Put all this together, and we seem to have arrived at the very threshold of our objective, the time of Ignatius of Antioch, when an unimpeachably episcopal ministry has clearly emerged into the light of day.

The fallacies in this argument are many. In the first place, it does not look as if the Twelve were meant to rule the Church. It is much more likely that they were meant to *be* the Church, or at least the nucleus of the Church. Next, the picture we are given of the Twelve exercising apostolic authority in the early Church is not confirmed by our earliest evidence, the Pauline epistles. Paul respects the authority of the Jerusalem church and of its leaders, one of whom, James the brother of the Lord, was not an apostle in the traditional sense. But Paul claims full authority for himself in the churches he himself founded. Another difficulty is that never at any time do we find the Twelve, or any one of the Twelve, passing on anything that looks like ministerial authority to anyone. The various commissionings described in Acts 6.6 and 13.3 do not look like acts of ordination. Paul never directly addresses οἱ προϊστάμενοι in 1 Thessalonians or the household of Stephanas in 1 Corinthians as if they were ministers whom he had ordained. When he gives instructions to his churches he never singles out those who might appear to be ordained ministers. He expects the community as a whole, not merely a group of ministers, to listen and take action. In both the Paulines and the Deutero-Paulines we find lists of functions (1 Cor. 12.28-30; Eph. 4.11), but the way in which the lists pass without a break from functions that look to us as if they might be offices to functions that cannot possibly be official makes one doubt whether the clergy/lay distinction existed when the lists were made. It is true that Luke, as we have seen, represents Paul as appointing presbyters; and in Acts 20.17-35 he represents Paul as calling a group of elders (whom Luke also describes as bishops) to Miletus, and there addressing them under the definite assumption that they had pastoral responsibility. But it seems likely that Luke is reading back into Paul's day conditions that prevailed when Acts was written late in the first century. We never meet the term 'presbyter' used for anyone in the Pauline churches. Clement's evidence is indeed important if he is writing before the end of the first century. But the evidence that was for long believed to connect him with the Flavius Clemens who was put to death by Domitian has recently been questioned. In some ways it would fit the evidence better if Clement belonged to the 120s, by which time of course some sort of an ordained ministry had been established everywhere. Apart from all this, we have surely demonstrated that when Paul wrote of 'apostles' he did not mean the Twelve, whom he never describes as apostles. Paul's apostles were not a limited college, and their aim was to pass on their function to the communities which they had founded, not to clergy whom they had ordained. In a word, the 'catholic' case for the theory that Jesus gave authority in the Church to the twelve apostles, who somehow or other conveyed that authority by ministerial succession to the first bishops, will not stand up to scrutiny. It is, admittedly, a possible explanation of the facts, but it is not so surely established that one can reasonably build a theology of the Church on it, or disqualify other ministries, and perhaps unchurch millions of Christians on the basis of it.

We now return to the question, can what Paul says about the apostolic ministry of his day throw any light by analogy on the ordained ministry that came into existence later? Can we see any connection between the gospel and this ordained ministry? We begin with one thing that both ministries have in common: they exist for the sake of the Church. This may seem obvious, but there are circumstances in which the ordained ministry is tempted to believe that it exists for the sake of its own honour and glory. Simply to be a minister of the Church is enough justification for the office. Or perhaps it is suggested that simply to celebrate the eucharist (the peculiar prerogative of the priest), whether there is anyone else to share in it or not, is some sort of an achievement. We think of those benighted priests who believe they have attained some great feat if they climb to the top of an inaccessible mountain peak and celebrate mass there. No, the ordained ministry exists for the sake of the Church, in order to enable the Church to carry out that ministry which Christ gave it. Thus there is no point in being called a bishop if one never exercises episcopal functions. Or again, the mere fact that as a priest one has celebrated mass, no matter how many times, is nothing to be proud of. The ordained ministry exists for the sake of the Church, just as the eucharist exists for the sake of the Church.

From this it follows that the ordained ministry must not be separated from the Church, and this means the contemporary, local church. This has in fact happened in the course of the centuries. By the year 1500, for example, in the West the ordained ministry was claiming complete domination over the Church. No non-cleric had any rights, in theory at least, as far as concerned ruling the Church or deciding its doctrine. The ministry claimed a God-given privilege to rule and direct the Church in every way, on the basis of the apostolic lineage which it claimed to have received from Christ, without any suggestion that it was responsible to the rest of the Church, i.e. the laity. In the ensuing centuries this claim was pushed to absurd lengths, reaching its climax in 1870 at the First Vatican Council, when the pope virtually claimed the right to rule and direct the Church on his own initiative without reference to anyone else. Ever since Vatican II Roman Catholic theologians have been understandably anxious to modify and explain away this appalling claim. But something very like the same claim is sometimes made by Anglicans:[25] on the basis of an alleged succession from the apostles, it is claimed that the bishops have a right to ordain and consecrate whom they will without reference to the rest of the Church. Such a claim is belied by the history of the first hundred years of the Church, incompatible with Paul's conception of the apostolic ministry, and destructive of the Church's life in practice. In circumstances such as prevailed in the early sixteenth century in the West, when the clergy had secured a stranglehold on the government of the Church and refused to allow reasonable reform, the only alternative was disruption and schism. Only in the most desperate circumstances is so drastic and painful a remedy justifiable.

In fact what happened at the end of the first century was that the ordained ministry began to take over most of the functions which Paul assigns to the apostolic ministry. The community was gradually eclipsed. In a certain measure this may have been inevitable, just as in a certain measure it was inevitable that the eucharist should take the place of the *parousia* hope in the Church's life. But we have observed that for the first three centuries the eucharist still held an eschatological dimension, something which the liturgical movement has recovered for us in our day. Should we not say, then, that the ordained ministry should have an eschatological dimension? The apostolic ministry certainly had such a dimension in Paul's day: it existed in order to enable the people of God in the new age to live out the dying and rising of Christ. The eschatological element in the ordained ministry of today ought to consist in its awareness of being an enabling, pioneering force, an integral part of the people of God, never content unless the people of God is fully exercising its God-given ministry, fully aware of its calling in the new age.

Of course Paul's apostolic ministry was exercised in local communities: we do not find anywhere in the genuine Paul the thought of a catholic ministry operating within a catholic Church. For this we have to wait for the Deutero-Paulines and Ignatius. It is the great glory of the Epistle to the Ephesians that its author had very clearly in his mind the idea of the universal Church, even though we must wait till Ignatius before we meet the word 'catholic'. But can we apply Paul's concept of the apostolic ministry to the catholic Church? We can easily see how a true ministry will operate within a local community to energize it and make it aware of its calling. But can this happen on a wider scale? Only if the ministry in the catholic Church is made responsible to the catholic Church in the same way in which Paul's apostolic ministry is related to the local church. Paul expected each local church to respond to the ministry by ordering its own affairs rightly. If the catholic Church is to respond to a catholic ministry, that Church must be enabled and encouraged to order its own affairs. Ignatius still had some such vision as Paul's as regards each local community: he wanted to see bishop, presbyters, and deacons, and the community as a whole acting together. But the idea that this might operate at a wider level did not make much progress. Cyprian, we know, was very careful to consult his fellow-bishops and fellow-presbyters on the various momentous issues which he had to face.[26] Constantine presumably was regarded as representing the laity when he presided at Nicaea in 325. Only today perhaps, when modern methods of communication enable us to organize representative government in a way never feasible before, are we able even to approximate to the application on a wider scale of what Paul thought right for the relation of the ministry to the local church. Perhaps, if we were writing a treatise in defence of episcopacy, this is where a word might be put in on behalf of the office of bishop. But we must not enlist Paul among its sponsors!

Ministry then is to be exercised in the Church and must always be held responsible to the Church. This does not mean of course a rigid Congregationalism. The phrase 'in the Church' can perfectly legitimately mean 'in the diocese'. But we should heed Schillebeeckx's thesis[27] that ordained ministry was originally intended to be exercised in some specific place, and was not to be regarded as a rank, or status, or privilege. A parallel with the eucharist is relevant here: one normally holds a local eucharist, a parish eucharist perhaps. Here the local Christian community in celebrating the eucharist acts on behalf of the universal Church. One can likewise have a deanery eucharist, or a diocesan eucharist. But is it meaningful to extend it any further than that? It is hardly possible to hold a provincial eucharist or a national eucharist. Perhaps the same limitation might profitably be set to the scope of the ministry: an ordained minister can act within a parish, or a deanery, or a diocese, but one can hardly be meaningfully commissioned for a wider sphere than that. The concrete and personal nature of Christianity would make it undesirable, except in the case of a very few individuals.

Another element in the eschatological dimension to the ordained ministry is its relation to the cross. As we have seen, this was central to Paul's conception of the apostolic ministry. The ministry is called to be a pioneer of the Christian life, in suffering and if need be in dying. But here least of all is it vicarious. It leads this sort of life so that the rest of the Church may lead it. As we have seen, this is an element in the life of the ministry that was well preserved in the post-Pauline period, both in the Pastorals and in Ignatius. History proves also that when persecution comes it is usually the ordained ministry that bears the brunt of it. Despite many shining examples of lay witness and even martyrdom, this is eminently true of the Church in Communist countries today. As long as ordained ministers are true to their vocation, this is an eschatological element in the ministry that will never be forgotten.

Before we turn to questions of validity and priesthood, there is one more point to be made. We have said that the ordained ministry must be responsible to the Church and must not dominate it, as it has in the past. This does not mean that the ministry must be merely the executive instrument of the Church, its willing tool, existing merely in order to carry out the Church's will, a sort of ecclesiastical civil service. This was not Paul's relation to his communities. The ordained ministry must on occasion be ready to condemn, to judge, to oppose the local church. But if it does so, it must not claim some superior authority not available to the rest of the Church. It must not regard itself, as it has in the past in some parts of the Church, as above criticism. Paul was given his ἐξουσία to build up the Church, and used it freely, but he did not claim anything more than what the Spirit gave. Only on the few occasions when he was able to cite a word of the Lord on his side does he give us the impression of not being willing to listen to other Christians. So when a member of the ordained ministry speaks in condemnation of the Church, he must submit to the condition which applies to all Christians when they speak what they believe is in accordance with God's will. They speak by faith; they await God's judgment. They do not claim any infallible knowledge not in principle available to any other Christian.

We have tried to show that Paul's concept of the apostolic ministry can throw some light on what the ordained ministry should be and do today. We now propose to explore a rather more specialized area. Can Paul's writings help us with modern questions about the celebrant of the eucharist, the concept of validity, and the notion of the priesthood of the minister? Since all these questions arose after Paul's day, it would on the face of it seem unlikely. But perhaps something can be gleaned.

As far as the person of the celebrant is concerned, there is no evidence whatever in Paul's writings to suggest that it mattered in the slightest. We may well quote E. Schillebeeckx here:[28]

> If we remember that the early eucharist was structured after the pattern of Jewish grace at meals—the *birkath hamazon*—at which just anyone could preside, it is evident that the leaders of house communities *ipso facto* also presided at the eucharist, and this is also evident from the texts written at the same time as the last part of the New Testament. In the earliest stratum of the Didache the 'prophets and teachers' preside at the eucharist; in a later stratum they are joined by presbyters and deacons who do so by virtue of their office.

In the Pastorals, as we have observed, presiding at the eucharist is not mentioned as one of the activities of either presbyter or bishop. In Ignatius for the first time do we find anything like a demand that the celebrant be rightly authorized. We quote the whole section in Lightfoot's translation (*Smyrn.* 8):

> (But) shun divisions as the beginning of evils. Do ye all follow your bishop, as Jesus Christ followed the Father, and the presbytery as the apostles; and to the deacons pay respect, as to God's commandment. Let no man do aught of things pertaining to the Church apart from the bishop. Let that be held a valid eucharist which is under the bishop or one to whom he shall have committed it.[29]

> Wheresoever the bishop shall appear, there let the people be; even as where Jesus may be, there is the universal Church. It is not lawful apart from the bishop either to baptise or to hold a love-feast; but whatsoever he shall approve, that is well-pleasing also to God; that everything which ye do may be sure and valid.[30]

The principle of Christ's presence in the eucharist is expressed in Matt. 18.20: 'For when two or three are gathered together in my name, there am I in the midst of them'. All that is essential in order that he be present is that the people of God in any place should genuinely intend to celebrate the eucharist. This is not, however, to imply that it does not matter whether an authorized minister presides or not. The eucharist is the Church's rite. It is therefore very appropriate that the Church's authorized representative should preside at the eucharist. We can at least sympathize with Ignatius, who was probably faced with a situation in which a number of factions within the churches in Asia Minor were celebrating the eucharist as a token of their independence of the bishop. But God is not the sort of God who would refuse to be present because the president was not duly authorized. The insistence that the eucharist should be presided over by an ordained minister is a necessary safeguard lest the eucharist should degenerate into a purely private devotion, like the Catholic saying his rosary or the Protestant having his quiet time.

Paul does however give some countenance to the concept of validity in connection with the eucharist. In 1 Cor. 11.17-22 he is dealing with misbehaviour at the celebration of the rite: instead of observing a common feast, the well-off members of the congregation are bringing their own food and eating it by themselves, leaving the poorer members with little or nothing. In these circumstances, says Paul, it is not the Lord's supper that they are celebrating: 'When you meet together, it is not the Lord's supper that you eat'.[31]

Scholars are agreed that this is Paul's meaning. By their behaviour the Corinthians have shown that they have no real intention of celebrating the Lord's supper. Thus Robertson and Plummer say that it is not the Lord's supper, 'for conduct such as this excludes it'. Goudge: 'A supper could be eaten, but it would not be His when there was faction and selfishness'. Foerster[32] contents himself with saying that κυριακὸν δεῖπνον is the same as δεῖπνον κυρίου, on the analogy of τράπεζα κυρίου in 1 Cor. 10.21. J. Behm uses the word 'profaned' for what the Corinthians were doing to the fellowship of the Lord's supper.[33] Weiss says the meaning is: 'It is (morally) impossible to enjoy a Lord's supper ("ein Herren-Mahl") which truly deserves the name κυριακόν'. Barrett is somewhat fuller: it is not to eat a supper in honour of the Lord . . . The supper (as conducted in Corinth) brings no honour to the Lord (as it should do) . . . This was not to eat the *Lord's* supper, but their own'.

In fact it is a defect of intention, not a defect in the person of the celebrant. Now it is perfectly true that the *effectiveness* of the eucharist may be impaired by the way in which it is celebrated. Thus there may be an inadequate understanding of what the eucharist is. I have occasionally encountered this in a flagrant form. I remember attending a eucharist in South India where the celebrant made it apparent from his prayers that, though he knew Jesus had told us to do this, he had no idea why. There are many other ways in which the eucharist can be rendered less effective: the people may be totally excluded from taking any part in it except to be present. There may be gross casualness in carrying out the rite. But there is no support in Paul for the concept certainly found in Ignatius that absence of a duly authorized minister renders the rite no longer valid. We see in this dictum of his just the beginning of that sinister process whereby the ordained ministry obtained possession of the sacraments as if they were their own privileged prerogative and did not belong to the Church as a whole.

Of course it is always open to those who regard as invalid a eucharist presided over by someone whom they consider unauthorized to argue that the very fact of its being celebrated by an unauthorized minister damages the effectiveness of the rite. But 'effectiveness' is not the same thing as 'validity'. The former admits of degrees; the latter poses an absolute 'either/or'. Only a defect in intention can lead to an absolutely invalid eucharist, something that, as Paul says, is not the Lord's supper. Irregularity in the orders of the minister does not imply absence of true intention. Much though we may desire that the eucharist should be presided over by a duly authorized minister, we are not justified in disqualifying the eucharist of any body of Christians as long as we are satisfied that they truly intend to celebrate it when they come together.

Finally, can we find any justification in Paul or in the tradition which immediately succeeded him for describing the Christian minister as a priest (ἱερεύς, *sacerdos*)? At first sight it would seem most improbable. The ordained minister, when he does appear at the end of the NT period, is never called ἱερεύς. The name only begins to be applied to Christian clergy at the beginning of the third century, first to the bishop and then to the presbyter. In the NT itself one can detect a deliberate intention to dissociate the Christian ministry from the Jewish Levitical priesthood. Only at a period much later, when the synagogue was widely separated from the Church, did it become usual to institute comparisons between the two. For NT Christians there was only one sacrifice: Christ had offered himself once for all. The Apologists of the second century boasted that Christians had no sacrifices, no temples, and no priests. It is true that in Rom. 15.16 Paul uses priestly language of his own ministry. But he makes it clear that his ministry consists in preaching the gospel to the Gentiles. He never even faintly suggests that this has anything to do with the eucharist. In Rom. 12.1 he also uses priestly language of the Christian's own dedication of his life to God in Christ.

This may perhaps give us a slight clue: in the NT Christ is the great high priest, but the Church is also described as a priesthood, not in Paul, but in 1 Pet. 2.5, 9; Rev. 1.6; 5.10; 20.6. The 1 Peter passage is of particular interest for two reasons. First, the author indicates what are the spiritual sacrifices which Christians are called to offer. It is the daily sacrifice of themselves to God through Christ in the Spirit. This affords a link with Rom. 12.1. Second, in 1 Pet. 2.9 we are told what our duty is as God's possession: we must proclaim the mighty acts of him who called us out of darkness into his marvellous light. But, when we first have any detailed account of what Christians do when they celebrate the eucharist, proclaiming the mighty acts of God is precisely what we find them engaged in doing. The great thanksgiving prayer, centre of the spoken part of the primitive eucharist, is precisely that.

At the eucharist, then, the Church is performing a priestly act: it is offering itself and it is offering its praises. All is done of course to God through Christ in the Spirit (Eph. 2.18). In as far as he who presides at the eucharist represents the Church he is engaged in a priestly activity and can be legitimately described as a priest. Indeed, since the Church as a whole has a priestly relation to the world, the Church's minister as the Church's representative has a priestly rôle to play. But this priesthood of the minister, seen most clearly perhaps at the eucharist because this is the rite where the Church expresses most clearly its own being and nature and relation to God, must not be regarded as something peculiar to himself apart from the Church. Apart from the Church's priesthood, he has none of his own. At the eucharist he has no sacrifice of his own to offer apart from the Church's sacrifice. He does not represent Christ to the Church by some direct gift not mediated through the Church. There is no justification whatever in the NT, or for a very long time after it, for the concept of a sacrificing priesthood as set out in Leo XII's Bull of 1896 *Apostolicae Curae*. Nor must we object if some parts of the Church prefer to describe the minister as 'presbyter'. This term has a foundation in the NT, which the term 'priest' conspicuously lacks. The reason why the Church of England continued to use the word 'priest' at the time of the Reformation was in order to demonstrate its intention to continue the orders of the mediaeval Church un-interruptedly. At the same time the Ordinal of the Book of Common Prayer made it equally plain that the term was to be cleansed of the mistaken associations which had accrued during the Dark Ages.

There is no *theological* justification to be drawn from Paul's letters for refusing ordination to the priesthood to women. Or rather, if we attempt to accept Paul's theology here we shall find ourselves in very great difficulties. He objected to the leadership of women in any sphere because Eve was formed out of Adam and was therefore necessarily subordinate to him (see 1 Cor. 11.2-16). Only if we are prepared to accept Gen. 2.18-25 with the same literalness that Paul did will we be free to use his argument. In any case, Paul's argument proves far too much for our comfort. If we object to the ordination of women on Pauline principles, we must object just as strongly to women head-teachers, women judges, women cabinet ministers, and women monarchs. We would find ourselves in the company of the Old Believers of Russia. If we concentrate on what Paul says about the apostolic ministry, we will find no obstacle to women having a part in what is its nearest equivalent today, the ordained ministry of the Church.

*****

We have come a long way since we began our quest with those mysterious verses in 1 Corinthians 4. But I believe we have pursued what is the right methodology for a biblically based theology today. We began from a problem not unconnected with modern questions which we found in scripture. We have examined this problem to the best of our ability by critical methods. We have ended by trying to determine how far our investigations have a bearing on some of the theological questions facing the Church today, and we have found, I hope, that they do throw some much needed light on our questions. Perhaps it is an indication of the correctness of our method that it has produced theological conclusions which might well form the basis for a fruitful ecumenical dialogue between Catholics and Protestants in the West.

NOTES

Notes to Chapter 1

1. 'I Corinthians 4[13b] and Lamentations 3[45]', *ET* 93 (1982), 7, 214.

2. E. Güttgemanns, *Der Leidende Apostel und sein Herr: Studien zur Paulischen Christologie* (Göttingen, 1966).

3. M.D. Hooker, '"Beyond the Things which are Written": an Examination of I Cor. iv.6', *NTS* 10 (1963), pp. 127-32.

4. J. Weiss, *Der Erste Korintherbrief* (Göttingen, 1910), my translation.

5. H. Conzelmann, *I Corinthians, a Commentary on the First Epistle to the Corinthians* (ET: Philadelphia, 1975 of German edn, Göttingen, 1969).

6. F.J. Ortkemper, 'Wir verkünden Christus als den Gekreuzigten (I Kor 1,23)', *Bibel und Kirche* 23 (1968/1), pp. 5-12, my translation.

7. H. Lietzmann (ed. G. Kümmel), *An die Korinther I und II*, 5th edn, (Tübingen, 1969).

8. A.J.M. Wedderburn, 'ἐν τῇ σοφίᾳ τοῦ θεοῦ 1 Kor 1.21', *ZNW* 64 (1973), pp. 132-34.

9. A. Robertson and A. Plummer, *A Critical and Exegetical Commentary on the First Epistle of St. Paul to the Corinthians* (Edinburgh, 1911).

10. H.L. Goudge, *The First Epistle to the Corinthians* (London, 1903).

11. J.F. Stenning, *The Targum of Isaiah* (Oxford, 1953).

12. U. Wilckens, art. σοφία, in *TWNT*, VII (Stuttgart, 1964), pp. 518-42.

13. P. Billerbeck, *Die Briefe des Neuen Testaments und die Offenbarung Johannis erläutert aus Talmud und Midrasch* (vol. 3 of full work) (3rd edn; Munich, 1961), *in loc.* 1 Cor. 1.20.

14. K. Müller, '1 Kor 1,18-25, Die eschatologischkritische Funktion der Verkündigung des Kreuzes', *Biblische Zeitschrift* 10 (1966), pp. 246-72.

15. I have discussed this Synoptic logion in an article 'Two Consciousnesses: the Modern Version of Chalcedon' in *The Scottish Journal of Theology* 37 (1984), pp. 471-83, where I have argued for its authenticity.

16. W. Bender, 'Bemerkungen zur Übersetzung von 1 Korinther 1.30', *ZNW* 71 (1980), pp. 263-28.

17. R. Penna 'La δύναμις θεοῦ—Riflessioni in Margine a I Cor. 1.18-25', *Rivista Biblica* (Brescia) 15 (1967), pp. 781-94.

18. I have argued for this in my book *The New Testament Interpretation of Scripture* (London, 1980), pp. 21-96.

19. J. Héring, *La Première Epître de Saint Paul aux Corinthiens* (Neuchâtel and Paris, 1949).

20. B. Schaller, 'Zum Textcharacter der Hiobzitate im paulischen

Schrifttum', *ZNW* 7 (1980), pp. 21-26.

21.   C.K. Barrett, *The Second Epistle to the Corinthians* (London, 1973). A. Plummer (*A Critical and Exegetical Commentary on the Second Epistle of Paul to the Corinthians*, Edinburgh, 1915) paraphrases with *nostro ministerio*.

22.   *Sic* R. Bultmann, *Der Zweite Brief an die Korinther* (ed. E. Dinkler; Göttingen, 1976).

23.   H.L. Goudge, *The Second Epistle to the Corinthians* (London, 1927).

24.   H. Schlier, art. ἀμήν in *TDNT*, I, pp. 335-38.

25.   R.H. Strachan, *The Second Epistle of Paul to the Corinthians* (London, 1935).

26.   J. Héring, *La Seconde Épître de Saint Paul aux Corinthiens* (Neuchatel and Paris, 1958).

27.   H. Lietzmann, *An die Korinther I/II* (ed. W.G. Kümmel; 5th edn; Tübingen, 1969).

28.   T.F. Torrance, 'One Aspect of the Biblical Conception of Faith', *ET* 68 (1957), pp. 111-14.

29.   O.C. Whitehouse, *Isaiah xl-lxvi* (London, n.d.); B. Duhm, *Das Buch Jesaia* (Göttingen, 1922); J. Skinner, *Isaiah Chapters xl-lxi* (Cambridge, 1954; reprint of 1916); G.H. Box, *The Book of Isaiah* (new impression, London, 1916); R.N. Whybray, *Isaiah 40-66* (London, 1975).

30.   F. Delitzsch, *The Prophecies of Isaiah*, II (ET: Edinburgh, 1890).

31.   P.E. Bonnard, *Le Seconde Isaïe; son Disciple et leurs Editeurs* (Paris, 1972), my translation.

32.   E.J. Kissane, *The Book of Isaiah*, vol. II (Dublin, 1943).

33.   J. Ziegler, ed., *Isaias in Septuaginta Acad. Litt. Gottingensis*, vol. xiv (Göttingen, 1967).

34.   W.H. Brownlee, 'Messianic Motifs in Qumran and the New Testament, II', *NTS* 3 (1957), pp. 195-201.

35.   See E. Hill, 'The Construction of Three Passages from St. Paul', *CBQ* 2 (1961), pp. 298-99. He tentatively suggests that δόξα might almost mean 'the doxology', the act of praise, perhaps a technical term for a part of the service, like the Sanctus in later liturgy. At any rate it includes, he holds, the meaning 'the glory we give to God in worship'.

Notes to Chapter 2

1.   Some MSS have inserted here those elements in the logion which Luke records and Matthew omits; but it is a pretty clear example of copyists being influenced by their knowledge of Luke's text.

2.   This follows the Syriac; the MT has ואני תפלה 'and I prayer'.

3.   *Midrash on the Psalms*, ed. W.G. Braude (New Haven, 1959), II, p. 203.

4. J. Jeremias, *Die Sprache des Lukasevangeliums* (Göttingen, 1980), p. 142.

5. R. Bultmann, *The History of the Synoptic Tradition* (ET Oxford, 1968 of the 2nd German edn, Göttingen, 1931), pp. 96, 105.

6. C.G. Montefiore, *The Synoptic Gospels* vol. II (2nd edn; London, 1927).

7. *Op. cit.*, vol. I, on Matt. 5.44.

8. H.W. Beyer, art. εὐλογεῖν in *TWNT*, II (Stuttgart, 1950), pp. 751-63.

9. In this section I draw freely on my article in *ET* referred to above (ch. 1, n. 1).

10. C.H. Toy, *Proverbs* (Edinburgh, 1904).

11. F. Hauck, art. περικάθαρμα in *TWNT*, III (Stuttgart, 1950), p. 434.

12. G. Stählin, art. περίψημα in *TWNT*, VI (Stuttgart, 1959), pp. 86-91.

13. See *Gottingensis* vol. XV (Göttingen, 1976).

14. A. Sperber, *The Bible in Aramaic*, III, *The Hagiographa* (Leiden, 1968).

15. There is more vocabulary in common in the Hebrew than in the Greek. The MT of Lam. 3.30a is יתן למכהו לחי. The MT of Isa. 50.6a is וגוי נתתי למכים ולחיי למרטים.

16. E.-B. Allo, *Première Epître aux Corinthiens* (2nd edn; Paris, 1956).

17. W. Straub, *Die Bildersprache des Apostels Paulus* (Tübingen, 1937), p. 50.

18. We argue in Chapter 6 (pp. 115f.) that these words mean 'God has appointed us', not 'God has exhibited us'.

19. *Op. cit.*, p. 99.

20. H.D. Betz, *Nachfolge und Nachahmung Jesu Christi im Neuen Testament* (Tübingen, 1967), p. 174.

Notes to Chapter 3

1. I assume that Col. 1-3 is post-Pauline, so Col. 2.3 is no exception to this statement.

2. The LXX has translated the MT quite accurately איכה נחשבו לנבלי־ חרש מעשי ידי יוצר.

3. W. Schmiedel, *Hand-Commentar zum Neuen Testament*, II (Freiburg, 1891).

4. H. Windisch, *Der zweite Korintherbrief* (Göttingen, 1924).

5. Compare also W. Straub, *Die Bildersprache des Apostels Paulus* (Tübingen, 1937), p. 60, where he concludes that the emphasis is on the value of the treasure compared with the worthlessness of the containers, and that there may also be a suggestion of the fragility of the containers.

6. G.H. Box and W.O.E. Oesterley (eds.), 'Sirach', in R.H. Charles,

Apocrypha and Pseudepigrapha of the Old Testament, I (Oxford, 1913).

7. A.H. McNeile, *The Gospel according to St. Matthew* (London, 1938).

8. F.W. Beare, *The Gospel according to Matthew* (Oxford, 1981).

9. J.M. Creed, *The Gospel according to Matthew* (London, 1930).

10. E. Klostermann, *Das Lukasevangelium* (3rd edn; Tübingen, 1975).

11. *History of the Synoptic Tradition*, pp. 77, 84, 93.

12. This is Lagrange's conclusion. See M.-J. Lagrange, *Evangile selon Saint Matthieu* (7th edn; Paris, 1948): 'le plus pur rythme, sémitique, lentement balancé'.

13. A. Plummer, *A Critical and Exegetical Commentary on the Gospel according to St. Matthew* (London, 1909).

14. M.-J. Lagrange, *Evangile selon Saint Luc* (3rd edn; Paris, 1977).

15. E. Schweizer, *The Good News according to Matthew* (ET London, 1975; German edn; Göttingen, 1973).

16. Billerbeck quotes as parallels Tobit 4.8f. and *Apoc. Baruch* 14.12. But the parallel is not very close. Tobit tells his son that almsgiving will ensure protection by God in time of danger. The other quotation runs: 'The righteous await the end cheerfully and enter into that life without fear, because they have with them a treasure of works which is preserved up in the storehouses'. This is much closer to the sentiment of Luke 12.32, but not very close to that of Jesus himself.

17. The Hebrew in each place is עצב.

18. The EVV end ch. 8 at v. 22 and make what is v. 23 in the Hebrew and Greek into 9.1.

19. These comments are made in Bultmann's commentary. We refer to his article in *TWNT* below.

20. B.M. Ahern, 'The Fellowship of his Sufferings', *CBQ* 22 (1960), pp. 1-32.

21. N. Baumert, *Täglich Sterben und Auferstehen, der Literalsinn von 2 Kor 4,12–5,10* (Munich, 1973), pp. 72-73.

22. C.M. Proudfoot, 'Imitation or Realistic Participation', *Interpretation* 17 (1963), pp. 140-60. In fact, as we indicate below, this translation is lexicographically improbable.

23. See R. Bultmann, art. νέκρωσις in *TWNT*, IV (Stuttgart, 1942), p. 899.

24. J.H. Moulton and G. Milligan, *The Vocabulary of the Greek New Testament* (London, 1951).

25. P. 6 R.

26. J. Dupont, *Gnosis: La Connaissance Religieuse dans les Epitres de Saint Paul* (Louvain and Paris, 1949), p. 107.

27. I have fully expounded this passage in *Jesus Christ in the Old Testament* (London, 1965), pp. 145-46.

28. F. Buhl (ed.), 'Psalms' in R. Kittel's *Biblia Hebraica* (Stuttgart, 1945), suggests on the basis of the Greek διό that the Hebrew may originally have

read לכן for כי.

29. It is interesting that the Vulgate has the same arrangement as the Greek. It runs as follows (115.1): 'Credidi propter quod locutus sum; ego autem humiliatus sum nimis'. It has thus inverted the sense of the Greek, indicating that the psalmist believed because he spoke. But it is no nearer to the meaning of the MT.

30. Quoted in Billerbeck, *in loc.*, 2 Cor. 4.13.

Notes to Chapter 4

1. I have expounded this passage at greater length in *Jesus Christ in the Old Testament*, pp. 147-52.

2. *Tractate Berakoth* 8a, ed. M. Simon (London, 1948) in the *Babylonian Talmud*, ed. I. Epstein (London, 1838), p. 38.

3. I have already discussed this question in *Jesus Christ in the Old Testament*, pp. 153f. and cf. my *Studies in Paul's Technique and Theology* (London, 1974), pp. 14f. I originally brought it up in an article in *Hermathena* 73 (1949), pp. 69-72, called 'The Interpretation of the Second Person Singular in Quotations from the Psalms in the New Testament'.

4. M.-J. Lagrange, *St. Paul: Epitre aux Romains* (Paris, 1915; reprint 1950); O. Michel, *Der Brief an die Römer* (5th edn; Göttingen, 1966); C.E.B. Cranfield, *The Epistle to the Romans*, II (6th edn; Edinburgh, 1975); E. Käsemann, *An die Römer* (Tübingen, 1973).

5. W. Sanday and A.C. Headlam, *A Critical and Exegetical Commentary on the Epistle to the Romans* (5th edn; Edinburgh, 1902).

6. D. Worley, 'He Was Willing', *Restoration Quarterly* 18/1 (Abilene, Texas) (1975), pp. 1-11.

7. The alternatives τῆς ἀγάπης τοῦ θεοῦ and τοῦ θεοῦ τῆς ἐν Χριστῷ Ἰησοῦ are not well supported in the MSS. The latter is obviously influenced by v. 39.

8. עורה and קומה respectively in the MT.

9. I have discussed the significance of Paul's use of Psalm 44 more fully in *Studies in Paul's Technique and Theology*, pp. 36-38.

10. See *Tractate Gittin* (ed. M. Simon; London, 1936 in *BT*) 57b, pp. 267-68. See also Billerbeck, *in loc.*

11. W.G. Braude (ed.), *The Midrash on the Psalms* (New Haven, 1959), I, p. 149 (on Ps. 91).

12. G. Delling, 'Die Entfaltung des "Deus Pro Nobis" in Röm 8,31-39', *Studien zur Neuen Testament und seiner Umwelt* (1970), IV, pp 76-96.

13. In neither case is the LXX accurately rendering the MT. In v. 6 'the Lord has laid upon him the iniquity of us all' would be a more correct translation; and in v. 12 'he poured out his life to death' is nearer the sense.

14. G. von Münderlein, 'Interpretation einer Tradition: Bemerkungen zu Röm 8,35f', *Kerygma und Dogma* 11 (1965), pp. 136-42.

15. In fact the Book of Wisdom provides an exception to this; see Wisdom 12.20-22.

16. H.W. Beyer, art. διακονία in *TWNT*, II (Stuttgart 1950), pp. 87-88.

17. P. Fiedler, 'Röm 8,31-39 als Brennpunkt paulinischer Frohbotschaft', *ZNW* 68 (1977), pp. 23-24.

18. περίστασις is used once in the LXX in Ezek. 26.8 for 'a roof of shields', and in 2 Macc. 4.16 for 'difficult situation' which those who have rejected the law have brought upon themselves. On the other hand Symmachus uses περιστάσεις in Ps. 33.5 (MT 34.5; EVV 34.6) to translate מגורותי 'troubles', where LXX has παροικιῶν. The word מגורה means 'horror' from a root גור meaning 'to be afraid'. The LXX has derived it from גור 'to be a stranger'. Symm. has got the right sense.

19. J. Behm, art. νηστεία, in *TWNT*, IV (Stuttgart, 1942), p. 926.

20. G. Bertram, art. παιδεύειν in *TWNT*, V (Stuttgart, 1954), p. 623.

21. Collange rightly dismisses the alternative reading πειραζόμενοι for παιδευόμενοι.

22. *History of the Synoptic Tradition*, p. 110.

23. E. Lohmeyer, *Das Evangelium des Matthäus* (ed. W. Schmauch; 3rd edn; Göttingen, 1962).

24. W. Nauck, 'Freude im Leiden: zum Problem einer urchristlichen Verfolgungstradition', *ZNW* 46 (1955), pp. 68-80.

25. J.S. Pobee, *Persecution and Martyrdom in the Theology of St. Paul* (Sheffield, 1985), pp. 28, 55, 67.

26. W.C. Allen, *A Critical and Exegetical Commentary on the Gospel according to St. Matthew* (3rd edn; Edinburgh, 1912).

27. E. Schweizer gives the reference 1QM 14.6-7; see also F. Beare, *in loc.* Matt. 5.3.

28. E. Bammel, art. πτωχός, in *TWNT*, IV, pp. 903-904.

29. F. Hauck and W. Kasch, art. πλοῦτος, in *TWNT*, VI (Stuttgart, 1959), p. 327.

30. *Abodah Zarah*, ed. I. Epstein (in *BT*; London, 1935), p. 107.

31. W.G. Braude (ed.), *Pesikta Rabbati* (New Haven and London, 1968), *Piska* 29/30, A5, II, pp. 576-79.

32. Vol. II, pp. 364f.

33. *Pesikta de Rab Kahana*, ed. W.G. Braude and I.J. Kapstein (London, 1975), *Piska* 16, p. 292 and especially Supplement 5.4, p. 484.

34. D.L. Mealand in 1976 published an article '"As Having nothing yet possessing everything" 2 Kor 6,10c' in *ZNW* 67, pp. 277-79, in which he claimed that Paul's epigram 'having nothing yet possessing all things' originated in Hellenistic popular ethics. He quotes Pseudo-Crates *Ep.* 7, ἔχοντες μηδὲν πάντ᾽ ἔχομεν. As a matter of fact Hans Windisch had already noted this remarkable parallel (see Windisch, comm. *in loc.*). Mealand's

conclusion is (p. 279): 'It is hardly surprising that a rhetorical commonplace should appear in the Pauline Epistles, in view of the use Paul makes of the diatribe style . . . Paul uses occasional ideas and sentences of this kind. But he builds them into a theological and ethical framework which is quite different from that of the philosophers'. All this is no doubt true, but I find it hard to believe that Paul deliberately borrowed from a Cynic philosopher. Mealand quotes similar sentiments from Philo (p. 278). It seems to me more likely that any influence on Paul from Cynicism came through a Jewish milieu.

35. On pages 43-44 above we have already discussed this to some extent.

36. V.P. Furnish, *Theology and Ethics in Paul* (Nashville and New York, 1968).

37. D.L. Dungan, *The Sayings of Jesus in the Churches of Paul* (Oxford, 1971), p. 3.

38. B. Fjärstedt, *Synoptic Tradition in I Corinthians* (Uppsala, 1974).

39. Fjärstedt, pp. 139f.

40. D.C. Allison, 'The Pauline Epistles and the Synoptic Gospels: The Pattern of the Parallels', *NTS* 28 (1982), pp. 12-32.

41. C.M. Tuckett, 'I Corinthians and Q', *JBL* (1983/4), pp. 607-19.

42. *Art. cit.*, pp. 607-608, 610-11, 619.

43. O. Betz, 'Die Menschensohnworte Jesu und die Zukunftserwartung des Paulus (Daniel 7.13-14)', in *Jesus und das Danielbuch in Arbeiten zum Neuen Testament und Judentum*, II, ed. O. Betz (Frankfurt, 1985), p. 142.

44. A.J.M. Wedderburn, 'Paul and Jesus: The Problem of Continuity', *SJT* 38 (1985), pp. 189-203.

Notes to Chapter 5

1. J.B. Lightfoot, *St. Paul's Epistle to the Philippians* (London, 1890).

2. R.A. Lipsius, *Die Briefe an die Galater, Römer, Philipper* (Freiburg, 1891).

3. E. Lohmeyer, *Die Briefe an die Philipper, die Kolosser, an Philemon* (8th edn; Göttingen, 1961).

4. See Pobee, pp. 55, 67, 92, 96.

5. J.-F. Collange, *L'Epitre de Saint Paul aux Philippiens* (Neuchâtel, 1973).

6. R.P. Martin, *Philippians* (London, 1976).

7. In Polybius ἐξανάστασις can mean a removal or deportation; elsewhere in profane Greek it can mean a getting out of bed, or even, in the papyri, a woman's ornament.

8. See O. Betz, art. στίγμα in *TWNT*, VII (Stuttgart, 1964), pp. 657-64.

9. Martin Luther, *Commentary on Galatians*, ed. P.S. Watson (London, 1953).

10. *Ioannis Calvini in Novum Testamentum Commentarii*, ed. A. Tholuck, V (Berlin, 1834) (my tr.).

11. M.-J. Lagrange, *Saint Paul, Epitre aux Galates* (2nd edn; Paris, 1925).

12. *Op. cit.*, pp. 59-60, 162.

13. H. Schlier, *Der Brief an die Galater* (Göttingen, 1962).

14. *Op. cit.*, pp. 126-34.

15. J. Bligh, *Galatians: A Study of St. Paul's Epistle* (London, 1969), pp. 496-97.

16. W. Klassen, 'Galatians 6.17', *ET* 81 (1969-70), p. 278.

17. U. Borse, 'Die Wundmale und der Todesbescheid', *Biblische Zeitschrift* 14 (1970), pp. 88-111.

18. 'Durch die Leiden seines Aposteldienstes hat Paulus Anteil am Tod Jesus' (p. 102).

19. G. Ebeling, *Die Wahrheit des Evangeliums* (Tübingen, 1981), p. 353.

20. Pobee, p. 95.

21. H. Koester, 'The Purpose of the Polemic of a Pauline Fragment', *NTS* 8 (1961/2), pp. 317-32.

22. A.F.J. Klijn, 'Paul's Opponents in Philippians iii', *Nov. T.* 7 (1965), pp. 278-84.

23. J. Gnilka, 'Die antipaulinische Mission in Philippi', *Biblische Zeitschrift* 9 (1965/2), pp. 258-76.

24. H.D. Betz, *Nachfolge und Nachahmung Jesu Christi im Neuen Testament* (Tübingen, 1967).

25. M.E. Glasswell, 'New Wine in Old Wine Skins; VIII Circumcision', *ET* 85 (1973/4), pp. 328-32.

26. The MT is שפכה כרות. κατατομή is only used once in biblical Greek, in Symm.'s rendering of Jer. 48(31).37, where it apparently means 'ritual cutting off of hair'. Paul seems to be the first to use it of cutting the flesh. This makes a ref. to Deut. 23.2 less likely. But see H. Koester, art. κατατομή in *TWNT*, VIII (Stuttgart, 1969), p. 111, where he argues that Paul's opponents in Philippi did urge circumcision on their converts.

27. A.T. Lincoln, *Paradise Now and Not Yet* (Cambridge, 1981), p. 89.

28. Dupont, p. 321.

29. Bultmann, art. γνῶσις, p. 709.

30. Wilckens, art. σοφία, p. 520.

31. Güttgemanns, pp. 63-64, 68-69.

32. R. Jewett, *Dating Paul's Life* (London, 1979).

33. I have not tried to fit Galatians into this scheme, even though Galatians has contributed something to our understanding of it.

34. I agree with H.D. Betz that the attack on Libertinism in Phil. 3.18-19 does not refer to the Judaizers but to a different category of people in

Philippi.
35. *Op. cit.*, pp. 52, 58.
36. O. Michel, art. κυών, κυνάριον, in *TWNT*, III, pp. 1100-1104.
37. F. Lang, art. σκύβαλον in *TWNT*, VII, pp. 446-48.
38. *Art. cit.*, p. 264.
39. *Op. cit.*, p. 90.
40. T.A. Burkill, 'The Syrophoenician Woman; the consequence of Mark 7. 24-31', *ZNW* 57 (1966), pp. 23-37, and 'The Historical Development of the Story of the Syrophoenician Woman (Mark vii: 24-31)', *Nov. T.* 9 (1967), pp. 161-77.
41. *Nov. T.* 9 (1967), pp. 172-73.
42. A. Dermience, 'Tradition et rédaction dans la péricope de la Syrophénicienne', *Revue Théologique de Louvain* 8 (1977/1), pp. 15-29.
43. G. Salmon, *The Human Element in the Gospels*, ed. N.J.D. White (London, 1907), p. 142.
44. E.P. Gould, *A Critical and Exegetical Commentary on the Gospel according to St. Mark* (Edinburgh, 1896).
45. A.E. Rawlinson, *St. Mark* (6th edn; London, 1925).
46. H.B. Swete, *The Gospel according to St. Mark* (3rd edn; London, 1927).
47. B.H. Branscomb, *The Gospel of Mark* (London, 1937).
48. V. Taylor, *The Gospel according to St. Mark* (London, 1952).
49. J. Jeremias, *Jesus' Promise to the Nations* (ET London, 1958; German edn: Stuttgart, 1956).
50. *History of the Synoptic Tradition*, pp. 39, 64, 155.
51. S.E. Johnson, *A Commentary on the Gospel according to St. Mark* (London, 1960).
52. M.-J. Lagrange, *Evangile selon Saint Marc* (4th edn; Paris, 1966).
53. E. Lohmeyer, *Das Evangelium des Markus* (10th edn; Göttingen, 1937).
54. J. Schmid, *The Gospel according to St. Mark* (ET Cork, 1968 of 5th German edn).
55. B. Flammer, 'Die Syrophoenizerin Mk. 7.24-30', *Theologische Quartalschrift* 148 (1968/4), pp. 463-78.
56. E. Haenchen, *Der Weg Jesu* (2nd edn; Berlin, 1968), p. 27.
57. E. Schweizer, *The Good News according to Mark* (ET Richmond, Virginia, 1970).
58. E. Klostermann, *Das Markusevangelium* (5th edn; Tübingen, 1971).
59. J.D.M. Derrett, 'Law in the New Testament; The Syro-Phoenician Woman and the Centurion of Capernaum', *Nov. T.* 15 (1973), pp. 161-86.
60. G. Schwarz, 'ΣΤΡΟΦΟΙΝΙΚΙΣΣΑ ΧΑΝΑΝΑΙΑ (Markus 7.26/ Matthäus 15.22)', *NTS* 30 (1984), pp. 626-27.

Notes to Chapter 6

1. The LXX has ἡ ταπείνωσις αὐτῆς.

2. *Comm. on 2 Corinthians, in loc.* 10.5. There is in fact no direct verbal connection between our passage and Genesis 11 in the LXX. There the builders are described as wishing to build a πόλις and a πύργος, neither of which words is used by Paul. But the resemblance of thought is undeniable.

3. A.J. Malherbe, 'Antisthenes and Odysseus and Paul at War', *Harvard Theological Review* 76/2 (1983), pp. 143-73.

4. H.D. Betz, *Der Apostel Paul und die sokratische Tradition* (Tübingen, 1972).

5. R. Le Déaut (ed.), *Targum du Pentateuque. I. Genèse* (Sources Chrétiennes; Paris, 1978), *in loc.*

6. See J.W. Etheridge, *The Targums of Onkelos and Jonathan ben Uzziel on the Pentateuch* (new impression; New York, 1968), *in loc.*

7. *Sanhedrin* 109a, vol. II, p. 748 (ed. H. Freedman; London, 1937). This Rabbi Shila was a Babylonian Amora of the third generation. Rabbi Jeremiah b. Eleazar is also an Amora of the third generation, but a Palestinian. In the same passage in *Sanhedrin* R. Nathan is cited as saying that they wanted to make themselves a god. R. Nathan is nearer NT times, being a Tanna of the second generation.

8. *Midrash on the Psalms*, I, 17, on Ps. 1.13.

9. *Midrash on the Psalms*, I, 545, on Ps. 68.11; cf. *Pesikta Rabbati*, P. 14.10, 284.

10. *Pesikta de Rab Kahana*, 4.4, 75.

11. For a justification of this statement see *Studies in Paul's Technique and Theology*, p. 146 n. 25.

12. See *The NT Interpretation of Scripture*, pp. 135-41.

13. W. Heidland, art. ὀχύρωμα in *TWNT*, V (Stuttgart, 1954), pp. 590-91.

14. O. Bauernfeind, art. στρατεία in *TWNT*, VII, p. 710.

15. F. Hauck and S. Schulz, art. πραΰτης, in *TWNT*, VI (Stuttgart, 1959), pp. 650f.; O. Preisker, art. ἐπιείκεία in *TWNT*, II (Stuttgart, 1950), pp. 586f.

16. W. Heidland, art. λογισμός in *TWNT*, IV (Stuttgart, 1942), p. 290.

17. *Op. cit.*, p. 92.

18. G. Bertram, art. ὕψος, etc. in *TWNT*, VIII (Stuttgart, 1969), pp. 611-13.

19. The Vulgate has the same sense as the LXX 'leva manus tuas in superbias eorum in finem'.

20. *Art. cit.*, ὕψος etc., p. 611.

21. *Greek-English Lexicon of the New Testament, based on Grimm's Wilke's Clavis Novi Testamenti*, ed. J.H. Thayer (4th edn; Edinburgh, 1905).

22. αἰχμαλωτίζοντες, the only significant phrase that we have not yet examined, comes into consideration in Part III of this chapter.

23. J. Moffatt, *A New Translation of the Bible* (revised edn; London, 1934).

24. For an extended study of Col. 2.14-15 see *Studies in Paul's Technique etc.*, pp. 1-12.

25. G. Delling, art. θριαμβεύειν in *TWNT*, IV, pp. 159-60.

26. A.-M. Denis, 'La fonction apostolique et la liturgie nouvelle en esprit', *Revue des Sciences Philosophiques et Théologiques* (Paris, 1958), pp. 401-36.

27. L. Williamson, Jr, 'Led in Triumph, Paul's Use of *Thriambeuō*', *Interpretation* 22 (1968), pp. 317-32.

28. P. Marshall, 'A Metaphor of Social Shame: ΘΡΙΑΜΒΕΥΕΙΝ in 2 Cor. 2.14', *Nov. T.* (1983/4), pp. 307-17.

29. R.B. Egan, 'Lexical Evidence on Two Pauline Passages', *Nov. T.* 19 (1977), pp. 34-61.

30. T.W. Manson, '2 Cor. 2.14-17: Suggestions towards an Exegesis', in J.N. Sevenster and W.C. Van Unnik (eds.), *Studia Paulina* (Haarlem, 1953), pp. 155-62.

31. In 6.2 it is the saints and not the apostles who are to judge the world.

32. It is also found in Theodotion's version.

33. The Aramaic is והשלמה.

34. *Op. cit.*, p. 1.

35. *Op. cit.*, p. 54.

36. G. Kittel, art. θέατρον in *TWNT*, III (Stuttgart, 1956), pp. 142-43.

37. This is the LXX translation of בני אלהים in Job 1.6; 2.1.

38. Cited by Kittel in *op. cit.*, p. 43.

39. *Ignatius Epistles*, ed. J.B. Lightfoot (London, 1891), p. 118.

40. *Op. cit.*, p. 45.

41. It has often been pointed out that as a Roman citizen Paul was exempt from the punishment of being thrown to the beasts. Defenders of the literal interpretation reply however that as a Roman citizen he was exempt from being beaten with rods; but by his own testimony this happened to him three times.

42. Appian *Bell. Civ.* 104.2.61, quoted in Grimm–Thayer, *sub* θηρίον.

43. J.B. Lightfoot, *op. cit.*, p. 121.

44. R.E. Osborne, 'Paul and the Wild Beasts', *JBL* 85 (1965), pp. 225-30.

45. In the MT 'beasts' is בהמות, LXX θηρίων.

46. A.J. Malherbe, 'The Beasts at Ephesus', *JBL* 87 (1968), pp. 71-80.

47. *Ta'anith*, ed. J. Rabbinowitz (London, 1938), p. 48.

48. MT אל תתן לחית נפש תורך; cf. also Ps. 68(67).31 (EVV 68.30). E. Kamlah ('Wie beurteilt Paulus sein Leiden? Ein Beitrag zur Untersuchung seiner Denkstruktur', *ZNW* 5 [1963], p. 218) suggests that Paul's language in

1 Cor. 15.32 is influenced by Ps. 22.13-14.

49. Aram. חיוא.

50. D.R. MacDonald in an article in the *Harvard Theological Review* 72 (1980), pp. 266-76, has advanced an ingenious theory that the story of Paul's fighting with beasts in Ephesus was a legend originating in the Corinthian church, instigated by the painting in the amphitheatre referred to in Osborne's article, which itself was based on an Androcles legend. Paul really means 'If, according to your absurd belief about me, I really had fought with beasts in Ephesus, what good would it have done me, if Christ is not risen?'. But in order to establish this thesis he has to treat the phrase ἣν ἔχω ἐν Ἰησοῦ Χριστῷ τῷ κυρίῳ ἡμῶν as a gloss without any MS support whatever, not to mention the extreme unlikelihood that Paul, if such a legend had grown up in so short a time, should refer to it in so allusive and cursory a manner.

51. *Op. cit.*, pp. 99-100.

52. So Goudge, Héring, Bultmann, Barrett, Collange (p. 296).

53. J.M. Court, 'Right and Left: The Implications for Matthew 25.31-46', *NTS* 31 (1985), pp. 223-33.

54. A similar equivalence is found in Hos 11.8 in connection with Aquila's version. The MT has אמגנך; LXX offers ὑπερασπιῶ σου, and Aquila ὅπλῳ κυκλώσω σε. Here both Greek translators have mistaken the root מגן 'to deliver up' for מגן 'shield'.

55. Etheridge, pp. 201-202.

56. *Ibid.*, p. 203.

57. Of course the most extensive treatment of the Christian's armour occurs in Eph. 6.13-17. But I regard this as having been written by a member of the Pauline school in the generation after Paul's death.

58. This point is made by Haenchen in *Der Weg Jesu*, pp. 146f. and E. Klostermann, *Das Lukasevangelium* (3rd edn; Tübingen, 1975), *in loc.* Luke 11.21-22.

59. *History of the Synoptic Tradition*, p. 61.

60. *Ibid.*, p. 105.

61. I have elaborated this point in *The NT Interpretation of Scripture*, pp. 28f.

62. M.-J. Lagrange, *Evangile selon Saint Luc* (3rd edn; Paris, 1927).

63. A. Plummer, *A Critical and Exegetical Commentary on the Gospel according to St. Luke* (5th edn; Edinburgh, 1952).

64. G. Kittel, art. αἰχμαλωτίζειν in *TWNT*, I (Stuttgart, 1949), p. 196.

65. The RSV translators are no doubt right in reading עריץ for צדיק.

66. G. Kuhn (ed.), *Sifre zu Numeri* (Stuttgart, 1959), pp. 596-97.

67. See *Studies in Paul's Technique etc.*, pp. 1-12.

68. *Tractate Sotah*, ed. A. Cohen (London, 1936), pp. 73-74.

69. Or 'in strength'. The Aramaic is בתוקפא.

70. J. Bonsirven, *Textes rabbiniques des deux premiers siècles chrétiens*

(Rome, 1955).

71. M. Mansoor, *The Thanksgiving Hymns* (Leiden, 1961). The Hebrew is

וסגרו דלתי שחת בעד הרית עול
ובריחי עולם בעד כל רוחי אפעה

72. M. Delcor, *Les Hymnes de Qumran* (Paris, 1962), *in loc.* He translates the passage thus:

> Les portes de la Fosse se sont renfermées sur celle qui est enceinte de
> l'Iniquité,
> et les verrons éternels sur tous les esprits de l'Aspic.

Notes to Chapter 7

1. *Synoptic Gospels*, I, p. 205.
2. D.E. Nineham, *St Mark* (London, 1963).
3. E. Best, *Mark: The Gospel as Story* (Edinburgh, 1983), pp. 85, 87.
4. *Op. cit.*, I, pp. 256-57.
5. *History of the Synoptic Tradition*, pp. 63, 68.
6. Güttgemanns, *op. cit.*, pp. 373-80.
7. *Paradise Now and Not Yet*, p. 179.
8. J. Schaberg, 'Daniel 7.12 and the New Testament Passion–Resurrection Traditions', *NTS* 31 (1985), pp. 208-22.
9. See Güttgemanns, pp. 173-74.
10. *Op. cit.*, pp. 317, 319-20, 322.
11. A. Schulz, 'Leidenstheologie und Vorbildethik in den paulischen Hauptbriefen', *Neutestamentliche Aufsätze*, ed. J. Blinzer *et al.* (Regensburg, 1963), pp. 265-69.
12. 'Our lowly body' RSV.
13. H.D. Betz, *Nachfolge und Nachahmung Jesu Christi im Neuen Testament* (Tübingen, 1967).
14. The word is διάκονος in Rom. 15.8 and δοῦλος in Phil. 2.7.
15. *Op. cit.*, pp. 161-67.
16. H.D. Betz, *Der Apostel Paulus und die sokratische Tradition* (Tübingen, 1972); the argument as summarized below runs all through the book, but note especially pp. 96, 100. I have already referred to this book on p. 224 above.
17. B.M. Ahern, 'The Fellowship of His Sufferings', *CBQ* 22 (1960), pp. 1-32.
18. See above, p. 89.
19. *Op. cit.*, pp. 67, 92.
20. These passages are discussed on pp. 26f. above.
21. See pp. 32f. above.

22. See pp. 47f. above.
23. *Op. cit.*, p. 99.
24. *Op. cit.*, p. 106.
25. See note 48, p. 225.
26. See above, pp. 22-23.
27. See above, pp. 27, 32.
28. See above, p. 33.
29. See above, p. 57.
30. See above, p. 59.
31. See above, p. 67.
32. See above, p. 122.
33. *Art. cit.*, p. 17.
34. *Art. cit.*, p. 225n, p. 226.
35. *Art. cit.*, p. 147.
36. *Op. cit.*, pp. 109, 110.
37. See above, p. 50.
38. See above, p. 85.
39. See above, p. 108.
40. See above, pp. 115f.
41. The reference in 2 Tim. 1.6 I take not to be historical.
42. If the reading Ἰουλίαν for Ἰουνιᾶν in Rom. 16.7 is correct, a woman is described as an apostle.
43. Dupont, *op. cit.*, pp. 240-44. A better parallel perhaps would be Jer. 24.6, where the MT uses the two verbs הרס for 'throw down' and בנה for 'build' which are rendered by the LXX with καθαιρεῖν and ἀνοικοδομεῖν respectively. In Jer. 1.10 καθαιρεῖν is not used. In 24.6 it is God who does the throwing down and building up. Perhaps an equally good parallel occurs in Ps. 28.5: 'he will break them down and build them up no more', where these two verbs are used in the Hebrew and the LXX uses καθαιρεῖν and οἰκοδομεῖν. In favour of this passage is the ending of the psalm, especially in the LXX: 27.7c in the LXX runs καὶ ἀνέθαλεν ἡ σάρξ μου (a mistranslation of the MT, which is לבי 'my heart'); and 27.8b is καὶ ὑπερασπιστὴς τῶν σωτηρίων τοῦ Χριστοῦ αὐτοῦ ἐστιν. An early Christian would understand these two verses as referrring to the resurrection of the Messiah. Ps. 28.9b runs: 'be thou their shepherd, and carry them for ever', which would be quite appropriate to the pastoral context of 2 Cor. 10.8. We may well conclude that the connection with Jeremiah is far from certain.
44. *Op. cit.*, pp. 316-18.
45. An allegorical interpretation of this text is however amply witnessed to in Jewish exegesis. See *Studies in Paul's Technique etc.*, pp. 161f.
46. In J.N. Sevenster and W.C. Van Unnik, *op. cit.*, p. 19.
47. *Art. cit.*, p. 22.
48. D.M. Stanley, 'Become Imitators of Me: The Pauline Conception of Apostolic Tradition', *Biblica* 40 (1959), pp. 859-77.

49. *Art. cit.*, p. 267.

50. *Op. cit.*, p. 28.

51. *Der Apostel Paulus und die sokratische Tradition*, p. 100.

52. *Op. cit.*, p. 55.

53. See above, p. 17.

54. See above, pp. 27f.

55. See above, pp. 41f.

56. See above, pp. 68f.

57. See above, pp. 71f.

58. See above, p. 96.

59. See above, pp. 123f.

60. *Art. cit.*, p. 11.

61. *Art. cit.*, p. 222.

62. *Op. cit.*, p. 373.

63. See D.L. Dungan, *The Sayings of Jesus in the Churches of Paul* (Oxford, 1971), pp. 3, 131.

64. N. Walther, 'Paulus und die urchristliche Jesus-tradition', *NTS* 31 (1985), pp.498-522.

65. See above, pp. 130f.

66. This is certainly Bultmann's conclusion: see *History of the Synoptic Tradition*, pp. 159-60, 328.

Notes to Chapter 8

1. For my reasons for holding this, see my commentary on *The Pastoral Epistles* (London, 1982), pp. 2-13.

2. *Art. cit.*, p. 329.

3. C.M. Nielsen, 'The Status of Paul and his Letters in Colossians', *Perspectives in Religious Studies* 12/2 (1985), pp. 103-22.

4. See *Studies in Paul's Technique etc.*, pp. 3f.

5. When I wrote this book in 1974 I believed that Paul was the author of Colossians. I have since become convinced that it was written by a disciple of Paul's.

6. See above, pp. 124-25.

7. J.B. Lightfoot *The Epistle to the Colossians* (2nd edn; London, 1897).

8. T.K. Abbott, *A Critical and Exegetical Commentary on the Epistles to the Ephesians and the Colossians* (Edinburgh, 1909).

9. M. Dibelius, *An die Kolosser; An Philemon*, ed. D.H. Greeven (3rd edn; Tübingen, 1953).

10. C.F.D. Moule, *The Epistles of Paul the Apostle to the Colossians and to Philemon* (Cambridge, 1958).

11. *Art. cit.*, pp. 27, 28, 29.

12. *Art. cit.*, pp. 157, 158, 160.

13. *Art. cit.* p. 229, n 55.

14. *Op. cit.*, p. 100. For the reference see above, pp. 141f.

15. E. Lohse, *Colossians and Philemon* (ET Philadelphia, 1971 of German edn, Göttingen, 1968).

16. J.H. Houlden, *Paul's Letters from Prison* (London, 1970).

17. *Colossians: The Church's Lord and the Christian's Liberty* (Exeter, 1972), pp. 62-63.

18. *Colossians and Philemon* (London, 1974).

19. *The Letter to the Colossians: A Commentary* (ET London, 1976 of German edn, Zürich, 1976).

20. J. Gnilka, *Der Kolosserbrief* (Freiburg, Basel, Vienna, 1980).

21. *Op. cit.*, pp. 106, 110.

22. I assume that the author of Ephesians is not identical with the author of Colossians.

23. References to the *parousia* appear in Col. 3.4; Eph. 4.30, but they can hardly be described as a leading feature of the thought of the Epistles.

24. I must express my gratitude to my former student the Revd David Cherry B.A. for drawing my attention to the possibility of this alternative translation.

25. The Tg. has 'the generations that were from the beginning' דריא דמלקרמין.

26. H. Sasse, art. αἰών in *TWNT*, I, p. 208.

27. F. Büchsel, art. γενεά in *TWNT*, I, pp. 660-61.

28. In his commentary on Colossians of 1974.

29. I have elaborated this point in *The NT Interpretation of Scripture*, pp. 28f.

30. See P. Trummer, 'Einehe nach den Pastoralbriefen', *Biblica* 51 (1970), and 'Mantel und Schriften (II Tim. 4.13)', *Biblische Zeitschrift* 18 (1974).

31. ἀγωνίζου τὸν καλὸν ἀγῶνα τῆς πίστεως. This cannot bear the sense so commonly given it 'fight the good fight'. ἀγωνίζου must mean 'maintain the contest', not 'fight the battle'.

32. I have argued the case for this in my commentary on the Pastoral Epistles (pp. 32f.).

33. This suggestion was originally made by W. Lock in *The Pastoral Epistles* (Edinburgh, 1924) and was accepted by C. Spicq, *Les Epîtres Pastorales* (2 vols; 4th edn; Paris, 1969).

34. For a fuller exposition of this passage see my commentary *in loc.*

35. J.A. Kleist, *The Epistles of St. Clement of Rome and St. Ignatius of Antioch* (Westminster, Maryland and London, 1946).

36. H. Paulsen, *Die Apostolischen Väter II* (2nd edn of W. Bauer's original, Tübingen, 1985). All quotations in Greek from Ignatius are from J.B. Lightfoot, *The Apostolic Fathers*, Second Part, vol. III (2nd edn; London, 1889).

37. See *Paradiso*, Canto VII, 21-51. The doctrine is of course taken from

Thomas Aquinas.
38. E.g. there is a reference to Eph. 5.29 in *Polycarp* 5.1.
39. My translation.
40. The word for 'comparison' or 'example' is of course τύπος.
41. The words in brackets are supplied by Lightfoot.
42. Cf. also *Trallians* 7.1.
43. MT כי הוא אמר ייהי.
44. The MT is corrupt:

ואנכי מעשיהם ומחשבותיהם באה
וקבץ את־כל־הגוים והלשנות
ובאו את־כבודי

The LXX followed by RSV has inserted 'I know', and assumes (as does G. Kittel in *Biblia Hebraica*) that באה should be בא. The Tg. offers 'And before me are all their deeds and their thoughts revealed'. The Vg has a compromise rendering: 'Ego autem opera eorum et cogitationes eorum venio ut congregem cum omnibus gentibus et linguis'.
45. Could these αἰῶνες be superhuman powers? Cf. Col. 2.15.
46. The MT has

הנה אשא לגוים ידי
ואל־עמים ארים נסי

The Tg. offers: 'Behold I will reveal my might among the nations, and will raise up my ensign among the kingdoms . . .'. It thus makes the passage rather a display of God's power than an account of God calling the nations to himself.
47. Lightfoot has inserted the word αὐτοῦ after the words ὑπὸ τῆς χάριτος.
48. 'The Theology of Suffering in the Pastoral Epistles and Ignatius of Antioch', in *Studia Patristica*, ed. E.A. Livingstone (Oxford and New York, 1982), pp. 694-96. Shortly after my sending this book to the publisher appeared W. Rebell's article, 'Das Leidenverständnis bei Paulus und Ignatius von Antiochen', *NTS* 32 (1986), pp. 458-65. His conclusions agree closely with mine.
49. Except when he is writing to the church of Rome, where, one suspects, monoepiscopacy had not yet emerged.

Notes to Chapter 9

1. R. Bultmann, *Der Stil der Paulischen Predigt und die Kynischestoische Diatribe* (Göttingen, 1910).
2. Paul only quotes Greek poetry once: 1 Cor. 15.33, where the quotation is used proverbially and paraenetically. Of course I do not regard Titus 1.12 as Pauline.

3. Bultmann himself refuses to speculate as to how the diatribe influence reached Paul (p. 107).

4. *Der Apostel Paulus und die sokratische Tradition.*

5. As we have seen, however. A.J. Malherbe has recently maintained that Paul was influenced by this tradition, although, unlike Betz, he is fully aware of the OT background; see pp. 102f.

6. See above, p. 64.

7. See my commentary on the Pastoral Epistles (London, 1982), p. 35.

8. See my 'Hodayoth xv and John 17: A Comparison of Content and Form', *Hermathena* 118 (1974), pp. 48-58.

9. M. Werner, *The Formation of Christian Dogma* (ET London, 1957).

10. For two examples of this see Rom. 10.5-8 and Eph. 4.7-10. And for a defence of my assertion see *Studies in Paul's Technique etc.*, pp. 146, 293-94 and *The NT Interpretation of Scripture*, pp. 135-41.

11. In reproducing the translation of Werner's words I have changed a good many of the capital letters for nouns which the translator has preserved, no doubt under the influence of the German original.

12. See above, p. 22.

13. See Güttgemanns, *op. cit.*, pp. 252-55.

14. See 1 Tim. 5.17 and commentaries.

15. 1 Tim. 3.15; for the argument in favour of rendering ἐδραίωμα as 'foundation' rather than 'bulwark' see my *Studies in the Pastoral Epistles*, (London, 1968), pp. 5-20.

16. Compare also Jude 3, 'the faith which was once for all delivered to the saints'.

17. There is a striking parallel in Judaism in the belief, still held by most orthodox Jews, that the Pharisaic *halakha* goes back to Moses.

18. I have argued in *Studies in the Pastoral Epistles* pp. 97-109 that references to the eucharist can in fact be found in the Pastorals. And there are surely distinct, although indirect, references to the eucharist in the Fourth Gospel.

19. This is without prejudice to the question whether it was a desirable development or not.

20. Compare 1 Thess. 5.2-3; Matt. 24.36-44; Luke 17.24.

21. Compare Heb. 9.27.

22. This is not to claim that there may not be something to be said for some notion of an analogy for the papacy to be found in the NT, on the same lines as the Pauline analogy which we propose below. But the Petrine analogy is much more remote, and is better used to explore the value of the present institution than to justify its existence on scriptural grounds.

23. K. Kirk (ed.), *The Apostolic Ministry* (2nd edn; London, 1957).

24. I have in mind in particular the work of the distinguished member of the Taizé Community Max Thurian, *Priesthood and Ministry* (London, 1983). I suspect that the recent report on the question of the ministry issued

by Anglicans and Roman Catholics (ARCIC, London, 1982) and the Lima Report, *Baptism, Eucharist, and Ministry* (ET Geneva, 1982), actually imply some such theory of the origin of the ministry.

25. The great William Temple himself made it in his Convocation Address of 1943.

26. Archbishop Benson considered that the series of councils held by Cyprian on the question of re-baptism were failures because he did not consult the laity. See E.W. Benson, *Cyprian, his Life, his Times, his Work* (London, 1897), pp. 424-31.

27. See E. Schillebeeckx, *Ministry—a Case for Change* (ET London 1981 of Dutch original, Bloemendaal, 1980); and *The Church with a Human Face* (ET London, 1985 of Dutch original, Baarn, 1985).

28. *The Church with a Human Face*, pp. 119-20.

29. ἐκείνη βεβαία εὐχαριστία ἡγείσθω ἡ ὑπὸ τὸν ἐπίσκοπον, οὖσα, ἢ ᾧ ἂν αὐτὸς ἐπιτρέψῃ.

30. ἀσφαλὲς . . . καὶ βέβαιον.

31. συνερχομένων ὑμῶν ἐπὶ τὸ αὐτὸ οὐκ ἔστιν κυριακὸν δεῖπνον φαγεῖν (11.20).

32. W. Foerster, art. κυριακός in *TWNT*, III, p. 1095.

33. J. Behm, art. δεῖπνον in *TWNT*, I, p. 34.

INDEX

INDEX OF BIBLICAL REFERENCES

OLD TESTAMENT

APOCRYPHA AND PSEUDEPIGRAPHA

NEW TESTAMENT

INDEX OF AUTHORS

JOURNAL FOR THE STUDY OF THE NEW TESTAMENT
Supplement Series